Conversations with

AMERICAN WRITERS

Conversations with
AMERICAN WRITERS

The Doubt, the Faith, the In-Between

Dale Brown

WILLIAM B. EERDMANS PUBLISHING COMPANY
GRAND RAPIDS, MICHIGAN / CAMBRIDGE, U.K.

Published 2008 by
Wm. B. Eerdmans Publishing Co.
2140 Oak Industrial Drive N.E., Grand Rapids, Michigan 49505 /
P.O. Box 163, Cambridge CB3 9PU U.K.

Printed in the United States of America

12 11 10 09 08   7 6 5 4 3 2 1

Library of Congress Cataloging-in-Publication Data

Brown, W. Dale.
Conversations with American writers:
the doubt, the faith, the in-between / W. Dale Brown.
p.   cm.
ISBN 978-0-8028-6228-0 (pbk.: alk. paper)
1. Authors, American — 20th century — Interviews.
2. Authors, American — 21st century — Interviews.
3. Religion and literature — United States. 4. Authorship.
I. Title.

PS129.B76   2008
810.9¢0054 — dc22

2007051227

www.eerdmans.com

In gratitude to

Jerry, Jane, Bill, Jennifer, and Craig:

Five friends I have

and none of them snakes

Contents

CONTENTS

Introduction

E diting this collection of interviews has been more fun than you'd expect. I was brought back to the sounds and smells of airports, restaurants, and hotel lobbies where these conversations began. And I was reminded of the walks, the follow-up chats, and the enduring friendships that have often emerged from these interviews. Re-reading them, I was taken up again by the weight of the ideas here, feelings about writing, about church, about contemporary culture, and about God. Like Nick Carraway, I've had a "consoling proximity" to famous folks. And they have been so very kind. So allow me to begin by thanking them.

For more than twenty years now, I have traveled around the country interviewing writers with a particular ear for what they have to say about wrestling with the sacred in their writing. Very few of them admit to preaching, but most of them, in one way or another, *are* preaching up a tempest. Some of them start from their problems with the faith. Others admit to being deeply enmeshed in faith, but take very different tacks in their writing about it.

This book follows on my earlier collection, *Of Faith and Fiction,* a grouping of some of the thirty-five or so interviews I have prepared during my career at Calvin College. Now I am pleased at this new gathering of voices. All but one of these novelists has been to Grand Rapids for a Festival of Faith & Writing. Most of them have shown up on the syllabi of my courses in contemporary American literature. They have helped me think about writing, faith, teaching, and more. And I am pleased to share the complete interviews with you here.

I have a friend who is a preacher. He calls now and then on those sermon preparation days to talk about books and, sometimes, movies. It is usually a Thursday or a Friday when he goes looking for a story that will "preach." I think he wants to find a film or a novel or a poem that he can weave into a sermon as a part of his weekly attempts to clarify the lives of his parishioners, a way to bring the gospel from unexpected directions. He's not just trying to be relevant, and I doubt that he'd ever use an illustration sourcebook. He's not looking for the sentimental story we've come to associate with the winding down of a bad sermon. Instead, I think he wants to draw from the powers of art as expressed in current books and films, plays and music — deep wells that just might help to sustain faith.

So when he asks, "Will this story preach?" — he means something good. But alas, his use of the word "preach" is an anachronism these days. Nobody wants to be preached at. Preachers who pound podiums, like parents who point fingers, have gotten bad press, and an artist who preaches is in suspicious company. Frederick Buechner says that ordination was a terrible career move. Ordination opened the door for his dismissal from the room: what sort of books would you expect a minister to write?

Talking with these writers over the last decade, I've been struck by the sudden wakefulness on the question of message-writing. Almost universally, they lean back in their chairs, recoiling at any notion of writing with a didactic purpose. "Never," they insist. They share our dread of preachiness; to be so categorized is to be identified with the wrong subculture — apocalyptic scribes and television moralizers. It used to be a marketing issue, I think. To be narrowly defined as a message-maker was to have one's audience significantly restricted. But Jenkins and LaHaye, Peretti and the rest, appearing alongside Grisham and Cornwall, have put to rest the monetary excuse. Serious writers, in the main, see their seriousness as linked to maintaining the surprising position that their fictions have no particular point.

We like our literature cloudy, our messages ambiguous, and the point of the story elusive. And so we have been trained. Postmodern literary theory, with its insistent implication that a story can mean nothing and, paradoxically, everything, has probably fueled a reactionary rise of interest in message narratives. But pinky-finger-bent, literary culture remains snooty about these tale-tellers with a point. The least whiff of a message, and we're talking Hallmark made-for-television and mass market book-bin pulp. Sales are one thing, literary merit another.

Frequently in this book, I raise the specter of correspondence between Walker Percy and Shelby Foote that gets at a common view of the literary scene. Shelby Foote says, "I seriously think that no good practicing Catholic can ever be a great artist; art is by definition a product of doubt; it has to be pursued. . . . Most people think mistakenly that writers are people who have something to tell them. Nothing I think could be wronger. If I knew what I wanted to say, I wouldn't write at all. What for? Why do it, if you already know the answers?"

In this view, literature is about the sin, the darkness, the fallenness — always the question, never the answer. (Unless, quite inconsistently it seems to me, the answer is that there is no answer. That didacticism is canonized.) Happy stories are for simple folk who haven't the literary sophistication to read books without models on the cover. And didactic stories are for those who aren't bright enough to have been overwhelmed by ambivalence.

I sometimes wonder what Homer or Dante or Shakespeare would make of our literary scene. But here's the great irony. All those writers who shudder at the suggestion that they preach? They're just kidding. Lucky for us. Contemporary writers are no less preachers than their kindred in previous epochs. The freight may be different, but it is still freight. And it is worth our lives, perhaps, to discover just what the crates contain.

In the stories of the writers who follow here, readers will find the same old consolation and instruction, pleasure and preaching, that good literature has always provided. Furthermore, the teachings that emerge in stories like these are equally powerful for the churched and the unchurched, the ardent practioner of faith and the darkest doubter.

Most of the writers in this volume, I concede, will not be anywhere in the vicinity of the Christian bookstore. They, nonetheless, "give us more to be Christian with" as Henry Zylstra put it long ago in a marvelous little book called *Testament of Vision*. My simple contention is that we need these truth-tellers whose work often falls in the cracks between the front-of-the-bookstore popular fiction and the carefully Christian works in the religion section. My hope is that your encounter with these folks will add good books to your reading lists for years to come.

I offer this collection with my thanks to those who encouraged me in the Festival of Faith & Writing work for a dozen years, to my family for their support, to my valued friends in the profession who have edited and suggested and shaken their heads with me. I want especially to thank the many student assistants who transcribed tapes with the background of restaurant noises, departing jet announcements, barking dogs, and crying children. They've worked with foreign accents, tape failures, and allusions that took them to Google again and again. Thank you Amanda Van Heukelum, Leslie Harkema, Stephanie White, and Maria Beversluis. And thanks to Erica Boonstra for help in preparing the gathered manuscript. My thanks, too, to the many students in my classes who motivated this work to begin with. Finally, my thanks to Eleanor, who taught me something about intensity; to Jan, who has tutored me in the ethics of trying and trying again; to Ron, who instructed me in paying attention to "what sticks"; to Ernie, whose humility continues to rub off; to Sheri, who educated me in pushing through despite the cloudiness; to Silas, who brought me to a deeper appreciation of place; to Phil, who taught me about courage; to Terry, who modeled the basic business of getting up and doing the work everyday; to David, who taught me about walking in the woods; and to Lee, who mentors me still in generosity of spirit.

DALE BROWN
King College
November, 2007

ELEANOR TAYLOR BLAND

Busy Lady

1944 — Born in Boston, Massachusetts
1992 — *Dead Time*
1993 — *Slow Burn*
1994 — *Gone Quiet*
1995 — *Done Wrong*
1996 — *Keep Still*
1998 — *See No Evil*
1999 — *Tell No Tales*
2000 — *Scream in Silence*
2001 — *Whispers in the Dark*
2002 — *Windy City Dying*
2003 — *Fatal Remains*
2004 — *A Cold and Silent Dying*
2005 — *Shades of Black: An Anthology*
2006 — *A Dark and Deadly Deception*

Lives in Waukegan, Illinois

Eleanor Taylor Bland has about fourteen things to say at once. And she has at least that many things going on in her life from one hour to the next. If you've heard her speak, you know how she fills a room. A full time writer since 1997, she also finds time for boards, committees, causes, and church. In addition to the thirteen novels

she has published since 1992, this writer has edited and contributed to anthologies, cranked out short stories, and found time to be involved in her community. A pioneer among African American writers working in the genre of mystery fiction, Bland centers her stories of Marti MacAlister, streetwise cop, and her partner, Vic Jessonovik, in the fictional town of Lincoln Prairie, Illinois, a version of her own city, Waukegan, Illinois. In our conversation, Bland talked of the genesis of her many novels, the complications of a serial story, interactions with readers, battles with cancer, connections between faith and fiction, and the various social issues that inform her fiction. To sit with this slight woman is to encounter enormous energy and resolve. She has lived many lives, but the fire still burns. She knows what she is about, and her words here help explain a career that has endured despite the vagaries of the book industry and personal challenges. How she stays on top of such an eventful career is a mystery only partly clarified during the morning we spent talking in Chicago.

DB The news has been mostly bad lately — hurricanes and Iraq and more. Do you keep track of all this?

ETB I watch the news.

DB Does it depress you?

ETB I often turn off the television. I turn off things that involve animals; I turn off a lot of things that involve real suffering. After a while the stories become so difficult to hear. It's very difficult to listen to other people's pain. I get very involved in other people's pain.

DB How does that affect your writing?

ETB I actually did write about a hurricane, because I was in one once. But, when I write, I don't want the reader to hit the "off" button. So I want to do enough to create some empathy. If I can make a character real, I'm satisfied. If I can make the reader see a stranger walking down the street and recognize them, I've done well. Coming here, I passed an elderly man who had a cup and was begging for money. If I can make you see that man and wonder how he got there, then I've done what I intend to do. I'm about creating character. I don't usually deal with tragedy directly. I don't do violence. It doesn't matter what kind of violence; I just don't do it. I want to register the impact on the person. How does what happens affect this person? That's where I think I'm going to get the empathy that I want from the reader.

DB So paying attention to your life provokes art?

ETB I pay attention. I'm the one who drives down the street and looks through your windows. I'm the one who eavesdrops on your conversations.

DB Eudora Welty said that the worst thing about getting old was that she couldn't hear well enough anymore to eavesdrop.

ETB I do that constantly, because that's how you learn.

DB Do you write better in one mood than another?

ETB No. I look at it two ways. First, the writing is something I do for myself. And then, because I publish, I look at it from the other perspective. I try to see it as a job, as well. Because that's what keeps you writing. If I didn't have that perspective, I couldn't do a book a year. I'd write whenever I was in the mood. I don't think there's a writing mood.

DB And you've maintained a book a year for twelve or thirteen years now?

ETB Yes. And some of my readers read them twice: once to find out what happened and a second time to simply enjoy the story.

DB Your first book was *Dead Time*?

ETB *Dead Time* was actually the second book. *Slow Burn* was the first book that I wrote, but no publisher wanted it. With *Dead Time,* I decided to give them what they wanted. They didn't know what they wanted, of course. No other black women were writing mystery fiction then. The only black writer that anybody knew was Walter Mosely. It was wide open for me to pretty much do what I wanted to do. But when I did *Dead Time* I wrote to their specifications. I had almost sold *Slow Burn.* I decided to get one book out, at least, and then worry about what would come next. When the editor had read *Slow Burn,* she thought the book was too much Marti MacAlister and the family, not enough police procedure, and not local enough. She wanted Ed McBain; that's what her experience was. So in *Dead Time* I gave them a straightforward police procedural. She called me up, and she said "We need Marti." It was the funniest thing.

DB   One interesting difference between the two books is the religion element. There's less religion in *Dead Time*. There's the "Thank you, Jesus" line at the end. But in *Slow Burn,* there's a whole lot more about the role of the church. Did your editors comment on that?

ETB   They don't seem to have noticed. The preoccupation with religion is part of Marti, of course. I'm Catholic; Marti is a Baptist. And I love to play with that. Editors have never commented on it, to tell you the truth. I think it's integral enough to Marti, even though you don't see her in church, that people just don't notice. The biggest problem I had was when, around the third book, they decided it was time she had a love interest. So Ben was kind of around from the third book on. But I have never met a woman who has lost her husband, particularly by death, as Marti loses Johnny, and then jumps into bed with somebody else. I simply have never come across that kind of woman. The women I have known are women who have grieved and mourned for a long time. I wanted Marti to be a person, a real person, and do what real people do.

The editors wanted a love interest. We actually had a meeting, and they were not excited that Ben and Marti were going to have a celibate relationship. But given the circumstances and the fact that there are teenagers in their home, I regarded their behavior as appropriate. They're Christian. That's appropriate behavior for them. So the editors went along with it. I have actually had readers come up to me and tell me that they love that about the books. Women, especially, love that, because they don't like the idea of running out and looking for a replacement. Widows and even widowers know that about mourning. They know that grief doesn't go away. They know they don't forget. I've never gotten any negative feedback about it.

I'll tell you something funny. When I began to write about Ben and Marti getting married, I was at a conference in Philadelphia, and there some fans told me, "You can't do that. You just can't let Marti get married. You can't do that." And I said, "Why not?" And they said, "Because then Ben will have to die." So I gave that a little thought. I did a little reading, and that's really true. Within the mystery genre, marriage partners always get killed off. So after the book where Marti and Ben get married, there's the chapter about the car accident, where Ben gets the child out of a wrecked car. I did that to demonstrate to the reader what his role will be in their relationship. He is not her partner; Vic is her partner. Ben is an important resource. Marti turns to him for insight, but he stays on the fringes of the various investigations.

DB   You're right about the genre. I think of the James Lee Burke novels. Dave Robicheaux is always losing wives.

ETB   Sure. I just decided that Marti and Ben would have a very stable relationship.

DB   How do you know so much about the Baptists?

ETB   I was born and raised Catholic, "cradle Catholic" as they call it. But my ex-husband's family is all Baptist. And the difference is like night and day. It is the funniest thing. Catholics greet one another solemnly and quietly at church. If you go to a Catholic funeral, you can expect formality. Even though we believe this person goes to God and death isn't an ending, we are solemn and serious. No emotional outbursts. But a Baptist wake is hysterical. The family discusses the corpse: "His hair doesn't look right, they put on too much makeup," and on and on. They literally critique the body. Then some folks have to hoop and holler and scream. My first Baptist funeral was for a woman who was somewhere between ninety-eight and a hundred and two. Nobody was sure. My one brother-in-law, God rest his soul, had had a few before he came to the service, so about every five minutes he would say, "How sweet it is!" Baptists wear the white gloves, and the nurses wear their caps. They're all dressed in white and walk around with Kleenex. I absolutely love a Baptist funeral.

DB   Some of your stories actually depend on doctrinal and theological understandings such as disfellowshipping in the Baptist church as opposed to excommunication in the Catholic Church.

ETB   Churches have always fascinated me. I was always getting into

6

trouble when I was a kid, because, if I could get into a synagogue, I'd go. Any kind of Eastern church, I'd go. I loved the ritual.

DB   And Denise Stevens, the deacon, is one of your main characters.

ETB   Yes, beginning with *Gone Quiet*. In the Baptist church and in the black community we're finally starting to acknowledge pedophilia and homosexuality. The only homosexual in the Baptist church, historically, is the choir director. He has some mystique, so he's allowed to be gay. Usually everybody knows, but nobody says it out loud. In general, if there's going to be a gay person in the church, that's him. So I play with things like that in my books. Pedophiles are everywhere, though. We don't like to admit it; we don't want to acknowledge sexual things. So I just did it. I told the truth. I like to turn the story around to change people's perspectives and confound their stereotypes.

DB   Generally speaking, the religious people in all of your books are good people. How do you avoid the stereotyping that often comes with the mystery genre?

ETB   My religious characters are misguided sometimes, but I try to avoid the religious fanatic thing. My oldest son is schizophrenic. In his positive phase he has a very beautiful spirituality. And when his medication isn't quite right, he deviates off into problems. Once, at church, he thought he had a curse on him. So he gave sixty-five dollars a month to the church so they wouldn't invoke the curse on him. I just cannot do religious fanaticism, because I think that the church has been, occasionally, a driving power in community, a real positive force. I'm selective about what I pick on. I give it to the juvenile system all the time, because they deserve it. Illinois currently has fourteen hundred juveniles in adult facilities. Fourteen hundred!

DB   Your books are certainly issue-oriented. You deal with homelessness and all sorts of social issues. Do you think of your writing as political?

ETB   I don't know a writer who isn't political. I know many who won't admit to being political, but we are all political. You put us together in a room without microphones, and we are political.

DB   Do you find yourself worrying about becoming too religious or too political? Some reviewers have labeled you as "goody-goody." And you even find a way to engage such issues as, say, the Persian Gulf War, which comes up via a character in one of your books.

ETB Lots of writers deal with war, because a lot of us are against this current war. I think it is legitimate to ask if we are right in our notions of defining democracy and telling other countries to get in line.

DB How does that come into your books?

ETB I do it in a very personal way.

DB You don't sit down and say, "I'm going to write an anti-war novel"?

ETB No, no.

DB You say, "I'm going to write this Marti novel, and these opinions may find their way in."

ETB Right, exactly. I'm going to write a book about Marti, and I'm going to put people in there who have opinions. I'm really not trying to convert anybody to anything. I don't think that's my job. If I was going to do that, I would be writing something different. I simply want to open readers' eyes. I want them to look at things from a different perspective. Marti has a conversation with Ben about the Vietnam War, for example, because her first husband was in Vietnam, and it changed him. Johnny became so quiet; he wouldn't talk to her about it, he didn't like to go where there were trees, he had all these little idiosyncrasies, and he had nightmares. At one point, Marti asks Ben why his experience in Vietnam was different. Ben says, essentially, "I was *helping* people; I wasn't killing them." When I write about post-traumatic stress syndrome and the problems of homelessness, the issues that veterans have to deal with, I think it comes down to the fact that these were people who had to kill. They had to kill children and women. This is what they had to do for their country. This was not something they would have chosen. It was something they were required to do. That's what I'm trying to get at.

DB Some writers who work within the mystery genre talk about themselves as entertainers. I'm sure you want your novels to be entertaining, but by talking about political issues, by veering away from stereotypes, and by your interest in religion, you seem to be going beyond entertainment.

ETB I've been writing since I was a little kid. I began to read the mystery genre only two years before I started writing my own stories. I didn't go into it to preach. I didn't know what I was doing. We didn't have workshops and all this stuff when I started. I just had to sit down and do it. I had no guide; I had no role model. There was no black woman who was doing it. I didn't read Mosely. He was from a different generation, writing about a different time period than I wanted to read about. I knew I wanted real people in my books. I wanted Marti to be contemporary. I wanted her to be like people I knew. I wanted her to be a really strong black woman, not a doormat. I wanted a genuinely strong person.

I know women who have raised children by themselves after divorce or after the death of a spouse. They have put two, three, or four children through college. They have gotten up every day and gone to work. They have done what they have had to do to raise children who can make a positive contribution to the community and to this world. Those strong women are the kinds of women I knew that I wanted to write about. I used my middle name, "Taylor," because that is my father's name, not because it is my maiden name. He died when I was young, and he always thought I could do anything. So everything I do — a book, a degree, a certificate — has "Taylor" on it. That's my way of honoring him. So I couldn't put three hundred pages of fluff on a shelf. It had to be more than entertainment. It had to have value.

DB Each of your books has several introductory pages where you acknowledge friends and your sources.

ETB I definitely go to anybody when I need technical help. And I have super fans, people who come up to me at book signings and hug me. They say nice things. One bookseller I know goes out of the way to sell books for me. And sometimes I get a super copy editor, and I really want to acknowledge them, too. And there's my family. I'm at that age where people are dying, so I often have memorials in my dedications. I am fortunate because I've always had somebody there telling me I could do it. And I acknowledge that in my dedications. It's a fun thing, and I do get a lot of comments about those first pages. I love it. Those are the last pages that get written, and I don't want to leave anybody out. But I always do. The publishers actually leave three pages blank for me now.

DB   The publishing business has changed a great deal in your lifetime. Are you expected to be active in the marketing of your books?

ETB   I don't tour anymore. I do a lot by phone and by mail. Book tours are very good to introduce you to people when you are starting out. Going to Barnes and Noble is good for some sorts of books. But everybody buys romance novels now. For mysteries and genres like science fiction, you really have to get to know your booksellers. Probably 50 percent of the reason I'm in print is because I have sellers who go out and promote me. The other 50 percent is because I have people who have bought the books and continue to buy them. I'm careful to identify the audience I want to attract. That's where I'm at now. I'm making changes with Marti. In marketing language, you go up, you plateau, and then you go down. So I'm trying to avoid the downward trend by making changes that will take Marti to another level.

DB   Are Marti and Vic outgrowing Waukegan?

ETB   No. Waukegan is critical. Marti will definitely stay in Waukegan. What I'm trying to do is not change her base but expand her base. A lot of writers are taking their characters and moving them to another city, because they have played one place out and want to put new life into things. But Marti will stay where she is and will continue to be on the same course, but she will work for a task force on an as-needed basis. That gives me some new geography. The new book actually deals with World War II a bit. There's a lot of stuff coming out about the Holocaust, and I wanted to incorporate that. There were so many people who were targeted for death, so many countries that were destroyed. I wanted to broaden the focus that way this time.

DB   This will be your thirteenth novel?

ETB   Yes, *A Dark and Deadly Deception*.

DB   Do you write your own titles?

ETB   They've let me lately. The first two books, the ones with two-word titles, were worked out via phone calls with the editor. Then I just started branching out, and astonishingly enough, they let me. I've named the last four, at least, and nobody's messed with them.

DB And Marti is on a statewide task force in the new book?

ETB Yes. And it was fun. All of them are fun. I know it doesn't sound like fun to kill people, but you have to remember that I don't kill these people on stage. I don't go through the graphic motions. Readers can figure out the details for themselves. I try to write about the interesting stuff afterwards, like the Indian bones in *Fatal Remains*. I talked to that professor in Tennessee, and he had the archeology down to a science. I told him what I wanted to find, and he told me where I would find it, and under what conditions. I'm very meticulous when it comes to things like that, but I don't tell the reader too much. It is the joy of discovery that turns the pages.

DB You've got a lot of genealogy in that book, too.

ETB If you're African-American, it is tough to go back beyond 1835, but that search was fun. I have a research assistant now who is invaluable to me. I can just sit in my rocking chair while she taps away on the computer. She comes up with the odd and interesting peripheral stuff that I often work into the story.

DB What will you bring into the new book?

ETB The new book is going to get us into World War II Romania. They have about one million orphans in Romania. In the novel, World War II artifacts from Romania turn up in Waukegan. And I've learned new things about Waukegan. For example, there's a place near Waukegan that was called Frog Island back in the 1940s. It was where all the black people lived. They called it Frog Island because it was wet there, and they got a lot of frogs. It has been developed now, but it's still there. It was a poor community in the 1940s. Just recently, during a renovation in downtown Waukegan, builders came across a building with a false ceiling. They discovered a whole second story with old wallpaper, all these old pictures, an old beauty shop, and a dental shop. So I bring all of this stuff into the book. Marti actually goes out to Los Angeles, because Los Angeles is involved in the story. The novel opens with a bit actress being killed.

DB   Thirteen novels now and all with the same lead characters and the same setting. How do you keep track of all this?

ETB   Well, remember it is Lincoln Prairie, not Waukegan. I need to be able to manipulate things to fit the crime. I usually start with the crime and work it out from there. So I need an environment that I can manipulate. I don't have to put things precisely where they actually are; I don't have to make them look precisely the way they really look. People love guessing about my characters and settings. The retired chief of the Waukegan County Sheriff's Department will see me in the grocery store, and he'll say, "I've got a couple questions for you." He'll be figuring out where in Waukegan I've gotten the idea for some locale in one of my books. If I need a little information, I just call him. I've got all kinds of sources like that. They're invaluable. I love the police department, though. Marti gets a new lieutenant in the last book. I decided I had to shake things up a little in the police department.

DB   Dirkowitz, the grenade guy, is gone?

ETB   Yes, Nicholson is still there. She's the boss, and Marti gets into more trouble with her. They just don't get along. In the book I'm getting ready to write, I will sort of resolve that conflict.

DB   You seem to enjoy bringing office politics and personality conflicts into your books.

ETB   That's because I worked in a business environment. The problem is that I truly like the Waukegan police department overall. It starts at the top. We've got a good chief and a good deputy and it works its way down, so I can't say nasty things about them. I bring water in from somewhere else, so I can have a bad cop.

DB   Nicholson's pretty nasty.

ETB   Yeah, she's a pistol, and she doesn't get any better.

DB   When did you know that you had a series and not just a single novel on your hands?

ETB   It's kind of funny. I have trouble with endings. I would have sixteen two-thousand-page manuscripts, but I could never end them. Readers think I have thirteen books out there that are a couple hundred pages each, but I really have just one long book. When I was a kid, I never read short books. I loved to immerse myself in a time period and the life of a character. That's what I wanted to write.

DB You say you didn't read very much in the genre. Did you read Ruth Rendell?

ETB Oh, I love the Brits.

DB Others?

ETB I started out reading Dick Francis, because somebody put me onto him. He's very good at the craft. I get really involved with Peter Robinson. Then there was a series about Charlie Salter that went by the wayside. He was in Canada. Mostly I read the veterans like P. D. James. Now I'm reading a woman named Patricia Sprinkle. We're having a Sprinkle marathon right now at my home. She's a Presbyterian minister. I'm also reading Margaret Maron.

DB Did you ever read the old Rex Stout series?

ETB Yes, some of them.

DB You face a problem not unlike the one Stout dealt with in his more than fifty books. You have Denise Stevens walk in, for example, and you describe her hat. That hat will come up in six consecutive books. Stout will do the same thing, as with Nero Wolfe's library and the globe in the corner. The way a series works is always interesting. It's like revisiting a familiar place. Readers get back into characters they already know.

ETB Yes, and then a continuator comes along. Someone like Bob Goldsborough extends the Wolfe series and picks up those familiar threads.

DB It seems to me that the master stroke in your series is the relationship between Vic and Marti. What makes that team tick?

ETB I didn't want them to be what is known in the business as a "cat and dog team." I didn't want them to have the generational gap issue. There is plenty of that. So their initial problem was that Vic didn't think women should be cops. What happens with any team of police officers is that they ultimately have to depend on one another. Your life depends on your partner. You never know if some situation could turn nasty, so the person with you has to be totally reliable. That's what I wanted to develop between Marti and Vic, despite the differences between them. In recent books, Vic is getting more like Marti. They are like a married couple. Ben, Marti's husband, is sort of an outsider. He is part of her support system, but Marti is getting more of Vic's characteristics, and he is getting more of hers.

DB You've gradually humanized Vic by introducing Mildred, his ill wife. And in one of the recent books, there is actually pretty distinct conflict between Marti and Vic, because the villain is Vic's mentor.

ETB That's probably the only one where they really have significant conflict. They do disagree about things; Vic is blunt and gruff. In the new book, there's a character who's going to be forced to work with Vic. He's this kid who's been to college and studied criminology, and Vic pokes fun at him. *A Dark and Deadly Deception* has to do with art, and Vic makes all these jokes about sculpture and stuff. Vic's new partner is really serious about all that, but he finally realizes that Vic is having him on. They are going to have fun in the next one. They provide comic relief.

DB How far ahead are you thinking in the series?

ETB I have actually plotted two more books.

DB Do readers come up to you and complain about any of your characters?

ETB One day I was at a library giving a speech, and a woman came up to me and said, "You know, I'm really concerned about Joanna, Marti's daughter." I'd always thought that Joanna was pretty normal. But I gave her an issue in the book that is coming out that she has to deal with. Marti comes across Joanna and Joanna's boyfriend in the basement. Marti and Joanna have what I refer to as a "Jesus meeting," but it's a friendly discussion. Basically, Marti tells Joanna that the family must come together and work to resolve their problems, and that Joanna doesn't need to get affection from someone else. That would just gloss over family problems. A librarian at Northwestern University once asked me if Vic's wife was going to be all right. She was totally serious. I have a sense of how involved readers become with these characters, and I really respect that.

DB Do you get attached to your characters?

ETB Oh yes. I don't see how I could ever let go of any of them. I have actually made a commitment that nobody important in the stories will get killed off. I recognize how involved my readers are.

DB What effect has your race had on your career?

ETB African-American writers are largely invisible, especially in the mystery genre. I'm trying to get a project going to identify what the situation is and to study that situation. We don't get our books reviewed, though we have some really gifted writers out there. Everything goes by sales, of course, and as soon as one publishing company merges with another, they drop the bottom 15 percent. That eliminates a lot of minority writers. Nobody pays much attention to you until you do three books and get a dozen reviews. They are not going to pay attention to you, because they don't know if you are going to stay around. I was just lucky.

When I first started, it was just me on a table with Walter Mosely. Many bookstores have changed now, but, when I was first published, I was slotted in the African-American section. It wasn't until people started asking for me that bookstores started putting my books in the mystery aisle.

DB Toni Morrison says that it's not about being an African-American, its about being a writer.

ETB You want to be a writer first. But also, I am African-American, German, Scotch, Irish, and Polish. My biological son is Mexican and Cherokee on his father's side. So, I've always had to live in a multicultural world. If we are going to survive as a people, we are going to have to see each other as multicultural. We have to do that. Not just multicultural, but multi-lingual, multi-religious, and more. We have to see each other that way.

DB In an interview with CBS, you said that your books aren't about race. You don't sit down to write about this diversity thing; it is simply one of these issues that come up.

ETB Sure. I often don't know why things happen the way they do in my books or in life. I just go along and see what happens.

DB In one of your interviews you say, "I don't tell my characters who they are; they tell me."

ETB I don't want to know. To the extent it is possible, I want to do what the reader does. I want to turn the page. I don't outline too much beforehand. I give the publishers a plot line. I've given them plot lines for the next two stories, which I may or may not stick to. I don't know yet, because I haven't met all the characters. When I meet the characters, I just bring them on and they tell me who they are. For example, there's the book where Marti finds out how Johnny, her first husband, died. That Diablo character just showed up in the last paragraph of a chapter. I didn't know who Diablo was until the end of the book. He told me his name was Diablo, and I thought, "If you do something, you stay, and if you don't do anything, you go." He turned out to be critical to the book. In the third book, Belle showed up. I was having tea one afternoon, and I heard Belle say, "I'm the only one who loved him." There was no Belle in the book. I said, "What's your name?" and she said, "Belle." And there she was. That doesn't happen in every book, but it happens periodically.

DB   What is the role of humor in your books?

ETB   Nobody thinks I'm funny! Well, I guess some people do. I'm a Bostonian, and I'm used to that dry Irish wit. I realize that I'm not a stand-up comedian, but I couldn't write the books without humor. I absolutely couldn't write the books. The only book I've done about physical abuse of a child is *Keep Still*. I cried in that book, even though there is only one paragraph where you really see what happened to her. I have a difficult time writing anything about the physical dimensions of violence, so I need the funny stuff.

DB   And there's a psychic in that book.

ETB   She was in there for me. Given what is on television now, I could have had an angel appear, but I don't think Marti's character would have seen it. The psychic is in there to reassure me that the child is okay, so I could keep writing the story.

DB   You do mix the supernatural into several books. You don't go as far as John Dickson Carr, but you do allow for a certain mystery. You don't do that in the first couple of books, but later on it becomes noticeable.

ETB   There is a whole dimension out there that we just don't recognize. Marti is a Baptist, of course, and faith finds its way into the books there. Her mother has the mysterious ability to feel wellness and sickness in people. There is an aspect of being African-American that lends itself to some spirituality. We are much more open.

DB In *Gone Quiet,* perhaps the most Baptist of your books, you write about the potential for hypocrisy or even perversity in fundamentalism. It doesn't seem to me that you were straining to make that the center of the book, but was that part of what you were thinking about?

ETB I do poke a little fun at my community and the black church. But in *Gone Quiet* I'm not really poking fun so much. At the point that book was written, subjects like abuse and homosexuality were closed subjects. I'm saying the church could be dynamic. The church was so wonderful during the civil rights era. Now we're not reaching out; we're not becoming involved. At one point, everything that made the black community new was done within the church.

DB And the pretense, the closing off, is dangerous?

ETB Absolutely.

DB You sometimes draw on vocabulary related to your roots. What does "seditty" mean, for example?

ETB It means that you feel you are slightly above everyone else.

DB Talk about food in your books.

ETB I try to make food meaningful, like maybe a time of year when people come together to have a nice meal. Joanna does have a problem. She has lost her father and the family tolerates her behavior when she tries to get them to eat fish and chicken and no red meat and all the rest. Marti understands that this is one of Joanna's ways of working through her grief. She is also as attached to Ben, her stepfather, as she ever was to her dad, and she has a real fear of losing her parents. And Vic goes home sometimes to these marvelous Polish dinners that Helen, his wife, makes. I skip the Jello, though. If you go anywhere with Polish people, you eat Jello! I leave the Jello out, but I put the rest in.

DB I asked about whether readers complain about your characters. I have trouble with Marti's friend, Sharon.

ETB Probably because you're a guy. Women get her. All women know a Sharon. You can walk into an office or a business and see the most competent woman in the world, and then see her in a social setting and wonder where her brain has gone.

DB She reminds me of the person in a horror movie who always opens the door, even though everybody knows she shouldn't.

ETB And she does it every time. Her daughter is smarter than her. But I bring her back. Another character who has to come back is Isaac, the wino. I got more questions about him than any other character. He had to get his own book, because of the emotional reaction of my readers.

DB As detectives, Marti and Vic want to speak for the victims. They solve a crime by getting to know the victim. This is always the principle in your books. What attracts you to that form?

ETB I don't know. A couple of my books would be considered thrillers. The last one I did was a real puzzle book. I loved the puzzle aspect of it. I think the next two are going to be puzzle books, too.

DB You do seem to move between three genres: the suspense novel, the mystery novel, and even the romance novel. Are your editors okay with that?

ETB I am very fortunate. My editors are very accepting, and my agent likes what I do. But they say you should write what you know. I thought I was going to have to go back to college and learn something new, say about antiques, or photography, or something. What I am realizing is that what I know is the street. I know a lot about the situations my characters find themselves in. I write what I know, but I have also discovered that who I am folds into the prose as well.

DB What is the role of autobiography in these stories?

ETB Not a lot. If you see Marti, you see my sisters-in-law. When you read the story of Iris, when she goes to a woman she's stolen from and the woman forgives her, you are seeing my sisters-in-law. They are repeatedly forgiving and loving, right to the last ounce. They have done incredible things. I watched my sister-in-law, who turned eighty this year, as her mother got very sick. My sister-in-law cared for her at home for four years. Her mother lived on the love that her family had for her. I see remarkable people, and readers see them in my books with people like Sharon. It is not about right or wrong; it is about family.

DB You did a genealogical search for your father, right?

ETB Yes, I started to get into that. I actually found a cousin because of it. I found a cousin who is seventy years old, and it turns out we have so much in common. It is incredible, and we didn't even know each other existed until last year. But my father's trail dead ended. He died when I was thirteen, in 1958. My mother died in 1978. Both of them were totally estranged from their families. My mother was thirty-five when I was born, and my father was forty-six, so I got a little information about my family from my mother's side, but nothing from my father except that he had a sister named Ruth, and she got struck by lightning. I think my mother just told me that so she could put all the lights out when we had an electrical storm. The real mystery is my father. So the mystery writer actually has a mystery for a father.

DB You have an interesting ear for phrases. I remember running across the line about "noses wide open."

ETB I'm not a visual writer. I'm an auditory writer. When I am sitting at a computer, I am literally typing what I hear people saying in my head. Sometimes I have to stop and go back and put a little more in or take some things out. But characters are actually talking to me.

DB It sounds like a trance of sorts.

ETB No, I just listen. Some people are very visual, but even when I am reading a book, I hear it more than I see it visually.

DB Over the course of your books, we go from typewriters to computers, and Marti even gets a cell phone eventually. Yet, you don't often refer to contemporary political events. You don't talk about the Clinton or Bush presidencies, for instance.

ETB I try not to date the books too much. You want them to be specific on the one hand, but not time specific on the other. Sue Grafton always states the time period of her stories, 1978 or whatever, almost like a disclaimer. She has kept her characters there. I want mine to move along technologically, but I try not to date the book too much.

DB Yet, your struggles with contemporary problems are very much

19

in your books. Take the issue of whether or not Theo and Mike should go to private school.

ETB Oh, yes. I do have them in private school now, and they like it. Theo is brainy and Mike likes a good time. In the new book, they are doing their homework, and Marti is really impressed that Mike is excited about what they are doing.

DB Does that have any kind of autobiographical connection?

ETB I've had issues with the educational system in Waukegan. I finally just withdrew my son.

DB Some of those struggles obviously find their way into the book.

ETB Yes, they're real. And I have problems with the whole juvenile system in Illinois.

DB There is a phrase that shows up in the introduction to *Fatal Remains* and then in *See No Evil* about the danger of becoming blind to the good in the world. You worry about that for Marti. Obviously, you also think about that for yourself. You have become involved in all kinds of social issues where you see the grimy, the depraved, the ugly, and you write about these realities, too. How do you avoid becoming blind to the good?

ETB Maybe it is the church that makes the difference. Being Catholic and also a Carmelite, which is a contemporary order, I pray a lot. I'm on the parish council, and I'm on the social justice committee. We feed the poor, buy clothing for people, and things like that. I'm on several councils and boards. I'm on a county advisory board against sexual assault. I get really involved. And people talk to me. I can be sitting on the bus and a complete stranger will talk to me. I don't need blinders. I can look at the world. I deal with that in the books. What I do in the books would be difficult for me to do as a person, because I couldn't survive it. It would break my heart.

DB You have Marti and Vic giving clothing to homeless kids, so your empathy clearly relates to your gifts as a writer. It sounds like you are also nourished by your faith.

ETB I don't go to churches that are not involved in social action, because I think that is a responsibility of the church. But I do get strength there, yes.

DB   I suppose one of the basic ideas of crime fiction is that evil is always present. Nobody is safe. You are writing about fragility and imminent danger.

ETB   You have to acknowledge the real lives of your readers. For example, I have one book that deals with the abuse of the elderly. I've had three people come up to me and tell me they have seen such abuse. I've had people say that they have a child like that. I want people to know that this stuff is real.

DB   Are your recent books more ambitious, more complicated, more complex than the earlier ones?

ETB   Yes, because I've had more time since I retired from my CPA work in 1999.

DB   And the two bouts with cancer have certainly impacted your time for writing. The first time you were diagnosed was a while back, right?

ETB   They gave me two years to live in 1972. With my 2000 recurrence, they didn't give me any predictions. I had the same cancer as Cardinal Bernardin. Same doctor, same hospital, same surgery. I don't let the doctors give me statistics and things like that, but it's been almost five years, and I do know that now I'm in the elite four percent of survivors.

DB   Do you still use that phrase, "I'm a survivor"?

ETB   Usually I say "I'm a cancer patient." I don't believe you survive it. With that diagnosis in 1972, I knew I couldn't float along anymore. I made three decisions. One, I was going to work for Abbott Laboratories. Two, I was going to finish my degree. And three, I was going to publish a book. I did all three of them. I was at a point where I told myself to get up and do something. It still motivates me.

DB   *Booklist* called *Tell No Tales* the most complicated of your books. With *Whispers in the Dark,* critics talked about the "exclusion theme."

ETB   I usually find out what I've done when I read the reviews. But I've never really gotten a bad review. I'm not analytical, and I don't have an agenda when I write. I suppose I have a general agenda, of course, but I read the reviews to see what people liked.

DB What about the guy who referred to your books as "goody-goody"?

ETB Well, even that was a pretty good review. He was talking about DaVonte in *A Cold and Silent Dying,* how the villain becomes human in the end. I had to make him human. Suddenly I knew this wasn't the guy I thought he was, because he had become attached to this child. That just happened. But some people thought it was cliché and a predictable ending. When I finish writing a book, I can't see the trees for the forest. I have zero perspective. I put the manuscript down for a couple of weeks, then I pick it up and read it. When I think it's ready, I send it to my agent first. I can do the characters in my sleep, but plotting is where I get in trouble. I usually send my agent the first hundred pages, and he sends them back with comments. That helps me with the plot. Then I go ahead and write the whole book and send it to my agent again.

And I love my editor. The thing with editors and other writers is, the better you are, the harder they are on you. If I get a pat on the back in my writing group, the Red Herrings, I worry. I tell them that their job is not to pat me on the back and tell me what a good girl I am. I want this book to be the best book I've ever written. I see every book as a step up. I don't want to write the same thing; I want to improve. So I demand that they be honest with me. And they are. Now, they are polite as all hell. You should hear the nice ways they can phrase criticism. I get respect as an author, I do. But they are honest with me and I listen to them. If it's a criticism, I listen. I might agree with them. A lot of times I agree with them, but I know why I've written something a certain way, and I wouldn't change something because of a review.

DB What about the short stories? In a couple if them, you seem to be flirting with a new series idea.

ETB Yes, I really want to do something with Tori and the Vietnamese stories. That was my intention. I'm hoping that now that I have time I can do that. But at the time I was just cranking it out. I do short stories basically on demand. One of the Vietnamese stories, the hardboiled one, was for Sara Paretsky. She asked me to do it. She's mentored me, and I love her dearly, and we're really good friends. I wanted to give her something good.

DB You seemed to have some knowledge of Buddhism in those stories.

ETB Yes, I went to a college professor for help. And "Getting Robert" was for Mary Higgins Clark. I pulled that story out of *Dead Time* and rewrote it from a different perspective.

DB I liked "The Canasta Club." People end up dead over a card game.

ETB That is the one where Vic realizes that all the women in the rooming house are gay. It was an enlightening moment for him, a nice twist.

DB Do you have a writing target every day?

ETB No, I never got into that. I'm floating now. I keep telling myself every week to get down to it. It's probably time to sit down and get going on the next book.

DB When will *A Dark and Deadly Deception* come out?

ETB Soon. I'll do a few signings and some promotion, but book signings really don't work anymore. The economy is such that people aren't running out to buy books.

DB Books have become so expensive.

ETB Yes, you've got to find a gimmick.

DB Which of your awards has meant the most to you?

ETB Actually, I got one from *Booklist,* and I got one from Chester Himes. I was the honorary chairperson for our Meals on Wheels program in Waukegan. I got to give a fifteen-minute speech, and they gave me a little vase that was heart shaped at the top. Those are the things that I really love. Those things are meaningful to me. I like the reviews, and the rewards are always fun, but I most enjoy contributing to the community. I call myself a cheerleader. I try to get people involved, and I tell them how wonderful they are for getting involved. The books are such a pleasure to do; they are rewards in and of themselves.

DB Do you still enjoy going into a bookstore and seeing if they have your books?

ETB Yes, I do. Oh, yes, absolutely.

DAVID JAMES DUNCAN

River Mud, Mysticism, and Corvette Stingrays

1952 — Born in Portland, Oregon
1983 — *The River Why*
1992 — *The Brothers K*
1995 — *River Teeth*
2001 — *My Story as Told by Water*
2003 — *Citizen's Dissent* (with Wendell Berry)
2006 — *God Laughs & Plays*

Lives in Lolo, Montana

David James Duncan lives on a Montana trout stream with his wife, the sculptor, Adrian Arleo, and their two children, two dogs, and fish and fowl of various sorts. Duncan has received awards for his novels, *The River Why* (1983) and *The Brothers K* (1992), and for his various collections of stories and essays. Activist and author, Duncan manages to juggle two careers.

In the room where he writes, Duncan has gathered some of what you'd expect — a computer, piles of books, and the well-worn desk chair. But there's also the postcard pictures hanging from shelves, the clippings of wise sayings, and the baseball, signed by Mickey Mantle, that came too late for Duncan's dying brother years ago. And there's the river teeth, hardened knot remains of ancient trees in which Duncan sees a metaphor for the stories in us all.

Our talk there rambled from the books to the book business, from satire to religion, from grace to "L.A. Law." Several books came quickly to hand, as you will see here, and Duncan paid me the courtesy of taking my questions seriously. And on a later ramble through the woods, Duncan's playful seriousness continued to emerge. He knows about fishing and walking in what he calls "mink style." His own books take readers into fly-fishing and baseball, Vietnam, and the forests of the great Northwest. But he also forces an intense look at inner landscapes as he is so intent on his own.

DB Who are the people for whom you're an exciting discovery?
DJD Judging by the fan mail I receive, the common denominators seem to be literacy and iconoclasm. Reverence for nature, too, I suppose. But I felt a little hemmed in by fans of *The River Why*. It was published by Sierra Club Books. They normally produce nature books, and the climax of my book was a nature-based epiphany. But I wrote that book such a long time ago. I was twenty-six when I started it. I'm forty-five now. I can see *River Why* people coming. They have twigs in their hair and a certain mad gleam in their eyes. Often they seem to want me to be the protagonist of my book, not only be that protagonist, but be that protagonist at the height of his mystical understanding. It just makes me want to tell them butt jokes or something. I guess I received a thousand letters from *River Why* readers. But for me, that book feels like a completely grown-up child that's gone off to college and is living a life of its own.

The Brothers K, which I lived in so long, is more recent, and I still write in somewhat the same style. There was a huge Dickensian influence in *The River Why*. I gave the protagonist a British father and an Oregon ranchbrat mother, and made him schizophrenic. He could talk in sort of grandiose nineteenth-century British prose, like his dad, or he could talk like a Twainian hick. But he didn't really have his own voice. That was my strategy. He did not have his own voice until he began to sink roots into this river valley on the Oregon coast. Then his language began to change. As Gus reaches deeper layers in himself, his voice becomes distinct from his parents' voices. That was the strategy. I don't know how well it worked, but at least he doesn't sound like Dickens by page 200.

There was a completely different strategy with *The Brothers K*. I started off trying to remember childhood in as much detail as possible, but allowed it to be remembered with the flow and precision of an adult vocabulary. And because childhood takes place in kind of an eternal present, the narrative is in the present tense, up to the point where the father smashes the narrator in the face. That knocks him into a more omniscient, detached voice, narrating from the past tense.

DB   And now you've won a reputation. Are you comfortable with that?

DJD   When I was first asked to appear in public, I was terrified. The whole idea of an anonymous author really appeals to me. (I think I first read about that notion in an essay of C. S. Lewis, "The Personal Heresy.") I was at a conference years ago with a bunch of writers, and we were asked why we became writers. Mary Clearman Blew was there. She's a woman who grew up in a patriarchal ranching culture. She said she had felt invisible there. "I became a writer in order to become visible," she said. And I said, "I became a writer to become invisible." I was fairly enfranchised as a kid. Student body vice president in seventh grade. And my brother was president. Three-sport athlete. "Popular" and all that shit. But I began to yearn for a kind of unself-consciousness. Self-consciousness is the enemy to art and life. I take very literally the idea that "He who loses himself shall find himself." Writing is gratifying in that way. I come in here every morning, and remain lost to myself for most of the day.

DB   Does it seem inappropriate to talk about your writing, the themes, and the like?

DJD   No. But I'm working toward reacting exactly the same way to praise as I do to criticism. Neither is relevant to the basic self-forgetting process. When I'm in situations where someone is praising my stories, I'm just trying to get through it as fast as I can, to forget it as fast as I can. My friend Sherman Alexie, the Indian writer, is a very public figure. He gets trotted out in front of huge crowds all the time. When one of us is on the road and depressed, we sometimes call the other. He's said to me that all the attention makes you "feel dirty," and I think that's true. To be put on a pedestal puts you in a false position. And you can be placed on a pedestal so fast it makes your head spin. So the first thing I do when I come home is put on my green chest-waders and go stand in the river. The lowest place you can stand is in a river bottom, and rivers drown saints and reprobates without preference. So I get to the lowest point, and stand there until I forget myself, and let the dirt of admiration or too much attention wash away.

DB   Do you hear the negative stuff too — people wondering why you've written this or that?

DJD   I got some criticism just the other day. It wasn't nasty so much as a completely dismissive response to "Bird-watching as a Blood Sport," a recent essay in *Harper's*. I don't try to be a saint when I'm unjustly trashed. I allow myself to fume. Then I say, "Okay, now I'm being ridiculous." Then the irritation vanishes. When I try to pretend I'm unscathed, something stays in there. But I took that particular response with a grain of salt anyway, because I know that the editors of *Harper's* are fond of publishing the most prickly letters to the editor they can find.

DB   So you try not to pay too much attention?

DJD   To either side. Praise or blame. A bit of the Gospels I take literally is "Judge not." Just love, and let 'er rip.

DB   I talk to a lot of writers who don't like to talk about the meanings in their work. Do you simply wind up your characters and watch them go?

DJD   I'm a little more cerebral than that. I'm thinking about what the story means as I'm writing it, and I have outbursts of novelistic essay writing that are woven into the story. These essays are a kind of didactic prose, but I try to follow Milan Kundera's dictum. He says that the difference between didactic prose and a novelistic essay is that in a novel it should always end with a question that turns us back to the

28

story. It should always be open at the end. I do enjoy withdrawing from the plot, though, and allowing my (hopefully open-ended) mind to reflect on emerging themes, and play with these themes directly. I'm a bit of a European in this, I guess. Or a preliterate Hindu.

DB   Do you write on a schedule?

DJD   I was a binger until I had small children. Now I think of Peter De Vries's line: "I only write when I'm inspired. And I make it a point to be inspired at nine o'clock every morning."

DB   Is this a good time to be a writer?

DJD   I just read the most cynical piece I've ever seen on the writing life. It's by Lewis Lapham, in *Harper's*. Lapham sounds very bitter that writers don't have more power and fame, and strongly advises the young to pursue some more enfranchised and remunerative line of work. For me, though, being a writer has been a way of having a contemplative life, an inner life, a way of taking my place in the ancient tradition of quiet reflection. Like I said, my goal as a writer is invisibility. And Lapham might agree with me that it's a very good time for that.

Let me say, without irony, that for me personally, this has been a fine time to be a writer. In my late teens, in the late '60s, I became obsessed with the idea of vocation — of finding work, in that depressing war era, that would do no harm. I considered four possibilities. I thought about being a monk. But I loved sex! The second time I played golf I broke forty, so I grew interested in becoming the first voluntarily poor pacifist hippie golfer. I had visions of winning the Masters with long hair, a beard, bare feet, overalls and no underpants, doing for lovers of simplicity (and haters of polyester) what Tiger Woods has done for blacks. But when I was a senior, and a scratch golfer, I got kicked off the team for refusing to cut my hair. Me and Samson! The third possibility was jazz piano. But there were two trouble areas here. One was having to put up with the egos and substance abuse and sexual deviations and bad musical taste of the other members of one's band. And the other thing was, I hit a plateau. I was good at arrangements, accompaniments, orchestration. But my right hand had no speed for those wonderful riffs all jazz pianists can do.

That left writing — the thing I was worst at. Well, no. Being a monk would have been worse. But writing, I've discovered, *is* being a monk. Only in writing, I found, I could do those jazz riffs. And embrace the poverty. And escape the other band members. And wrestle instead with the best thoughts ever expressed and best yarns ever spun. And since, unlike Lewis Lapham, I've never wanted to have dinner at the White House or be considered a cultural oracle, it's been great. What I would say to aspiring writers is, keep your expectations as low as the mud on the bottom of the river, and you'll never be disappointed, except possibly by success. The best news is: my longing to proceed on to complete invisibility is right on schedule.

DB   But, like fly-fishing, writing is hard work?

DJD Writing and fly-fishing aren't hard work, to me. They're pursuits in which you can lose yourself. And holy for that reason. The fly fishers I know have a couple of different approaches. A lot of them are like great blue herons in their pace. They just arrive in one place, and stay there. Then there's the mink style fisherman who works rapidly along the bank. You just head upstream, and every new piece of water is a fresh occasion for childish, predatory hope. I go mink style, usually. I burn up a lot of calories, cover a lot of miles, see a lot of birds and wildlife, and my thoughts are pretty much just of things to do with the nuances of the current, trying to get the fly to float down that complex line of current to where I see a fish holding. It ain't profound, but it's very soothing for somebody who's spent the day in his head.

DB   And now you're working on *Letters from God* — a novel you've described as "a metaphysical comedy."

DJD Yes, that novel is on both front burners. It's a hard book to talk about in much detail, because it's a comedy that hinges on a device that's got properties that defy basic laws of physics. Any description outside the novel makes the whole thing sound ridiculous. But without a description, the novel is hard to talk about. It's like trying to talk about the holy grail to people who've never heard of the blood of Christ. That publicity problem aside, what I'm trying to do is create a modern coda to *The Divine Comedy*, which is an unassailable masterpiece, of course, but isn't funny. And nobody has any idea what it feels like in the original. Its metaphysics now feel so specific and arcane that they're just about inaccessible to Americans. People talk about the so-called dark ages, but the Middle Ages were intellectually rich compared to our era of TV-doped minds. I'm trying to get to some of that juicy stuff that's in Dante and other mystics in a way that's amusing. I want to move people toward thinking about the word "God" in a way that encourages them to drop all preconceptions and just look at the naked word. Is there a way to get people, through laughter, to reconsider the attributes they give this poor, abused being? That's what I'm trying to explore. And the other thing I'm trying to do in the novel is explore, with humor but *without cynicism,* some of the wonders of marriage and the erotic life. Although such work has been done beautifully in various places around the globe, it feels like fairly virgin territory here in America. My friend Barry Lopez has a story called "The Letters of Heaven" that touches on the mystery I'm trying to circle. But Barry, like Dante, is essentially a serious and reverent man. I find myself far too ridiculous to be all that serious. Once the self is effaced — in love for God, love of sex, love of fly-fishing — the self has vanished, and it no longer matters whether you're serious or not. I'm trying to write from this place.

DB   Will readers recognize it? Will they say, "Oh, this is like *The Brothers K*?"

DJD   I doubt it. I like the idea of remaking myself from scratch with a new book. You sit down with a stack of blank pages, and start from zero. I never want to write the son of *River Why.* I never want to write the sequel to *The Brothers K.*

DB   How do you feel about the Oprah effect? She is really making careers for writers.

DJD   Ironic, ain't it? I mean, if TV isn't the enemy of literature and the inner life, I don't know what is. Obviously there's some good TV. You can't make a safe generalization even about *that* disgusting medium. But commercial television and the whole Global Celebrity Village, virtual "friendships" with "stars" who may actually hate you. . . . Oh my. Don't get me started.

DB You know that your readers are often interested in the connection between your own history and the histories you invent in your books. How do you use your own story?

DJD Obliquely! The autobiography thing is overplayed. The best novels are not autobiography. They're more analogous to a work of art like a symphony, or a thick collection of poems, or a group of twenty-five or thirty paintings. Nobody expects a symphony to be anything but what it is: an imaginative work made of rhythm and tones. A novel is much closer to that than people realize. It is strange to me when people want me to be the protagonist of my books, want the events in the novel to be true in a physical, literal way. This approach misses the point. A novel is a symphony. The author is the composer and the reader is the conductor. And the imagination — of both the composer *and* the conductor — is the symphony orchestra.

I was in a music store in Portland and I saw this guy pick up a symphony score. I glanced over his shoulder as I walked by, and to my untrained eyes, the score looked like fifty pigeons had crapped on the paper. Even though I know how to read simple music, this score was so complex! But this man started reading it. And after a bit he was laughing and breathing hard, and waving his arms, and his chest was swelling. He had lost himself completely in rhythm and tones, just by staring at this dead, black, gobbledy-gook. And it struck me: this is exactly what all *readers* do. It seems incredible to me that we possess this power. To turn our attention away from this power and reduce the story to, "Okay, you went out behind your house and hooked this really big fish just like you say here in the story" is sad-making. It's like abandoning *The Odyssey* for *Outdoor Life*. And I think a lot of that prejudice comes from television. What does "Based on a true story" mean? Placing the emphasis on that buzz phrase is sad. People are missing the literary boat. And that boat is glorious. And what it sails on is your imagination. It's all about your own stupendous imaginative powers. Every man and woman's ability to create life where there is none.

DB Walt Whitman says we need a new reader who will engage in a "gymnast's struggle." You want a reader who will somehow enter the imaginative experience with you?

DJD There's no other kind. Readers all create their own imaginative worlds. The author is not there. The author has vacated the scene, and left behind a score. The conductor and orchestra are hiding in the reader. Who cares who the author was? It's the music that's alive.

DB So things can happen with one of your books that are far beyond anything you would have imagined yourself?

DJD I've had readers find things in stories I've written that I didn't see at all. Occasionally they've struck me as off the wall, but other times they've seemed completely valid. There's a little story in *River Teeth* that's a left-over from *The Brothers K*, a story about Irwin going into old growth forest to think about his father, who has died. One reader found the echo of Christ's line "Father, my Father, why have you forsaken me?" I hadn't noticed that at all, but it seemed undeniable to me after she brought it up.

DB Why did you cut that scene from *The Brothers K*?

DJD I felt that I had already achieved emotions in *The Brothers K* that are similar. The wake scene, and the scene where Kincaid drops the salmon on the stairs, because Irwin has appeared with sheets covered with the blood of their father. The tone of the old growth scene was redundant. I didn't want to try to put the reader in the same mood two times in a row, in one book.

DB What about the Seventh Day Adventist threads running through *The Brothers K*? That is at least partly autobiographical, isn't it?

DJD It's a symphony that plays blithely with some Adventist rhythms and tones. But I was never an Adventist. I was just a kid held temporarily captive by their cult. And I'm grateful Seventh Day Adventists taught me that religious zeal is one thing but spiritual truth is another. Robert Musil says, "There's no truth that stupidity can't make use of." I had no problem with Jesus. My problem was with the institution. I don't want to make myself sound more sophisticated than I was, but it did occur to me at a pretty young age that the people in the churches I attended seemed like some of the likeliest candidates to be the crucifiers of Christ, rather than his followers. The indoctrination never took hold. But I was impressed by the theatricality and rhetorical passion of some of the sermons and prayers. And though I don't ever remember thinking "this is the truth" or feeling my own heart touched, I do remember feeling touched by my mother's devotion.

In retrospect, I believe that a doctrinaire fundamentalist childhood, where you have a family member who buys the dogma completely, has a psychological effect like having a nail driven into your hand. You've heard the saying that if a parochial school gets hold of a kid from birth to age seven they have them for life. That's the nail hole. They'll be a Catholic. A jack Catholic, maybe, but still a kind of Catholic. My feeling is, we ex-Adventists, ex-fundies, ex-Catholics, need to wrestle the psychological nail hole away from the people who put it there and believe it into something beautiful. This has been my relationship to Christianity. It has not sufficed to make me a Christian, but it has sufficed to let me forgive and heal and grow.

DB   What about Scripture? You must have been steeped in The King James Version.

DJD   It's still right there beside my thesaurus and phone book. And I dip into it often. The Old Testament never took with me. I might almost say I hate it. Leviticus. Exodus 21. The only purpose of the Old Testament is to create the need for Christ, as far as I can see. I read the stuff on how hard you're supposed to beat your slaves, shake my head and say JESUS CHRIST! But I still find things in the Gospels that delight me. Not as often as the Zen and Sufi traditions, or fly-fishing and wilderness and rivers and children and birds and my wife delight me. But still, the Gospels have got some kick.

The climax of my relationship with the King James Bible occurred in 1965, when I was thirteen, and my older brother, the person I was closest to, died after a series of unsuccessful open heart surgeries. I've told the story in a memoir in *River Teeth* called "The Mickey Mantle Koan." What the memoir perhaps leaves out is that I was a pretty good, non-rebellious "Bible boy" up until then. Although I didn't like church, I didn't feel moved to any kind of radical rejection. But church, coupled with my brother's death, became a big part of my becoming who I am. There was a zealous young Adventist clergyman, fresh from seminary, who showed up at the hospital shortly before my brother died. The seminarian told me that if I prayed for my brother hard enough, with a pure enough heart, I could save his life. Very shortly after, he died. I have to struggle to remember what is actually inscribed in the marble on my brother's tombstone, but I sure remember that seminarian's words. And though I did pray for my brother, I was left with huge questions — about the meaning of life, the efficacy of prayer, the purity of my heart. That preacher saying that to me was immeasurably important. His glib certainty killed the glib certainties in me. Somehow what happened to my brother, the false promises of preachers, the hesitations in my own heart, the fact of death, God's seeming creation of that fact, dovetailed into the Vietnam era in my emotional experience. I hated that war more than most, because I had already been broken open by my brother's death. I thought *Great, here's a way to destroy young American men by the thousands, instead of one by one.* I became wild — a delinquent, I suppose. But I began to find some solace was when I was about fifteen or sixteen. I had an older friend who went to Stanford, and he started sending me his reading lists and books that he'd read. At sixteen, in high school, my grade point average headed for the basement, because I was reading Thomas Mann, Herman Hesse, Nikos Kazantzakis, Mark Twain, and too much Jack Kerouac, instead of doing homework. But I began to find some of the same questions that haunted me being asked by these novelists. And there was hope and consolation in that. I also remember Hesse as my first exposure to Eastern spirituality. The attraction was immediate and very strong. I really liked Buddhism and Hinduism right from the start.

I've explored the major religions in some depth. It's interesting to see how the different traditions talk to each other. For example, Buddhism after a few centuries became so monk-dominated that poor lay people were inundated with these begging monks. And they rebelled. It was like "Get outta here, ya bums. Grow some crops. We're Buddhists too." This was right at the time of Christ. I sometimes wonder whether in some inner way, Christ wasn't responsible for the shift in Buddhism from a contemplative tradition to a more lay tradition. Similarly, the time of Mohammed was when the Celtic monks began to make their peregrinations. The flowering of Islam and the flowering of Christianity took place at very much the same time, and I sometimes wonder whether Mohammed didn't have something to do with the things going on in Europe, in some inner way. This is some wild, mystical theorizing, but I have never felt a need to make the messiahs discrete or antagonistic. When I read Meister Eckhart and Rumi — a Christian and a Muslim — I'm hearing the same voice from two different sources.

DB   So you never felt you were "throwing the baby out with the bath water"?

DJD   The idea of the *only* Son of God is very problematic, because the only-ness is so hugely emphasized in the Protestant and Catholic traditions. We need the mystics! If you think about the Son of God in Eckhart, for example, it feels emotionally and spiritually the same as reading about the bodhisattva in Buddhism, or the mysterious female in Lao Tsu. It is all about inner reality. I have no problem with the idea of *oneness*. But *only-ness* is one of the things that keeps me outside the church. The Bodhi Tree of Buddha is exactly the same as the cross of Christ. To sit down there, motionless, baking, starving, until he defeated illusion was no less a feat than for Christ to be willingly crucified. They're both miracles of compassion.

DB   Despite your beliefs, *The Brothers K* was well-received by Adventists. Does that give you pause?

DJD   A bit. I went to Walla Walla College a couple years ago, and felt like I was right in the mainstream with the literary Adventists. It was an amazing experience, and good comedy, if you know the whole story. Back in college — which I paid for myself — I had a standing offer of a full scholarship to Walla Walla from my Adventist grandparents. When I refused, they disinherited me. Money was a huge carrot they put in front of their children. But all of us were stubborn. Both my sister and I refused free houses because we knew there were strings attached, *chains* attached. At nineteen, disinherited, I was working nights as a janitor and going to Portland State, studying English, history, philosophy, anything for which I felt passion. But the whole time I was going to Portland State there was this offer from my grandparents that, if I would transfer to Walla Walla College, they'd give me free ride, pay all my living expenses, and buy me a brand-new Corvette Stingray when I graduated!

My grandparents would have been dumbfounded to see me speak at Walla Walla College after *The Brothers K* came out. There's a formidable old church there, one of these places where the walls have been scarred by the fumes of all the fire and brimstone from the pulpit. So there I was with four or five hundred people in these pews, at the church on the campus where my grandparents had wanted me to go all along. And I read the church scenes from *The Brothers K*, which are, well — far from reverent. Yet the Adventists were rolling in the aisles! It was so strange. I told the Walla Walla faculty the story of my grandparents' offer. They responded by sending me an autographed softball and a little teeny Corvette Stingray. That's when I realized that, if my grandparents had just made it one of those Volkswagen Westfalia vans that pops up into a camper, I might have been off to Adventist college, chains or no chains.

DB Do you in any way envy the passion that once burned in that old church?

DJD The passion that dunked witches and exterminated Indian tribes and burned women and beat children? Not much. There's a lot of passion in any kind of ideologue. People who want things to be simpler than they are often generate great energy by their very simplicity. I think that there are positive things about fascistic religious movements from the original zealots to the Promise Keepers. But I am wary of that passion. Religious passion, chosen-ness, only-ness, gets people killed. Christ, for instance.

DB Do you worry about being cast back radically upon yourself and your own understanding?

DJD I'm not alone. I have a sangha, a group of spiritual brothers and sisters. I have a spiritual home, too.

DB Somewhere you talk about the Amish with some wistfulness.

DJD Sometimes I feel shamed by my culture. In fact, I don't consider it my culture. When people say "we," and mean America, I don't feel anything I can get a handle on. When someone says "we," meaning the people who live in the Columbia River Basin, then I start to resonate.

DB There's an almost Southern sense of place in your work, an awareness of geography and environment. And you've pursued these subjects in your non-fiction too?

DJD I've wanted my writing to be very much feet on the ground, so I do look at the ground my feet are landing on. There's a lot of people from urban areas, especially southern Californians, who come here to Montana to retire with their nest egg. To protect that egg, they vote down the taxes that provide for our schools. So the kids at our school this year had no band, no art, no sports, and had to go out on the street corners, to raise money a dollar at a time. I just read in Kabir about a cow trying to nurse from the calf. That's how "American culture" feels to me. The young and the poor feeding the rich. The enfranchised sucking dry the people they should be helping. It's an old story. And a sad one. The best way to resist such ignorance is to keep your feet smack on the ground.

DB You say somewhere that issues make bad literature. Is there a danger that some cause — anti-fundamentalism or environmentalism or whatever — might blunt the force of your stories?

DJD No question about it. My own ideologies are as reductionist and blind to grace as anybody else's. So I resist even those ideologues who seem to help me. For example, it was an interesting experience for me to have my first novel taken by Sierra Club Books, a house run by the Sierra Club, a white-collar, lawyer-heavy, environmentalist group. I didn't join the Sierra Club, but I got a pretty good look at what they were doing. When they would block ancient forest sales in Oregon, I was always grateful toward them. But I don't use the word "environmentalist" to describe myself. In 1988, George Bush ran for President insisting that he was an environmentalist. The same year Weyerhauser Corporation and Du Pont Chemical were insisting that they were responsible environmentalists. They can have the term. The word always seemed problematic. It's clunky, and it turns a blind eye to economic questions. By their fruits ye shall know them. By my fruits ye shall know me.

DB   What is your reaction to your reviewers, and the pressures of marketing and the like?

DJD   I was recently handed some reviews of *The Brothers K* that came from the Internet. Readers apparently type out these little book reports. One guy says, "Terrible. My dad even hated it." The rest give it 10s, the highest score. My reaction is: stay off the Internet!

DB   Don't you sometimes think about the success of a Grisham or a Cornwall, those writers who get 500,000-copy first printings?

DJD   It's amazing, how little I think about that. I was still a kid when I noticed the way a child will be playing along and really enjoying it, until she sees three kids playing over there, looking like they're having fun. Suddenly, what she was doing goes dead for her. She becomes obsessed with this other circle. I've always been the opposite of that. I've always felt that where I am feels enough like a center. The little exposure I've had to eastern literary communities makes me wonder if there isn't more jostling for position, more petty rivalries there. The scene seems dominated at the top by these gargantuan egos like Norman Mailer, who reminds me of Humpty Dumpty. I dread his big fall. I'm very much a West Coast writer in terms of who I know and where I go on book tours and where I get invited to give talks. And I think — though this could be an illusion that will be shattered — but things feel a little friendlier here. In the northwest of Montana, things feel *much* friendlier. We're all unsuccessful!

DB   You say somewhere the purpose of literature is not very different from the purpose of worship. How so?

DJD   In her book, *Nine Gates*, Jane Hirshfield answers this question so much better than me. Jane says that if a story or poem "is the harvest of true concentration, it will know more than can be said in any other way. And because it thinks by music and image, by story and passion and voice, poetry and story can do what other forms of thinking cannot: approximate the actual flavor of life, in which subjective and objective become one, in which the conceptual mind and the inexpressible presence of things becomes one. Letting this wideness into ourselves leads us into the self, but also away from it. Transparency . . ." (INVISIBILITY!) ". . . is what we seek in art, and in art's mind of concentration. . . . Free to turn outward and inward, free to remain still and wondering amid the mysteries of mind and world, we arrive, for a moment, at a kind of fullness that overspills into everything."

C. S. Lewis talks about literature giving us windows into other worlds, giving the benefit of other perspectives. For instance, you can debauch with William Burroughs without having to destroy your liver. My relationship with literature has changed through the years. Somewhere in my thirties, I began feeling somewhat guilty after reading a good novel. I had imbibed so many wonderful stories. When was I going to start telling my own? It began to feel slightly self-indulgent. Now I even resist the novels I'm very interested in reading. For example, I have not yet read *Snow Falling on Cedars*. I still hope to, but I'll probably have to get the flu to give myself permission. That's when I read novels. When I'm sick. When I'm well, and working, I find it helps to starve myself for narratives. Then my hunger for narrative is fed by the narratives I'm trying to create. When I was working on *The Brothers K,* I tried to read *Beloved* and *All the Pretty Horses.* I had to hide them, because what those two writers are up to is so powerful. I had to be wary of connecting too much to another's prose rhythms.

DB   Their rhythms might influence you?

DJD Norman Maclean talks about this. He says all prose should be rhythmical. He says the rhythms should be barely perceptible. He says the rhythms should become noticeable at times, "as when the author is fooling around and showing off." He says, "If an author writes out of a full heart and rhythms don't come with it, something is missing inside the author. Perhaps a full heart." When my writing is going well, it feels very similar to when I sit down at the piano and improvise. I'm just sitting at the keyboard, and there are rhythms guiding the narration. Although you might have quite a definite idea about where you want the story to go, the rhythms, the magic, the give and take of language, the character and voice, are all alive and changing as you go. There's a constant sense of discovery if you give these forces freedom. But it's a fragile process. When I'm on a roll, but stop to read some writer whose voice is idiosyncratic and strong, it's like listening to Beethoven while you're trying to be Bill Evans. If you're Bill Evans, Beethoven's the last guy you want blasting in your head.

DB Is there a stripe of the satirist in you somewhere?

DJD Yes. But with caveats. I learned my satire lesson the hard way, back in my twenties. I had just read *Zen and the Art of Motorcycle Maintenance*. Then I read a pretty funny satire called "Zen and the Art of Lawnmower Maintenance." Then I read Peter Matthiessen's *The Snow Leopard*. The Buddhist philosophizing in that book annoyed me at the time, I think because I was really trying to clear a space for my own inner quest. So I wrote a parody called "The Snow Leper" about these Buddhist lamas gathering on the slopes of the Himalayas. My parody has Peter Matthiessen and an anthropologist from New York watching through binoculars as the lamas gather on the slopes in preparation for their annual jet migrations to Boulder, Colorado, and southern California. And when it came time to polish and publish it, I started to feel like I was judging another man's spirituality. So I just reshelved it. But a couple years later, I was reading some book about the Zen tradition and found a parody of Basho, written by a Zen monk. "The old pond./Basho jumps in./The sound of the water!" It struck me funny. And I thought, okay, Peter Matthiessen's a Zen Buddhist and there is a tradition of parody and satire in Zen. So I mailed "The Snow Leper" to Peter. As soon as I did so, though, I knew I'd been really stupid. It made its way to Matthiessen, and I didn't hear back and forgot about it. Then, in a bookstore maybe a decade later, I picked up Matthiessen's *Nine-headed Dragon River*. The second chapter of that book is a beautifully honest look at the death of his wife, Deborah. I was blown away by it — standing in the bookstore with tears running down my face. And then I remembered the parody that I sent this man. I realized that *The Snow Leopard* was in fact the journey he took in his grief for his wife, when he was trying to put himself back together. And many of the things that annoyed me in the way he was talking about inner life and inner struggle were coming directly out of the grief he'd just gone through. You can imagine how I felt about my parody. I wrote Matthiessen a letter of apology, confessed to feeling like a worm.

Then in 1996 the Nature Conservancy invited me to New York to read at a fund-raiser, and one of the people I was reading with was Peter Matthiessen. I had visions of this grey-haired, distinguished-looking man punching me in the face. But as soon as I set eyes on Peter, I could see he was capable of great mischief himself. We became friends via birds and fly rods. Nowadays he makes a little pilgrimage to Montana every summer, and I've become one of his fishing guides. Anyhow, looking back I realized my motives were not pure when I wrote that satire; I just wanted it to be scathing. About anything at all. Peter had nothing to do with it. So I'm glad of the backfire.

DB So satire is too sharp-edged a sword?

DJD When aimed at another mere mortal, yes. And satirists end badly. Swift himself says so. Look at Twain. A sad man. He really suffered the effects of wonderful statements like "Faith is believing what you know ain't so." He lost a fortune, a wife, two of his children, and had nothing with which to answer his grief but his own wit. There's danger in the satiric life. My own strong satiric streak began to wither because of spiritual fear.

But I still find uses for it. When a corporate cyanide heap-leach gold mine threatened to kill the Blackfoot River, I wrote a little parody. It's about a guy who discovers that he has these mineral deposits in his knees, and an 1872 Surgical Law gives any doctor in the world the right to come to America, open his knees to get these minerals out, and leave him crippled for life. He's a nice rancher on the Blackfoot River in Montana as it happens. And there really *is* an 1872 mining law that's insane. My yarn is over the top, Swiftian satire. But I felt that, with an enemy as powerful as a giant mining corporation, any small havoc I could verbally wreak would be justified.

DB You use the word "sad-making" often. Do you feel a sadness about American culture?

DJD I've been called a "grief-stricken comedian" by some critic or other.

DB As opposed to?

DJD Well, it's a funny thing. I would say that one of the things my interior life has given me is faith, and one of the roots of faith is ultimate optimism. But *pen*ultimately, I'm a pessimist. I don't have happy pictures of what's going to happen in the immediate future. I feel very apocalyptic. Not *Revelation* sort of apocalyptic. But when I look at my children's world, I really need that ultimate optimism.

DB Both *The River Why* and *The Brothers K* have a good bit to say about community, about needing others, about being driven into real life with real people. Am I right?

DJD Yes. That goes all the way back to high school for me. I wanted to escape people. I wanted to erase high school. I wanted to try to purify myself. So I went up into the Cascade Mountains right after the senior all-night party, camped alone, and fasted for a week. I became kind of a fruitarian for a number of months. And I really did achieve a physical purity that I'm glad I tasted. When we were eating dinner as kids and didn't like what was on our plate, my dad would say, "You don't know what it is to be hungry." It was good to finally be able to say, "Yes, I *do* know what it is to be hungry." I continued to do smaller fasts. I'd live for a week on organic Valencia oranges and ride my bicycle fifty miles a day and play six sets of tennis. I had huge energy. But I weighed about 130 pounds when my normal weight should be more like upper 160s, and I'd moved into that crazy realm that Gus was in before he grounded himself, and that Peter was in, while in India. I started to find people intolerable for the thinnest of reasons. On a hiking trail I could smell people coming long before I saw or heard them. If they'd stopped at the Charburger before heading up the trail, I could smell their onions and beef. And the smell made me nauseous, made me hide off to one side of the trail. But to loathe the company of someone because they had a hamburger is not good! I got so incredibly sensitized from the light diet that my circuits could be blown by anything. I came to the conclusion that to be that sensitive in this culture is not workable. So when Thanksgiving came around, I choked down some turkey.

DB You've had extraordinary experiences? Spiritual experiences?

DJD Peter Matthiessen and I were talking about this while we were fishing a couple weeks ago. We both realized that we distrust anybody's extraordinary experience but our own. It's a double-standard,

I know. But I feel extremely uneasy around New Age-ism and loosy-goosy mysticism. At the same time, my faith has been dramatically shaped by experiences. Several times in my life I have set out with a thimble in my hand, asking for love, and ended up standing there with a lake of love landing on my head. What I was trying to do in *The River Why* was create a stage upon which such an event could believably take place.

DB　So the book is about Gus's discovery of grace?

DJD　That's what I was after in the chapter called "The Line of Light," where he's journeyed the river with the salmon that he can't possibly control. He knows right where it is because of the light line that connects them, and he later experiences some kind of vigilant, absolute love that is attached to him in the same ineffable way. The whole novel was built around that image. An image of paradox; it's an absolute paradox. There's no rational way to talk about it. We have freedom and no freedom at the same time. I can't think of a less irritatingly Zen way to say it. Anyhow, "The line of light" became the central image, and I went all the way back to the beginning of the novel to rewrite around it.

DB　So much seems to depend on Gus being able to trust his instincts and follow his heart. I'm thinking of Graham Greene's line, "The heart is an untrustworthy beast." Isn't there potential danger in this sort of self-trust?

DJD　The heart may be the only trustworthy thing in us. Graham Greene is using the word "heart" in a traditional British sense as a nexus of eros and lust. But I don't use the word that way. To me, the heart is an organ of fire and light. It's the seat of the soul. Graham Greene's definition is so different from mine; it's like Saint Francis's God versus Pat Robertson's God.

Here's some lines from Ruzbihan Baqli, a twelfth-century Sufi master, that describe the human heart for those of us who have not bought into the wretchedness of John Calvin or Graham Greene or whoever:

"I saw God on the streets with something hidden in his hand. I said, 'My God, what is this?' He said, 'Your heart.' I said, 'My heart has such a station that it lies in your hand?' He gazed at my heart, and it was like something folded up, so he spread it out. And my heart covered all the space from the Throne of God to the earth. I said, 'This is my heart?' He said, 'This is your heart, and it is the vastest thing in existence.' I said, 'Where are you taking it?' He said, 'To the world of eternity, so that I may look in it, and create wonders of reality in it, and forever manifest myself in it with the attributes of divinity.'"

It's a considerable plummet from this view of a human being to John Calvin, who says, "Whatever is in man, from intellect to will, from the soul to the flesh, is all defiled and crammed with concupiscence." In my view, John Calvin confused himself with his penis. The mystics and Ruzbihan suffer no such pitiful confusion.

DB You refer to yourself as a "devout non-Christian." Is that part of drawing a line between yourself and Pat Robertson?

DJD I draw a line between myself and a lot of what Christianity has been. My favorite Christian, Meister Eckhart, preached to communities of mystics who founded self-sustaining communities all over the Rhine Valley in Belgium, France, Holland, Germany. They ministered to the sick, taught kids, helped the dying. But they were hounded out of existence by Holy Mother Church. Their saints were burned at the stake; their teachings and writings were destroyed. When you say Christian, do you mean the people who were burned, or those who did the burning? I can't hear the word without hearing that crucial question.

DB What do you mean when you say that Christianity is tired?

DJD Well, look at Christmas, for example. Santa is an anagram of Satan, and acts like it. I can still feel the poignancy of my childhood encounters with the stories of angels and shepherds and the manger. Then I had the innocence of a child. Every year the stories get more tired. Every year I feel more coerced to buy a bunch of plastic baubles that children have shoved down their throats by corporations. That's Christmas. That's our holiday cheer; God help us. But there's still the inner life, still the practice of keeping one innocent word in your heart, fastening it to your heart, and not allowing your head to even analyze this holy word. "It is not a matter of analyzing or elucidating," as the anonymous writer of *The Cloud of Unknowing* says. It's very simple. "No one can truly think of God," he writes. "It is therefore my wish to leave everything that I can think and choose for my love the thing that I cannot think. God can be loved but not thought. He can be held by love, but not by thought." This is a *full-time job*, not a tired, late December holiday.

DB Why the big gap between *The River Why* and *The Brothers K*?

DJD I'm slower than a seven-year itch. And I got divorced between *The River Why* and *The Brothers K*. And then I fell in love, which was *really* hard. I feel deeply drawn to writing. But it doesn't compare to being in love!

DB You were writing *The Brothers K* for that whole ten years?

DJD I fooled around with three novels at once from 1983 till 1985. Then in 1986 I sold the prospectus for *The Brothers K*, and divorced. Then I fell in love, and enjoyed myself for a while, in 1987 and 1988. By 1989, I was in serious debt. Which helps! I wrote the last 450 pages of *The Brothers K* in a year and a half or two years, to get the paycheck. You know Aesop's fable about the ant and the grasshopper? I'm a grasshopper who is fortunately married to an ant.

DB When you were interviewed about *The Brothers K* by the *New York Times*, you focused on the K, the strikeout.

DJD I hear the term two ways. There's the baseball failure, and there's also striking out to find your fortune. Striking out into life. My peculiar definition of the term occurs around page 500. The K, as I define it, symbolizes the paradox I've been talking about all day: losing yourself in order to find yourself. My editor at Doubleday hated the title. She wanted to get rid of it. She said critics were going to crucify me because I was comparing myself to Dostoyevsky. I disagreed. *The Brothers Karamazov* is about a depraved father. *The Brothers K* is about an almost completely admirable father. I really wrote the book to rediscover the father. Homer Simpson is the father of our time, and there's one story after another about abusive, awful fathers. I felt my story was so different from what's going in *The Brothers Karamazov* that there was nothing to worry about. My pretensions were actually even greater. I was shooting for Tolstoy. I wanted to write a great big nineteenth-century baseball novel where the prose was contemporary, where the plot was tight, with sudden juxtapositions, and jumps that you almost never encounter in nineteenth-century Russian literature, jumps more like those in contemporary film-making. So I wasn't concerned about the title. But my editor hated it. So I got on my computer and constructed a public opinion poll. I gave all my editor's arguments, and gave people space to suggest alternative titles. I asked for opinions: "Is *The Brothers K* a good title or should it be different?" I sent it out to about fifty people, threw the fifteen who disagreed with me in the garbage, sent those who agreed to my editor, and said "Look! It's a landslide!" I cheated and won. In honor of spitballers everywhere.

DB   In both *The River Why* and *The Brothers K,* you use an episodic style. I remember being frustrated when Gus meets the girl who then disappears for seventy-five or a hundred pages. But you're back to that style in *The Brothers K.*

DJD   Maybe I'm too patient. Also, the amount of material I had was overwhelming. I felt inadequate to impose order on it. But I also had a strong sense of where the novel had to go. Two things helped me structurally. One of them was deciding to break the novel up into novellas. When my mountain of material became six discrete novellas using the same characters, it began to feel much more manageable. But I didn't come to that for a long time. I'd written hundreds and hundreds of pages before I came up with Book One, Book Two, Book Three. But as soon as I came up with Book Four, "The Left Stuff," a section that deals with the havoc that Everett creates, everything came into focus. The book called "The Brothers K" is the one in which all of the brothers go through their most intense, transformative, purgative experiences. The earlier section, called "Dogmatomachy," is about the warring dogmas in terms of social perspective, religion, attitudes toward baseball, and outlooks on life. These broads topics allowed me to order hundreds of disconnected pages of rough draft, sketches, and vignettes.

DB   The structure here feels a bit like Faulkner.

DJD   To me it feels more like the TV program "L.A. Law." Almost every episode of that show had three discrete stories told in glimpses of a few minutes. It kept your attention by moving, usually at a fairly tense point, to a completely different story. The whole idea of the braid, braiding the lives of the brothers, became very appealing to me and I have to admit the idea came while I was watching "L.A. Law." I learned something from television!

DB There's a marvelous honesty in the book. Even a fairly nasty character like Beal gets that beautiful moment when he hits the home run. Kincaid recognizes that it was the most remarkable moment of this guy's life. He dances; he breaks rules. But then he reverts to his sad piety and staunch dogmatism. And there's Everett's glorious radicalism that we both admire and mourn. I'm remembering the scene where he takes on the professor over Vietnam issues. And the professor makes good sense. Everett is embarrassing there. There's a two-sidedness throughout the book.

DJD I think the novel, perhaps more than any art form, has been able to capture the fact that life is paradoxical. No matter how much you aim for sweetness and light, no matter how compassionate your actions, everything remains paradoxical. It's inescapable. Paradox grounds fiction, gives it a human reality that people respond to. We try to deny paradox, but we're mired in it. The greatest democracy on earth is founded on slavery and genocide. "All men are created equal," but Indians and blacks aren't men? Or take one of the greatest heroes of the abolitionist movement, Ralph Waldo Emerson. In one of his essays he talks about the worthlessness of the Chinese. He says at least we've "taught the Africans to carry our wood." Then there's another essay where he calls the Chinese the ugliest people on earth. *Ralph Waldo Emerson!* This wonderful man who overcame incredible personal suffering, this lucid mind. Because of such paradoxes, I can't allow my characters to show forth a great glory without also living it down. It's what life on earth seems to do to all of us. So there's Papa, dying from his cigarette addiction, still wanting the simple pleasure of holding a cigarette, telling his appalled daughter, "Love thine enemies, my girl."

DB I grew up in a factory town, and I think you got that business right too.

DJD There's a James Taylor song called "Factory Worker." "And it's me and my machine for the rest of the morning, for the rest of the afternoon, for the rest of my life." I've tasted that life, too. Plastics factory. Truck driver.

DB I suppose that's another way everything comes back to the father. His factory work is part of the sacrifice. There's the difference between Christianity and Christ-likeness in the character.

DJD His life is an *attempt* at sacrifice. But it fails. What I love about the father is the scene where he throws the baseball out of the stadium. So beautiful, but so futile — like art! That scene, by the way, makes the novel, in an underhanded way, an *anti*-baseball novel. The book came within one vote of winning a Casey Award, an award given to the best baseball book of the year. What won was a wonderful photo documentary of the Negro leagues. And I think the judges were right. Baseball in my book works only as metaphor. My love of baseball has a ceiling. It doesn't extend to the Bigs.

DB Papa's throwing the baseball out of the stadium was a way of saying what?

DJD That there are other things more important than one's art. That people matter more. This was extremely felt for me. At the time I was working twelve hour days, eight and nine days at a time. My son would come to see me for three or four days. I would have to spend some time, a few hours at least, working so it didn't go cold, the awful way that it can. Novels are like bonfires. When they stop burning, they grow cold and wet. You've got to throw *everything* into them. So here I was trying to make the death of a fictitious father meaningful while my own son is playing Nintendo or drawing pictures in my study, just to be near me. It made me feel broken! I felt burned by the whole paradox of the novel's father-son relationship and my own.

DB Do you hear from many people who identify with Laura, the mother?

DJD I hear from people whose family situations are so similar that they're shocked.

DB I know some readers have identified with Laura's feelings of protectiveness, her desire to see her children saved.

DJD When I go to Christian colleges, I meet people who identify with Laura. But I don't think those are the people who write me fan letters. People who identify with Laura don't really want to congratulate the author of a book like *The Brothers K.*

DB They feel you painted her as only destructive?

DJD Maybe. But I feel she's completely vindicated. I feel that way about a person in my life now, a dogmatic person who loved me. When you know a person's *whole* story, everything feels different. If you were the victim of Laura's kind of father, you wouldn't want a God who was loving and compassionate. You'd want Jehovah to kick this guy's ass in the afterlife. Difficult people make sense, but the difficulty is getting to know their whole story.

DB Another way I think of the book is as a consideration of prayer. There's Bet's prayer, "Papa hurts." And Everett's, "Dear God, if there is a God." And Irwin, of course.

DJD I agree that it's a book about prayer. Thanks for noticing. But for me personally, this is troublesome territory, this specific prayer stuff. I was at a Christian college last weekend, and somebody prayed at this dinner that was held in my honor. They thanked God that I was there. I felt so embarrassed. I thought, *don't bother God with this shit.* I feel it's God who is always there, and *we're* all absent. So try to be present!

DB Another of my favorite scenes is the one that occurs out by the baseball field when Kincaid decides he's not meant to be a baseball player, when he realizes that the coaches are different from him.

DJD The moment when you give up on the rules. What he goes through with his coaches is what I went through with political leaders, school teachers, and clergymen. I heard what they were saying, but I knew that theirs were not the voices for me. I heard them, but if God lives in me, they were just a distraction. There's a resonance that comes from within that these people are missing.

DB I have a friend whose husband read *The Brothers K* in two days. She said he laughed for the first day and cried for the second.

DJD We're mortal beings. Sometimes that's funny. Sometimes it's sad. The idea of a mortal being with an immortal spark inside it seems strange. But I see it as a comical idea, too. I wrote about this a lot through Everett's voice. I had him arguing with Kincaid for a hundred pages past the end of the novel. I wrote way past where the novel now ends. Everett's theory was that the body is an atheist. And that the mind is such a waffler that even to call it an agnostic is more specific than what the mind wants, because the mind is just all over the road. And the soul is of course the unkillable point of pure faith and belief. But the soul, because it's immortal, cannot be put at risk. To encounter the cross, to march in Jackson, Mississippi, in 1962, to go to jail instead of Vietnam — these are hardly victories for the soul because nothing bad can happen to the soul! Bad things and suffering occur to the mind and body. So it's the agnostic and the atheist who get kicked in the teeth as the devout soul drags them along through an incarnation. I'm just fascinated by that. Of course the body and mind are enlivened by the soul and have to be grateful. But more often I have the heretical feeling that the soul owes the body the greater thanks. That this stubborn self-seeking, pleasure-loving *animal* has to accomplish *spiritual* deeds! What a joke!

DB *The Brothers K* seems poised on the issue of affirmation or negation. At one point, you refer to the search for meaning as "a twice-hammered thumb." But then this jubilant Joon character comes from nowhere.

DJD With Joon, I was actually thinking of a specific person, a wonderful man who was raised Adventist, a jack Adventist like myself, who lives in Hawaii. He's a beneficent man whose name is Jim Koon, so I reversed the letters and made him Kim Joon. I made him Korean so the name would fit and just sort of took off. Just about the time I get really disgusted with Christianity, which happens frequently, I meet some Christian by whom I am totally charmed. It's happened all my life. I feel really smitten sometimes by those people willing to live graciously beneath all the baggage of the church. I'm never going to deal with all that baggage. But some Christians' lives seem wonderful in a way that a knee-jerk rejection of Christianity doesn't begin to take into account. Americans will reject anything about which it's possible to be ironic. But you can be ironic about *everything!* It's no basis for rejection! For example, Mark Twain was ironical about religious faith. He lived in the Gilded Age and was half-nauseated by the kind of feel-goodism you find in, say, William Dean Howells. But I think Twain is somebody who allowed his powers of irony and his keenness of observation to talk him right out of any kind of spiritual consolation. A voice in our time who comes dangerously close to the same sort of thing is Edward Abbey. I love Ed, and I wouldn't want him to be much nicer than he is, but his quotes about God? One is "God is love? *Not bloody likely!*" Great comedy. But when I'm faced with crisis or with death, I'd prefer a different scripture!

DB   One of the characters in *The Brothers K* comes up with the notion that she believes in God, and God is not really a nice person. Out of shame, one becomes an atheist. You don't really want to reach the position where you believe God is cruel.

DJD   The situation is much more mysterious than "God is cruel." There's a line on my wall from a philosopher friend, Henry Bugbee. Henry defines sacrilege as any human act "denying our involvement in a mystery." By that definition, every televangelist, every fundamentalist preacher, and every atheist, too, is committing constant sacrilege through the denial of the mysteriousness of human life and the ways of grace.

DB   Your characters do get to that mystery. Joon accepts God's "No comment." Even Sister Harg joins in the pilgrimage to save Irwin. There's also this business of mystery and acceptance in the *River Teeth* stories. And "The Mickey Mantle Koan" from *Harper's* is in here. But talk about the story "The King of Epoxy." I read it as being about the writing life. There's something about the writer who "sacrifices everything for the nothing of beautiful words." You seem to capture the curse as well as the calling of the profession.

DJD   You're right about that story, "The King of Epoxy." Somebody once told me that Michael Crichton has a meter beside his computer that tells him how much he's earning. It's a little motivation thing. He makes maybe $30,000 an hour for sitting at his desk, and likes to watch it mount up. I don't know if it's true, but it's funny. I should have one too. *85 cents!* But it goes back to what I was saying before about the body. From the physical point of view, writing is tough. I have varicose veins in the sides of my knees and dorked shoulders and other problems to show for the number of hours I've spent sitting in this very posture. My body would be much happier if I were doing something wildly different. But my body doesn't rule this room. "The King of Epoxy" is my best attempt to express how it feels to me to write a novel. The sacrifice, the transformation. Most people never figured this out. One reviewer said that it sounded like Duncan drank fifteen cups of coffee and sat up all night, writing whatever came into his head. But I spent months cranking that story out. And I love its idea that the writer's or artist's life is a bridge that dissolves behind you as you go, and you really can't go back the way you came. That archeologist character is absolutely addicted to his work, and that leads to loss of self somehow. And "the nothing of beautiful words" alludes to the nothing that the mind can say about God, the nothing that's the emptiness in Buddhism. The nothing and the everything are a lot alike.

DB   Words like "iconoclast," "mystic," and "idealist" have been used to describe you. Are these close?

DJD   Well, there's a dichotomy in me between the credulous devotee and the complete skeptic. The devotee loves Love. The skeptic prides himself on his iconoclasm. No matter which of the two I'm being, there's that other side too. I invoke Kabir's great line: "Between the two of us, God, who's to blame?"

TERENCE FAHERTY

Doggedly Low Key

1954 — Born in Trenton, New Jersey
1991 — *Deadstick*
1992 — *Live to Regret*
1993 — *The Lost Keats*
1994 — *Die Dreaming*
1996 — *Kill Me Again*
　　　　Prove the Nameless
1997 — *Come Back Dead*
　　　　The Ordained
1999 — *Orion Rising*
2000 — *Raise the Devil*
2005 — *In a Teapot*
　　　　The Confessions of Owen Keane

Lives in Indianapolis, Indiana

Terence Faherty gave up the writing of computer manuals to take up the writing of detective novels. Over the last decade, he has introduced two new sleuths to the whodunit world, Owen Keane and Scott Elliott. Keane, featured in seven Faherty novels, is a failed seminarian and amateur detective whose quests generally turn out to be metaphysical. Unlike the Keane novels, which are more or less set in the contemporary era, the three Elliott novels evoke post–World

War II Hollywood and feature a former soldier working as a private security detective. Faherty's detectives tell their own stories through first-person narratives that turn out to be as much about their own idealisms and struggles as about this or that crime. Thus the beauty of the books.

Faherty, who has won a Shamus Award and been nominated for a prestigious Edgar, breaks most of the latest rules for the genre: there's no guts and little blood, nor forensic analysis of the crime venues, no dramatic sex scenes, not much shock and little violence. But Faherty's novels are page-turners, nonetheless, because he features a thoughtful exploration of character that includes a distinct spiritual questing, an attempt, as one reviewer says, "to track down God." These are mystery novels with something really big going on.

I spoke with Terence Faherty at his home in Indianapolis, Indiana. He had just finished the latest Elliott novel, *Raise the Devil*. We discussed his resistance to self-promotion, the vagaries of the writing business, Raymond Chandler, Dorothy L. Sayers, and *Casablanca*. We talked of how his Catholic faith informs the fascination in his stories with confession, forgiveness, and synchronicity and about how a writer of technical manuals gets into the murder racket.

DB So you have a website. What do you make of the burgeoning electronic culture? Is this a bad time to be a writer?

TF I'm only semi-literate in the electronic technology, but I am optimistic as a midlist writer whose early stuff is out of print. (And "midlist writer" has become such a bad term to have hung on you.) I'm hoping to get *Deadstick* and *Live to Regret*, the early Keane books, back into circulation because of the new publishing options.

DB You're thinking of e-books?

TF That or on demand publishing, where the publisher no longer has to stockpile physical copies. You order a copy of *Deadstick;* they print it and ship it. I see a lot of promise in that. No, it's not a bad time to be a writer. I think this will be an interesting time, especially for a writer trying to break in. The only thing that worries me about electronic publishing is that we could lose the gatekeeper function that publishing houses have historically filled. Although I probably shouldn't be worried about the big publishers. Whenever sweeping technological changes come along, we hear predictions that the big companies will be hurt. Usually, they end up being the ones who take over the new field. So I think the publishing houses will survive, and that's not a bad thing. The idea of Stephen King and everybody else firing out unedited books on the Internet scares me.

DB   So the danger of the Internet is that it is a mile wide and an inch deep; we could get too many words, too much information?

TF   That's already happening. The Internet is already the greatest distribution method for pornography that's ever been invented. And it could function the same way for misinformation or disinformation. As a society we've gotten to the point where we don't debate each other's facts so much as ignore or deny each other's facts. The Internet provides a tremendous amount of raw material but not much healthy debate. And it's eliminated some important checks and balances involving the verification of information.

In the case of electronically published fiction, the dropped step may be editing. My editor at St. Martin's Press has made a lot of important contributions to my books; working without her would be like working without a net.

DB   You've been a professional writer for how long?

TF   I was a technical writer for fifteen years and I've been writing fiction full-time since 1991. I began doing technical manuals back in the days when information technology was called data processing. Big companies would develop their own computer systems. I wrote operating manuals for a bank and then a power company.

DB   How did you manage that final jump in 1991?

TF   The novels were what I'd always wanted to do, and when I sold *Deadstick* I got a two-book contract. That's not an unusual deal; publishers like to get that second book cheap. I kept my day job at the power company and tried to write the second book evenings and weekends. But I kept thinking, "If this book fails, you'll always wonder if it might have succeeded if you'd worked at it full-time." I didn't want to have that question in my mind. We didn't have kids and economically it seemed feasible, but I was very naïve. I thought I'd either make it financially as a writer or they'd ask me to leave. I didn't know there was this area in between, this "midlist" business.

DB As a professional mystery writer, are you able to enjoy other people's mystery novels? Are you adept at solving other novelist's puzzles?

TF The career has impacted my reading. I used to read mysteries obsessively for relaxation, but now I can't really get into them. I'm either saying "He didn't do that very well" or "What is she up to with this?" I'm either jealous or irritated. So for relaxation I'm more likely to read historical fiction now or stay out of fiction altogether and read biography and history. Mystery movies have suffered the same way, though I was never very good at guessing the endings.

DB You're not like your detective, Owen Keane, who always figures out the mystery before anyone else?

TF No. Someone in *Orion Rising* comments that Owen always figures out the murderer when watching *Perry Mason* reruns, but that's no great feat. Those shows were a little heavy-handed. But Jan, my wife, tends to figure out a mystery show before me. For one thing, I'm distracted by the whole jealousy thing. We went to *LA Confidential,* a good movie, but I kept thinking what a great movie they could have made of *Kill Me Again,* the first of my Scott Elliott books, with the same actors, sets, and costumes.

DB Have you sold anything to movies?

TF No, I've never even been optioned.

DB I recently ran across a Spanish movie, *Passage to Lisbon,* that struck me as a rewrite of your novel *Kill Me Again.*

TF That would be amazing. I wrote that novel trying to stay out of legal trouble with the people who own *Casablanca.* I never dreamed I'd be inspiring someone to pirate me.

DB Do you try to respond to all your readers who ask questions via your website?

TF A fair number. I'm bad at getting on there and staying up with it. I'm ashamed to say that the whole self-promotion thing is something I don't have a real talent for. I'm a little embarrassed by it.

DB   A writer these days is expected to be involved in marketing and sales.

TF   Very much. And to do book signings. And to speak at conventions. And I find it challenging. All writers have horror stories about book signings. They can be anything from the best night of your life to simply two hours in the dentist's chair, and I've had both experiences. I've had people come in with every book I've written, and it touches me so much. But at that moment I feel like saying, "Turn around and get out of here." If you really love the books why would you want to meet the author? Where can the relationship go from here? Or there's the signing when nobody shows up. The bookstore owner is busy apologizing, thinking he's let me down.

I was in down in Louisville doing a signing for *Kill Me Again*, and the owner wanted me to do a reading. When I showed up, they had a podium and seats and one guy sitting there waiting for me to read. The owner insisted that if I'd start reading, others would show up. So I read a page or so and looked up and there was still just this one guy. And I had an overpowering urge to say, "Look, there's a bar down the street. I'll buy you a beer and tell you how this turns out." That was one of the negative ones. But I'd only driven an hour. I've driven a lot longer and done less.

DB   I read somewhere that you've said you "wanted to be Hemingway but couldn't make the weight." Is the mystery novelist still regarded so differently from the literary novelist?

TF   Oh yes. It's something I've struggled with. I think Raymond Chandler had a big chip on his shoulder about that. He could never be considered a serious novelist because he wrote in a specific genre. It kept me out of mystery writing for a long time, even though I loved mysteries.

Then I happened to read an essay on the mystery by Chandler and one by Dorothy L. Sayers that were opposite sides of the debate on whether the mystery could ever be a serious novel. Sayers said no and Chandler said yes and cited Sayers as an example of a writer whose writing was so good that she transcended the genre. Around the same time I attended a talk by four touring mystery writers: Liza Cody, Peter Lovesey, Paula Gosling, and Michael Lewin. They were all so articulate and so interesting that I came away thinking it would be an honor to be part of that fraternity. So I decided to give mystery writing a shot. But I know that we don't get the same critical attention.

DB You've experimented in other genres. You've done short stories.

TF Yes and I'm very proud of some of them. But the problem with my attempts at a Hemingway novel was that I just didn't have a story to tell. I come from an Irish, storytelling family and that's really all I've ever wanted to do — tell a story. But I didn't have much of a life story, and I'm jealous of the one I have. So I would write three or four chapters of a novel and hit a wall. Mystery stories gave me a built-in story framework. This murder has to be resolved, and I could hang so many other things within that framework.

DB But some reviewers label your stories "low key." You even have some books in which nobody really gets murdered. Do you feel some dissonance with Michael Connelly, Dennis Lehane, Patricia Cornwell, and the popular mystery novel these days? There's forensics, and lots of blood, lots of violence, lots of sex.

TF I've always felt out of step with that. I'm not only called "low key." One critic recently called me "doggedly low key."

DB Do you get pressure from editors to get with it.

TF Some. St. Martin's isn't a big blood and guts house, but there's been a little pressure for more action and more violence. Not so much for more sex but more romance, certainly. Keane has romantic encounters, but most of them are short-lived. I made a decision early on that my models for mystery were the older writers who were not very bloody. I'd never read much Mickey Spillane, for example, and he's fairly mild compared to a lot of people now. But I decided I simply would not compete with this very violent stuff. I couldn't. I do resent the fact that those books are considered more serious by the critics than my stuff, when in fact some of them are fairly routine in terms of plot and character. The extreme violence makes them seem cutting edge. I don't resent their sales. I accept the fact that they'll sell more. It's understandable. That stuff is written to read like a literary roller coaster ride and roller coasters are a lot of fun.

DB   But you've gotta get higher and higher. The thrill quotient keeps getting turned up?

TF   Yes. So they keep pushing the envelope. But I'm writing about an amateur sleuth, and I'm trying to be realistic in my own way. Owen Keane would just not be involved with slashers or serial killers. He's obsessive about mystery solving, but he's always sucked into a fairly quiet mystery.

DB   But your other detective, Scott Elliott, is closer to the hard-boiled genre. When you say you're thinking of the older writers, you mean Chandler and Ross Macdonald, not so much John Dickson Carr?

TF   Right. Elliott, my Hollywood historical detective, is a self-conscious attempt to move closer to the hard-boiled detective model.

DB   But in the second book he gets married. Despite Dashiell Hammett's Nick and Nora, that's just not done.

TF   There's a certain part of my nature that says if everyone else is going right I'll go left. I'd learned very early on that in this genre you don't marry off your protagonist, so I thought I had to try it. I wanted the Elliott series to be seven or eight books, taking him through his life fairly quickly, moving him from the young World War II veteran to an old man in Hollywood. He'd see his Hollywood destroyed over the course of his life. At the same time, I could tell the story of a marriage, the ups and downs.

DB   So he's still married in the new book, *Raise the Devil*?

TF   Yes. And his boss, Paddy Maguire, is close to retiring. Elliott is still carrying on his love/hate relationship with Hollywood, fighting his rearguard action for this unrequited love. I'm going to see how *Raise the Devil* sells before I decide if I want to continue his story. The Elliott novels were supposed to be a more commercial series to help support Keane. But the Keane novels have consistently outsold the Elliott ones, even though an Elliott, *Come Back Dead,* won the Shamus Award.

DB   So you have developed a loyal following with the Keane series.

TF   Yes, although Keane doesn't sell in huge numbers. They sell enough for St. Martin's to keep asking me to do another thankfully. That's one of the odd things they don't teach you in writing class. The publisher can make money at a sales level where the writer can't make a living. At least a publisher like St. Martin's, which doesn't spend much on promotion, can.

If your publisher invests more in marketing, then they naturally have a greater sales expectation. Simon and Schuster put more money into promoting the first two Elliott books, and they expected more in return than they got. Part of the problem was that I'd originally sold the series to Macmillan, and then they were bought out by Simon and Schuster. So I landed on a strange editor's doorstep like a baby in a basket, and there wasn't that kind of emotional commitment you get from an editor who has picked you out and really wants to see you succeed. This guy was a good editor, but he didn't have any real personal investment in me.

DB   So do you go back to Keane now?

TF   Actually I'm working on a non-series mystery, set in Ireland. It's currently called *The Unquiet*. The protagonists are two American brothers who go to Ireland to find the ghost town where their grandfather was born. And they get interested in an old, mysterious death. It was going to be the book that moved me a little further away from mystery and toward the mainstream novel, but my editor and my agent and everyone else pushed me to build up the mystery element. It's my own fault for not making a cleaner break with the book's first draft. I sort of had one foot on the dock and one in the canoe, as far as breaking with mystery was concerned. The original version of the book did have a mystery element. And one of the brothers is a mystery writer.

DB   Your agent reads everything?

TF   Yes. I'm with Curtis Brown. Agents have really become the first readers for publishing houses.

DB   If I may say so, you seem to sell yourself short. You've won the Shamus Award. You've been nominated for the Edgar Allan Poe Award. Doesn't that make you more confident?

TF   It has kept me going. It's like making a birdie on the last hole of a really terrible round of golf.

DB   So these awards are like academy awards for sleuth writers?

TF   The Edgar is the big one. It's given at a banquet in New York City every spring. The others are given for subgenres. The Shamus is for private eye stuff; the Agatha is for the cozy subgenre. And there are others.

DB   Do you get support and fellowship out of this?

TF   Sure, at the awards dinners and also at the conventions we have for fans of the mystery, the Bouchercon and the smaller ones. You bump into other writers having the same problems that you're having. You're reminded that you're not alone.

DB   I understand you carefully outline all your novels.

TF   I do.

DB   You pretty much have a book in place before you start?

TF   Right.

DB   That's not the way most writers do it, at least if we can believe them.

TF   Mention "outlining" and you immediately divide writers into opposing camps. Some writers say that no work of art can be planned out. Robert Olen Butler said that in the interview he did with you. I'd like to take him into the Sistine Chapel. Others just have this vague feeling that outlining is not as creative somehow. But whether an author outlines or not simply has to do with the way that author's mind works. I don't want to write eight or nine months on a project and not get a book out of it. I want to know going in that I have a story to tell. Also, as Ross Macdonald said, mystery is more dependent than any other form of fiction on a logical structure. You either have to have it in mind when you start or you have to do a heck of a lot of rewriting to make sure the logical structure is there. You can't have a reader finishing a book and feeling that the solution didn't make any sense or that the characters' motivation wasn't clear.

So I outline and at some length. I'll write a six- to eight-thousand-word plot summary. My editor at St. Martin's will read it and make suggestions. That's a way to avoid having a manuscript come back with an "I don't believe this" attached. Some of my plots hinge on points that are pretty offbeat. *Prove the Nameless,* for example, where the retired cop so identifies with the dead murderer that he begins to act on his behalf. One critic did not like that, incidentally. It was too much of a reach. Anyway, I want my editor to know where I'm going from the start. I don't want her to tell me after I've written the entire book that she doesn't believe the premise.

I feel that during outlining I'm being creative on the macro level, seeing the big picture. Then, day to day, I can be creative on the micro level. My outline may say only that Owen Keane goes to a Pocono resort and gets information about an old summer camp. That's all I have. So when I write the scene I have to come up with the character, Rose, who makes that scene work. But I don't have to start every workday wondering what Owen's going to do that day. I always know.

DB There's a linear quality to your approach to detective novel writing that is so completely unlike Owen Keane, the character. I knew you weren't Owen, but what is the role, if any, of autobiography in your books? Did you ever want to be a private eye?

TF Yes, as a kid. I'm more frequently asked if I ever wanted to be a priest, since Owen is a failed seminarian. The answer to that is no. I thought about it because I went to Catholic school in Trenton, New Jersey, and then to Boston College, just like Keane. He finished there, whereas I transferred. And that's where our biographies part company. But obviously everything that happens to me is part of these books. I was in an automobile accident and broke my arm. Keane, in the very next book, *Prove the Nameless,* broke his arm, and he was in an automobile accident in a later short story called "The Third Manny." I didn't want to waste the experience.

My story gets into the books though other characters besides Keane. I'm convinced that the mystery novel can be a serious, even literary, novel. But whether the mystery series can, that's another question. If you see the novel as the record of the most enlightening incident in the protagonist's life, an epiphany moment, and you have the same protagonist over the course of seven books, then you have a problem. Readers will wonder why this guy needs seven epiphanies. Is his memory bad? Is he not taking notes? To get around this, I use epiphany characters. Each book has a different character facing an epiphany. Keane may be the facilitator of this experience. Or the focal character may be the murder victim. Keane must understand this character's experience before he can solve the mystery. For example, in *The Lost Keats* a character named Michael Crosley learns, just as he's moving into adulthood, that he's totally misjudged his father. The realization undermines his own sense of identity, sets him up for the events that lead to his death. That whole revelation episode was autobiographical. I couldn't have it happen to Keane, so I aired it through another character.

DB An epiphany like that would have been the end of Keane?

TF Yes. I don't want him figuring out too much of his life.

DB I wondered about that exact issue with *Orion Rising* and, to some degree, with *The Ordained*. Your most recent Keane novel, *Orion Rising*, explains Keane's fascination with getting at the truth, his enrolling in the seminary, and his subsequent searches. The story of the brutal rape at Cleveland Park Circle is, as Keane admits, the private business of his life. With that solved, much of Keane is cleared up.

TF That's true. At the very least, the Mary Fitzgerald issue is resolved. I mean, we understand why he lost her, what he gave her up for, and he gets to say good-bye to her in a way. I'm unsure what's going to happen to Keane next. That's one of the reasons I've been working on a non-series book. I remember thinking at the end of *Orion Rising* that if I was hit by a bus the next day, people would say, "At least he got his series finished."

DB How did you happen on the character Owen Keane? There's a reference to the radio character, Mr. Keen, "tracer of lost persons," but Keane doesn't credit that.

TF I took a writing class back in 1978 and wrote a mystery story called "St. Jimmy." That was the first Keane and it pops up as a background story in some of the early books. This is the story of Keane meeting the kid at summer retreat who claims to have spoken to God. I came close to publishing it just this year, but it's a hard story to publish. There's not only no murder in it, there's no traditional crime in it. But I wrote that for the class and I gave Keane a lot of my own characteristics, as writers tend to do in their early work. When I began the first Keane novel, *Deadstick,* I wanted to give him a failure in his past to make him more interesting. I came up with the idea of his being a seminary dropout. That's the unforgivable sin for him, his moment of doubt, and it was somehow autobiographical for me. I was working as a technical writer in a power company, though I'd dreamt of being a novelist. I felt like I'd fallen away from a higher calling. And from Fiction Writing 101, I knew I couldn't just write about a technical writer who wanted to be a novelist. I had to step away from it. So I ended up with an amateur detective who once wanted to be a priest.

DB   But you know so much about the seminary business. You must have had your own altar boy days?

TF   I did. In fact the priest who was in charge of altar boys at our parish was named Keane. That's where I got Owen's last name, although I like the tie to the old radio detective. Owen's a tracer of lost persons too.

DB   Do you like the label "metaphysical detective" for Keane?

TF   Yes, a *New York Times* reviewer hung that on him. I liked it, so I quote it frequently.

DB   That reviewer was on the mark in seeing the whole series as an attempt at the large, spiritual questions. For Keane, the real mystery is not this or that murder, but his own interior mystery. Where does that come from?

TF   It's always been there since "St. Jimmy," the very first story. I knew from the start that Keane was going to be a guy who "can't distinguish between the large and small mysteries." (That's from a *Philadelphia Inquirer* review.) Keane sees the potential of solving the big mystery by finding clues in little human mysteries. Even with the first books I was trying to reach beyond genre writing and wanted a guy who was going to be interested in other questions beyond who did it. The metaphysical tag scared me a little bit because I felt the critics might be writing checks that the books couldn't cash. But I've tried hard to keep Keane from just becoming another amateur sleuth, to stay on the trail. I hope I've succeeded.

DB   Sometimes, as in *The Ordained* in particular, religion is really the subject. It's not a religious book but it's a book in which religion is *the* question. You even have novels where Unamuno shows up.

TF   Yes. I like him. He's ultimately a sad guy, just like Keane.

DB   There's often a theological stirring going on. Does this come from your Catholic background?

TF   I suppose. And maybe the questioning is the Irish part. But the religious schooling was a big influence, of course, not to mention my own quirkiness. I define a novelist as somebody who continues to ask questions, lives with mystery. My neighbor, the accountant, is only interested in those questions that have answers. (I realize that's a slight on those accountants who are in fact wondering over the same issues I puzzle over. But you see the point.) Keane represents my idea of the artist in society who continually asks questions that other people have resolved or don't care about in the first place. And he's between the two camps: the people who have dismissed those questions and the people who are certain of their answers.

Those two points of view are reflected in my favorite image from *The Ordained,* the image of a man lost in the snow. He thinks he's walking a straight line, but because one of his legs is shorter than the other, he's actually walking in a circle and so never gets anywhere. The story is introduced by Krystal Morell, the doctor who wants to be a believer but isn't. For her it's an analogy for her own despair. She thought she was directing her life toward a certain goal, but she's ended up back where she started. When Brother Dennis, the believer, hears the analogy of the man in the snow, he has a completely different take. He thinks it's a wonderful idea. This guy who's wandering aimlessly is forming this perfect pattern with his footsteps, a symbol of the eternal. The key is seeing it from the right perspective. God's.

DB   At the core of your work that question of pattern, or providence, seems to swirl. Is it really God that Owen Keane is trying to track down?

TF   He thinks it is. *And* I think it is.

DB   What about the bumbling?

TF   Keane is something of a bumbler. But one of the joys of every book is that moment at the end when everybody who sold him short finally realizes that he has more going on upstairs than they thought. I take the reviews that stress his bumbling a little personally because when I write these books I'm always thinking about what I would do in a given situation. Assuming I'm not a trained detective, and I'm not, how would I find certain information? Where would I go? Who would I ask? And that's what I have Keane do. He does tend to jump to conclusions; I'll admit that.

DB   He comes up with a potential conclusion that you know must be wrong because you've still got fifty pages to go.

TF   A dead giveaway. When you write a first-person detective story, your detective can't be what critics of the mystery call a Great Detective. The classic Great Detectives, Sherlock Holmes, Nero Wolfe, Hercule Poirot, all have other people telling their stories. Holmes is seldom on the wrong track, but Watson always is, and he can misrepresent the information presented to the reader, which is necessary for the mystery fiction to work. Because Keane tells his own story, he has to be wrong himself for most of the book. Many of the reports he gets, like the narrative of the disappearances in *The Ordained,* are distortions that Keane has to consider, at least for a while, to be the truth.

DB   So the reader has to take the missteps along with the detective. Somebody tells Scott Elliott that maybe his third read of the evidence will be the charm.

TF   Right. Elliott, another first-person narrator, also tends to follow a false trail. In *Raise the Devil,* Paddy implies that Elliott has been slow to spot the obvious. Elliott asks Paddy if he's accusing him of being "slow on the uptake." Paddy replies, "Neville Chamberlain was faster."

DB   One of the many great one-liners in your books.

TF   Some of them are what one critic called "relentless Chandlerisms." "She was higher than Eisenhower's hairline." That sort of thing. Those are fun for me.

DB   Having noted that the Keane novels are about a quest for God, we've moved close to the issue of the religious book. Your books, it seems to me, raise more intriguing religious questions than do many of the books sold in so-called Christian bookstores. But your books wouldn't be sold there because they contain bad words.

TF   Though not enough bad words to please my editors.

DB   What do you make of this?

TF   I find the little I've heard about Christian publishing to be fascinating. The idea that there are Christian books, especially those related to millennial and apocalyptic matters, that are selling so well. And that the secular bean counters have made a conscious decision to censor or ignore these books by omitting their sale numbers from the popular bestseller lists, like the *New York Times* list. Nonetheless, I hear the sales are phenomenal, and I suppose it is encouraging that readers are interested.

We're living in an interesting age to be identified as a religious person. If someone had told me in 1968 or 1969, when I was getting out of grammar school, that before I was fifty Christians would be a marginalized group, or on their way to being a marginalized group, I would have said there's no way that's going to happen. I thought it was interesting that many of the writers you interviewed for your first book were defensive about being labeled Christian. It's like they're afraid it will kill their sales, and they'll never again be invited to a dinner party.

I'm still a practicing Catholic and a member of the Holy Spirit at Geist Parish. In fact, I was a member of the liturgy team until they changed our regular mass to the youth mass and replaced all the gray-haired ushers with kids. Now I just sit in the congregation and complain about the music being too loud. But I am a Christian writer, I suppose.

DB   But have you ever been identified in that way, invited to speak for a church group or something?

TF   No. When I wrote the first Keane novel, *Deadstick,* I actually downplayed the seminarian aspect because I thought it would alienate readers. My editor encouraged me to build it up. She said it would be that thing that would set this series apart from others. So I was able to use the idea of Keane being "more interested in absolutions than solutions." (I stole the line from my brother, Tim, who read an early draft of *Deadstick* and made that comment.) The more I revisit the books, the more I see that Keane, the failed priest, is functioning as a priest in terms of facilitating people's absolutions, making and receiving confessions. Part of the tragedy in *Orion Rising,* for example, comes about because Keane fails to make public the confession of the real murderer.

DB What role does research play in your books? You live here on Geist Reservoir. Is that where you get the name for Gary Geist in *Prove the Nameless*? Your books have intriguing details: water in the oil will cause an airplane to crash, marijuana farming in the middle of corn fields, World War II weaponry, computer tricks, and UFOs. I'm always wondering if you're using historical fact or just making stuff up.

TF I've been drawn more and more into research over the course of the two series. As a writer, I'd rather make it up than look it up. I don't think people read fiction to get information they can get from an encyclopedia. They read because you've created a "vivid and continuous dream," as John Gardner says. That's something I think about when I'm writing. If you don't see the dream clearly and vividly, the reader never will. But you've also got to get things right, and it's a kick for me to work the history into the Elliott books, like the role of the Klan in Indiana in *Come Back Dead* and the Nazi and Communist issues in Hollywood in the 1930s and 1940s in *Kill Me Again*. And you can sabotage a plane by putting water in the oil. I ran across that in Ernest K. Gann's autobiography, *Fate Is the Hunter*.

DB So what do you do, run across that reference and jot it down somewhere?

TF Right, I squirrel it away. For example, the new book, *Raise the Devil,* also involves airplane sabotage. Older airplanes used to have external braces that were put on their control surfaces when they were parked to keep the wind from batting them about. If you tried to take off without removing these braces, which were called gust locks, you'd crash. I read that the first B-17 ever built crashed because they hadn't removed a gust lock. In fact, that was the cause of the accident that killed the University of Evansville's basketball team a few years back. So I squirreled that fact away and now it's useful.

Before I wrote *The Lost Keats,* I had been reading a biography of Keats and ran across a footnote indicating that John Keats had had a brother who'd actually moved to Kentucky. Keats apparently sent all of his poems to this brother. So I used that. My editor had me put an author's note at the beginning of the book explaining that historical detail. I was afraid that would give the mystery away, but she said people would want to know that I didn't make it up. I think that author's note was one of the reasons that book did so well. The *Publishers Weekly* reviewer liked that odd little fact.

DB Even your geographical details seem meticulous. Whether Keane is in New Jersey or Boston or on the Boston College campus, you seem to have gone there and walked the area.

TF I do, when possible, visit the site. I went back to Boston College, for example, after I finished the first draft of *Orion Rising* to check my memory. I deliberately moved one huge building to a new spot and called it by a wrong name. It was the theater, which I renamed for Leonard Nimoy, Boston College's most famous graduate. I almost always change something so readers will know that I'm not writing a travelogue. I'm creating a world and I'll bend it however I want. But I like to work with maps.

I went to Michigan City, which is right on Lake Michigan, when I wrote the chapter in *The Ordained* in which Keane visits the prison there. You get happy accidents that way. For example, I got lost that day, and when I finally spotted the prison, the first thing I saw was one of the watchtowers. But I was convinced I was seeing a lighthouse because of all the nautical references I'd already seen around town. I liked the idea that the area had set me up to expect one thing, a lighthouse, and it had turned out to be something else, a prison. I saw it as a symbol for the misdirection of the entire book. So I had Keane get lost and duplicate my experience.

DB But you didn't run into a woman who filled you in on prison life.

TF No. I'd met her before somewhere else. I needed her to explain how a prisoner can have influence outside the prison walls. And she gives Keane good advice about keeping his mouth shut. That's tough for Keane.

DB What about your fascination with old cars that comes into the Elliott books?

TF Oh yes, I have a collection of lanterns from antique automobiles, much older cars than Elliott would drive. I can't afford the whole car, so I hunt down these old driving lights. Elliott likes to have the latest nice car. Keane is the sort of guy who would drive the same car for the rest of his life.

DB A Karmann-Ghia?

TF In the early books. And it will come back if Keane does. He's never sold it. But the Elliott books are fun because he gets a new car every year, and he always picks an automobile company that's about to go out of business. So I get to play with all these beautiful old machines.

DB You have a fondness for opening a book with a dream sequence that suggests themes. Why that approach?

TF I started that with *Deadstick*. During my rewriting, I decided that the book started slowly. That's a general problem with whodunits, especially if you have an amateur sleuth. A leggy blonde can walk into Marlowe's office and start the ball rolling, but an amateur sleuth has to sidle sideways into his cases. So a whodunit can begin with a lot of exposition, which was the problem I saw with *Deadstick*. Instead of going for a structural fix, I wrote that brief prologue, something out of Keane's subconscious, jumbling together the elements of the story. It is a promise to the reader that something interesting is going to happen. But I don't give them enough information to give the mystery away. And I've used the same technique since, in *The Lost Keats* for instance. It is a way to be provocative. It's analogous to the little teaser that they used to show before the commercial break in a dramatic television series.

Sometimes I use the prologue to describe events that occurred before the time of the story, as in *Live to Regret*. In later books like

The Ordained and *Orion Rising,* I've been writing little two-minute mysteries that introduce Keane's tendency to compulsively solve mysteries. I use these often at readings. They play well at a Barnes & Noble.

DB   And you come up with fascinating characters. Where did the Skiles character, in *Deadstick,* come from?

TF   He was a guy that I was working with when I wrote that book. I frequently use a real person. I liked Skiles so much, his voice came so easily, that I wanted to use him again. So he reappeared in *Live to Regret.*

DB   He is vaguely Thoreauvian, a wise man on the hill. Yet there's something false about him too.

TF   His past is explained in a short story I just wrote called "Main Line Lazarus." I sent it to *Ellery Queen* magazine. I don't know whether they'll take it because it's tied so tightly to *Deadstick.* It starts two or three days after *Deadstick* ends when Keane goes back into the New Jersey Pine Barrens to find his Karmann-Ghia.

DB   What about your minor characters like Harry, Brother Dennis, Mary, and Sister Theresa? She gets one of the great speeches in *Live to Regret:*

"I mean — television — has changed the world. Absolutely changed it. You see it most in the kids. Name one subject that a nine-year-old of 1910 knew more about than his parents. You can't. There wasn't one. But ask the same thing of a nine-year-old today and the answer's obvious. Television. The kids watch hours and hours of it. They know more about the latest fads than their parents possibly could. That's what television really sells: fads, crazes, new styles. It's the chrome on the Buick, if you know what I mean. They can't come out with a new Buick every year, so they change the chrome. That's all television teaches kids, the latest chrome. No ideas, no substance. But it's enough to convince the kids they're smarter than their folks, that they know more about what's going on. That's the root of ninety percent of the problems these days. Parents can't pass on the important things they've learned because the kids think they know it all. But all they know is the chrome. They're specialists in chrome."

TF She's a tiger, isn't she? All of these characters are people I've known. Brother Dennis, from *The Lost Keats,* is based on a priest from my high school. He had a boxer's demeanor and the kids respected him, even though he was no great preacher. He looked like he'd been around. I mixed in elements of one of my brothers and got somebody that I liked and wanted to use again. And years later, when I brought him back in *The Ordained,* it was like he hadn't been away.

Keane is constantly meeting people that are having crises of faith or identity. It's like the Raymond Chandler stories. Everybody Marlowe meets in those novels is up to no good. They're shady people. It's unlike the world of Sherlock Holmes where most people are respectable and solving the crime is finding the one aberrant person in that society. By the time you get to Chandler, everybody is aberrant and Marlowe is just trying to find the one whose guilt matches a particular crime. With Keane, everybody is not necessarily on the same spiritual quest, but all of them are in the same boat spiritually.

DB Like Krystal Morell in *The Ordained*?

TF Exactly. Krystal actually reaches out towards this Adventist community at the end of the book, even though she is a rational character, a doctor. She has a void she needs to fill. In *Prove the Nameless,* someone compares Keane to the character in the Mel Gibson movie *The Road Warrior.* That nails it for me. In that movie, survivors of a nuclear holocaust are all driving around vehicles they've assembled from the bits and pieces of wrecked cars and trucks. The connection to the Keane stories is the idea that today people are cobbling together their own faith systems out of different pieces of what their parents gave them and what society gave them, and coming up with some real crazy combinations. Those are the kind of people that Keane is drawn to. And I'm drawn to them as a writer, I guess.

DB Do you know Loren Estleman's work? His world is like Marlowe's world. Amos Walker, his detective, goes around unearthing disreputable people in Detroit.

TF Yes. The detective story always reflects its society. It was born in the pre–World War I society that thought science was going to solve all our problems. It evolved to keep pace with the social disintegration of the century. Now we have vigilante detectives. It's not unusual for the detective to just blow the criminal away in the end of the story.

DB   I've wondered if the O.J. business has influenced the genre. Michael Connelly's recent book, *Angel Walk,* is one of many where the lines between the good guys and the bad guys are pretty fuzzy.

TF   That trend goes back at least as far as Mickey Spillaine. Remember *I, the Jury?* Mike Hammer is the judge, jury, and executioner. He's a step past the Marlowe type and, as you say, a model for many writers today.

DB   But you don't tidy up everything in your novels. In *Die Dreaming,* for example, Maureen gets away with it.

TF   Life is untidy. I couldn't defend these books as works of art if everything was tidy. Keane always solves a mystery, but he never really gets the answers he's after. There's always a sense of incompleteness. And because he's not an official detective, he doesn't feel obligated to hand everybody over at the end. Remember he doesn't turn in Professor Mott in *The Lost Keats.* He just gives up and goes away.

DB   It would seem logical that the further you go with a series the more you hedge yourself in. Each book inherits details from the last. Is that stifling in a way?

TF   Having Keane be fairly close to me in the biography department helps. I never have to worry about certain parts of his backstory. I've thought of keeping a journal of vital statistics about the major characters. Height, weight, color of hair.

But part of the challenge — and fun — of writing a series is trying to fit everything together, even the mistakes. During the editing of *Orion Rising* I wanted to check how I'd spelled Karmann-Ghia in *Deadstick.* (My copy editor wanted a different spelling.) Anyway, flipping back through *Deadstick* I found a reference to a one-page character named Manny who rents a parking space to Keane. That discovery bothered me because later, in *Die Dreaming,* Owen is working in a bar in Atlantic City and his supervisor's name is Manny. I hated that I'd used that unusual name twice without realizing it. I stewed about it for a couple of days and then decided I could fix it by writing a short story called "The Third Manny." In it Keane meets a Vietnamese kid, Manny Vu, who is smuggling guns for a Vietnamese gang. Keane is presented two opposing pictures of Manny. His family thinks he's a choirboy, and the police claim he's a gangster. In the course of solving the mystery, Keane comes to a third view of him. So the title works on that level but also allows Keane to reflect on having met three guys named Manny.

In the first novel, there are references to a mystery from Keane's college days. I didn't know then what it was. I just knew it had to be there, so I put in hints that didn't get explained until I wrote *Orion Rising,* eight years later. I mentioned Harry finding Owen weeping by the Chestnut Hill Reservoir, for example, and then used that as an incident in *Orion Rising.* If the reader gets the false impression that I knew eight years ago where all this was going, so much the better.

DB   That must be the fun of a series, these private jokes where you connect with a reader via something from an earlier book. Not everybody will get it but your special crew will. But you always seem to reshape the allusion, come at it from a new angle.

TF   Yes. You do have to do it in a different way every time or you'll bore the reader who has read every book. I want to reward the close readers, so I like the slight allusion.

DB   Is *Live to Regret* a book about forgiveness?

TF   A problem in many of the Keane books is how to get forgiveness from a dead person. That's Harry's dilemma in *Live to Regret,* and it's similar to Michael Crosley's in *The Lost Keats.* Just as Crosley has wronged his father, Harry has been unfaithful to his wife. She died before she could forgive him. So how does he get absolution? Keane tries to get Harry to forgive himself.

DB   The priest in that novel, Peter Marruca, has an interesting conversation with Owen on the subject of forgiveness. They debate the issue of whether forgiveness is divine or human. You leave that poised, I think. We don't know finally if there's providence at work or just people learning to get on with their lives.

TF   Yes. Harry thinks he has reached out and taken his dead wife's hand at the end of the book. When Owen tries to re-create the miracle for himself, a little girl — Harry's daughter — comes and takes his hand. He doesn't get the miraculous consolation that Harry got.

DB And in a later book, Owen resents Harry's mystical connection with Mary.

TF Sure. Harry and Owen are brothers. Spiritual brothers. I have three brothers myself, so I think about that relationship a lot. Harry and Owen didn't choose one another, but they appear to be stuck with one another.

DB In the Keane series, you seem increasingly comfortable with social commentary — as in Sister Theresa's speech about television and chrome.

TF I guess I'm more aware of what I can get away with now. While I was writing *The Ordained*, I caught an "X-Files" episode that contained a scene in which a murder victim writes a message in his own blood. In this case the guy had so much blood to work with he could have written the first chapter of a novel. Seeing that crystallized some of my thoughts about our popular culture and its tremendous violence. So I gave the book's villain, Curtis Morell, a speech about our very violent cultural expressions being a message written in our society's own blood and left for some future generation to figure out.

DB What does it mean that Curtis, the villain, gets these lines?

TF That he's intelligent, which makes him all the scarier from Owen's point of view. He's more challenging. His view is very dark, but he's right about some things. Our movies will be time capsules for future generations trying to understand our society, and a large percentage of the message we're sending them is unintended and unflattering.

DB Do you regard yourself as a pessimistic cultural observer?

TF Taken aback, at least: surprised a lot. Who would have guessed that cigars, martinis, and spiked heels would come back? And that tattooing would ever be big in a modern society? I like to use the idea of our accidentally re-creating the past as a motif in my work. In *Raise the Devil*, the new book, Scott Elliott is guarding a movie company that's filming a *Cleopatra* rip-off called *Warrior Queen*. It's the story of a queen of the ancient Britons who wanted revenge for some wrongs committed by the Romans but ended up getting everybody around her killed. And the movie company has the same thing going on, a powerful person bent on revenge who gets innocent people killed.

There's another instance of this in *The Lost Keats* when Curtis Morell dances around the burning barn, unconsciously re-creating an ancient ritual, at least to Keane's imagination. Morell has purposely abandoned society's rules, thinking himself superior to them, and has re-created a kind of savagery. This is a theme of writers like Flannery O'Connor. Her story "Good Country People" is a warning to be careful what you wish for in a post-Christian society, because you might get an evil more frightening than you could have imagined.

DB   When I think about *The Lost Keats,* I note the misdirection. The whole Keats business is really unrelated to the solution of the mystery. Do you think in terms of red herrings as you compose?

TF   No. It's not that mechanical. I simply go with what Keane believes at various junctures. As he comes to new understandings, layers of the onion peel away. And I don't try to work out themes when I'm outlining a book. I know what the mystery is about when I start writing but not necessarily what the book is about. Sometimes I have to reread the first draft of a book before I spot the themes running through it. That was true of *Die Dreaming,* the story of a guy who's willing to die before he'll let his dream of a perfect life be shattered.

For *The Lost Keats,* I knew I needed a sonnet that could pass as a Keats sonnet. I was so egotistical that I thought I'd write five or six sonnets and let my wife pick the one she liked best. I'd never written a sonnet, needless to say. After four or five weeks, I had four lines of one sonnet. I just could not get it done. Finally, I realized that, for the story to work, the sonnet had to be about the themes of the novel. It had to be about loss. Once I realized that, I sat down and wrote it in less than an hour. Sometimes I say that John Keats was looking down on me and getting so frustrated that he finally said, "Get out of the way, I'm finishing this." But that's overrating the final product.

DB   So outlining is about plot, not theme?

TF Sure, but I do have some theme possibilities in mind. In *The Or-dained,* for example, Keane is going back to the area where he failed in the seminary, so I had something in mind. But it didn't come together until I came up with that image of the circle in the snow.

DB What about all the religious themes as in *The Lost Keats*?

TF I was reading a lot of books on the priesthood as research for the novel and I ran across that idea of the dual nature of Christ, that he was both sacrifice and celebrant. That helped me to work out the book in terms of Keane and Crosley being two parts of the complete priest. Once I realized that, I started to see the themes of the book more clearly.

DB And yet, there are those who are very resistant to religion in that book. There's Karen at the halfway house, for example, and the deputy who makes a speech denouncing religious folk. You're anything but simplistic on the subject.

TF I hope so. But one thing about Keane is that, even though he failed himself, he'll stand with the believers of the world.

DB You suggest that Owen's problem is fundamentally religious; he simply cannot accept mystery. His curiosity is the key to his calling, of course, but Father Jerome recognizes that he sometimes over-reaches; he is unable to be pious and accepting like Michael Crosley.

TF Yes. And Father Jerome quotes some theologian as saying that the worst sin is curiosity. And that's Keane's fundamental character-istic. But where Crosley failed by being too pious, Keane's always going to err on the human side.

DB At the end of *The Lost Keats,* Morell predicts that Owen will for-give him. Is that the puzzle that finally motivates you to write *The Or-dained*?

TF It definitely came to mind when I started *The Ordained.* The question of unfinished business. I worried over how to get Keane back to Indiana for a story I had in mind. I've always been interested in the Adventist phenomenon of the 1840s and its potential for illu-minating our own time. The Adventists were as obsessed with the end times as we are, or at least have been recently, with the Millen-nium. And they were active in Indiana. I'd also run across information about drug smuggling that I wanted to use. Methamphetamine dealers were using small Midwestern towns as distribution points. That intrigued me. That's how books start cooking in my head. So I had to get Keane out to Indiana. I figured Curtis Morell would be coming up for parole, so I began to think of where their relationship had left off. And that's where the forgiveness angle comes in, of course.

I sometimes talk to classes about the research I did for *The Ordained*. I originally had the parole hearing in a big Perry Mason type courtroom with Keane sitting way in the back, maintaining emotional distance. Then I ran across a newspaper item about a guy who was up for parole for an offense similar to Morell's. I called the department of corrections and asked if I could go to the parole hearing. They said sure; anybody can come. The hearing was held in a very small room with three short rows of chairs. I felt self-conscious, sitting in the back row like Owen, as the room filled up with people from the small town where the victim had lived. There must have been forty or fifty people there to give support to the family of the murdered woman. They even brought in a big picture of her. I realized that I had to rewrite the scene so that Keane would be unable to maintain his emotional distance, so he'd be forced to relive the old tragedy emotionally.

DB *Die Dreaming* is a good book in which to see your sense of place. You've got books in New Jersey, Boston, New York, and Indiana. Does this reflect your own geographical travels? How can you be a regionalist if you're all over the map?

TF It's tough. It was a little bit of a mistake to set Keane in New Jersey. It was fun for me because it was a way of revisiting the state where I grew up. But marketing Keane would be much easier if I'd set his stories in the Midwest. And researching would be easier too. Now I have to travel back to the East Coast. When I speak here in Indiana, people are always nice to me about *Die Dreaming* and the other Jersey books, but the books they really like are *The Lost Keats* and *The Ordained* because they're set in Indiana.

DB Where is Rapture, the small town in *The Ordained*?

TF   I've met people who are convinced that it is a specific town, but it's really just a compilation of small-town Indiana.

DB   What about Traynorville?

TF   That's more like Anderson, Indiana. I changed the name to reflect the prominence of the Traynor family, and that gave me the freedom to make other modifications.

DB   These "modifications" are intriguing, like the way you both use and change *Casablanca* in *Kill Me Again*. How is it that you know so much about the Hollywood of the 1940s and 1950s?

TF   It's more research. There actually are guides to old Hollywood. And I read biographies of actors of the 1940s, but they seldom offer a lot of details about the nightclubs and studios. Some films of the period were shot in and around Los Angeles, so in them I find bits and pieces I can use. I found a book on Hollywood nightspots of the 1930s and 1940s and used it in the sequence where Scott Elliott visits the Mocambo in *Kill Me Again*.

DB   Your editors must have loved the *Big Chill* motif in *Die Dreaming*. Owen goes to his high school reunion. And you take the risk of a ten-year gap in the narrative.

TF   That was one of those great ideas that ends up being a lot of work. I had to age a whole cast of characters, fill in all those gaps, for a ten-year leap. I had to figure out what they'd been doing. How would they be different? That was the challenge of that book. It was even more fun and more challenging in *Orion Rising* to tell the old story and the new story at the same time, to overlay the two.

DB   The mystery genre, at least until the recent decade, has generally centered on justice as built into the universe. Going all the way back to *Hamlet*, at least, "murder will out." One critic refers to the genre as "ultimately Christian." And in your novels, particularly the Owen Keane ones, you use words like "synchronicity." Another word for "providence," perhaps?

TF   Perhaps. Some say the genre basically mirrors a Christian view of the world. Life is a mystery that will be solved by death: all things will be made clear in the end. It is a Christian way of looking at things to say that the universe has meaning even though we can't see everything clearly now. The mystery story reflects that mindset. Remember that the Christian plays of the Middle Ages were called Mystery Plays. I love that. Keane would love that.

My own favorite mystery story is the Ross Macdonald type where the dead hand of the past reaches forwards and grabs the present by the throat. Macdonald spent part of his childhood with his grandmother, a strict, religious person, a Mennonite. Some argue that that's where Macdonald got his sense of how sin will always find its way to the surface. His books are full of successful people who are brought low by something they did in the past, and that's the kind of mystery that I really like and like to write myself. The one twist that my Catholic faith adds to this is that these problems reach forward into our lives because of a failure to confess. That's the problem in *Orion Rising*. Owen could have halted the chain of events by being honest in 1969. But he was godlike in his choice to keep secret the criminal's identity. It is a Sherlock Holmes kind of presumption. That's what kicks him in the head at the end of *Orion Rising*.

And all my favorite mystery stories, like Macdonald's *Blue Hammer*, are first of all fine writing. Chandler and Macdonald were great stylists. Some of Chandler's plots may not hold up that well. There's a famous story that during the filming of the movie version of *The Big Sleep* the screenwriters called Chandler to ask him who had committed one of the murders. It wasn't clear from their reading of the book. According to the legend, he told them to just pick a character; he wasn't sure himself. But I'm drawn to Chandler's writing. And I'm drawn to great storytellers like Dorothy Sayers and Margery Allingham. When I sat down and wrote *Deadstick,* I took a Macdonald novel and analyzed how long his chapters were. Now, after ten books, I'm more likely to let a given story dictate its own best chapter length. But I've learned a good bit from Macdonald and the others.

In the best of these books, the mystery never ends up being about what time the train got into the little village station or the boiling point of mercury. It's always about the human beings. When Macdonald's detective, Lew Archer, understands the human beings, he sees the solution to the mystery. That's what I'm trying to do with

Owen Keane. When he has relived Michael Crosley's life to the extent that he understands it, he knows what happened in *The Lost Keats*. It's not about solving a death; it's about solving a life. That's a definition I picked up somewhere of the "metaphysical mystery."

DB   I remember a scene at the end of *Die Dreaming* where Owen reads the brochure of a Presbyterian school that describes itself as having "lost touch with its religious roots" and as being "aggressively humanistic." Owen says that's what happens to all of us. Is that the cynicism he wants to resist?

TF   Yes, it's the false sophistication of our society. We assume that growing as a human being means abandoning certain beliefs. That's a sophistication Owen tries to resist.

DB   In one of the Elliott books, set in the 1940s, you have Elliott make predictions about the 1950s and beyond.

TF   That's cheating, of course, since I know what's going to happen and he doesn't.

DB   But an instinct to play prophet?

TF   I suppose. It's more of my social commentary, having a character in the fifties predicting that the sixties will be a rocky time. I certainly don't see the 1960s as a totally wonderful time. I try to recognize the good and the bad.

DB   You talk about the "self-absorbed children of the sixties" in *Prove the Nameless*. It is a more philosophical book. Even the title suggests an elusiveness.

TF   I probably overreached a bit with *Prove the Nameless*. I recently read some essays on the mystery by H. R. F. Keating, the British mystery writer. He said it's all right to have serious themes in a mystery, but you should simplify the mystery plot accordingly, make it no more complex than it would be in a short story. You don't want to overload both elements of the recipe, mystery plot and serious themes. I thought *Prove the Nameless* was going to be my breakthrough book. Whenever I finish a book, I always think I've finally written the big one. But I really did think *Prove the Nameless* would establish Keane. The critical response wasn't what I'd hoped. And I'm afraid it was because the book was too dense, a novel with an intricate mystery plot as well as an ambitious set of themes.

DB But there's your usual preoccupation with the power of guilt and the need for forgiveness. And Barbara Lambert wants Owen to help her prove that the evil that took her parents wasn't random. And Owen takes on the challenge to demonstrate that Barbara's universe is not empty and illogical; real lies and actual obsessions brought on the chaos. Yet one critic didn't like the ending.

TF If it's the critic I'm thinking of, he thought I turned the screw one time too many. I had the readers' expectations directed toward one suspect and then pulled a switch at the end. And in his opinion it was a switch from a believable murderer to an unbelievable one. It wasn't a problem with the Barbara Lambert theme, the idea that she wanted a human murderer with human motivations. The critic just didn't like my choice of murderer.

The only criticism I really can't stand is the "no woman would do this" or "no man would do that" criticism. I like to think that there are things no man or woman would do; then I read the newspapers. There doesn't seem to be any limit to what people will do. For that criticism to be valid, it's got to be limited to the context of a particular novel. The critic doesn't believe this particular character would do this particular thing in this particular story. That's another way of saying that the author — that I — didn't do a good job of explaining the character's motivation. At the end of the book, I want the reader not only to believe this could happen but also that this is the only thing that could have happened.

DB In *Come Back Dead*, the Linda Traynor character moves the reader toward a psychological explanation. Do readers find these kinds of stories as satisfying as the old-fashioned, find-the-clue, mysteries?

TF Not all readers. The readers I'm after do. I do think the average reader would rather know that it was Colonel Mustard who did it in the library with the candlestick. That makes sense. But for me, the solution has to lie in the life that has shaped a human being in a certain way. When I read a story about a terrible crime, like a lot of people, I think how could this happen? But as a mystery novelist, I think how *could* it have happened: what things *could* shape a person to do this? That's the kind of story that I'm drawn to write. So Linda Traynor can both be the murderer and the character you're most drawn to in the book.

DB   After the first five books of the Keane series, why did you jump to a whole new character, new series?

TF   I'd written *Deadstick* before the idea of a series came along. The next three novels came quickly. I can do three books every two years if I stick to my thousand words a day. I got the idea of working to a word count from Louis L'Amour. He did four hundred words a day, and I thought I should be able to do a thousand. So I wrote three books in a hurry, and I was afraid of getting burned out on Keane. I always want to have a special idea for a Keane book. I never want to just be cranking them out. Like Keane is on a trip and his tire blows out and he winds up in a small town where the sheriff is corrupt. The cliché mystery novel. Anyway, I came up with Scott Elliott as a way of getting a break from Keane. At the end of an Elliott book, I'm really anxious to get back to Keane and vice versa. It recharges my battery even though I haven't taken a day off.

DB   Explain the title of *Kill Me Again*.

TF   There's a character in the book named Vincent Mediate. I got his last name from the sports pages where I often find character names. Sports and obituaries. Mediate is a movie producer with a dark secret in his past. Before the war he was a member of a pro-Nazi organization. He tells Elliott that he died when he toured the Nazi death camps during the war. Learning what these Nazis were really about was a kind of death for him. Now he wants to be punished, wants to die again. That's the story and the source of the title.

DB   You manage to weave your interest in film into the Elliott novels.

TF   I love old movies, and I do get to indulge that love in the Elliott books. Like my love for old cars.

DB   And you got to play with *Casablanca*.

TF   I wrote the book originally using *Casablanca* and Humphrey Bogart and Ingrid Bergman. Fairly late in the editorial process, after the book had been sold, I finally got around to asking if there was any problem using the characters from *Casablanca*. My publisher's lawyers decided that we needed permission from the current owners of *Casablanca*. I wrote them and got a very flat no. So I had about three months to come up with some way to save the book. I had to write a workable pastiche, something people would recognize as *Casablanca*, even though it would not be *the Casablanca*.

DB   And your detective is T. S. Elliott, not T. S. Eliot.

TF   I had a radio show in college where I did a fifteen-minute program every week. Thomas Scott Elliott was a continuing character, a pompous poet who would come on and read terrible free verse. So that's where I got the name. And I'm having fun with the literary allusions Chandler used when he picked the names Philip (Sidney) and (Christopher) Marlowe.

DB   And Elliott is the returning veteran with a Hemingway-like weariness.

TF   My father was a World War II veteran who survived physically but had emotional issues that he took a while working out, if he ever did. That was on my mind when I was watching, believe it or not, the Ken Burns series on the Civil War. At the end of that you almost feel as though you've been through the war yourself, and I wondered how could these guys just go back to their farms in Indiana or wherever and live the rest of their lives? That was the thought that attracted me to *Kill Me Again*. I could have my character answering that basic question. How do you live the rest of your life knowing that, at age twenty-five, you've done the most important thing you're ever going to do?

DB   Do veterans come up to you at book signings to say you got it right?

TF   Yes. I sometimes hear from people who lived through that time who say I got the feeling of it right. But that's what a novelist does. Imagining your way into a past era is no more difficult than imagining your way into the mind of a character of a different sex or race or anyone whose experience doesn't match your own. It may be that I'm fooling myself, but I don't think you can write fiction if you don't go into it believing that you can actually make that connection, that you can visit a time in which you've never lived. That possibility is what I love about historical fiction.

DB How are the two series alike? How is Elliott like Keane?

TF I set out to make Elliott totally different from Keane, because I wanted a break from Keane. I wanted a guy with less emotional baggage.

DB Doesn't Elliott have more ego?

TF He has more self-esteem, certainly. He's more comfortable around women and other confident men. Keane always feels at a disadvantage. But as I wrote the books, Elliott got more and more backstory and baggage and his own sense of failure. I ended up, unconsciously, creating somebody who might have been Owen's uncle. When readers started pointing that out to me, I had to admit to myself that there's a certain kind of person I want to write about, so I'm going to write about him consciously or unconsciously.

DB And there's the idealism in both characters.

TF I admire that. Elliott's much more a man of action than Keane. He's also been through enough that he doesn't want any more trouble in his life, but he's an idealist, yes.

DB And in the second Elliott book, your film is *The Magnificent Ambersons*?

TF Only I call it *The Imperial Albertsons.*

DB It's a veiled reference?

TF Yes, again to keep me out of legal difficulties. But I think it also helps the books for me to be able to reshape these movies as I see fit. In every Elliott book, I want the movie to work thematically with the mystery. *The Imperial Albertsons* is about a Midwestern family that gets ruined by the rise of the automobile: it's an inter-generational family story that ends up commenting on the mystery itself. In *Come Back Dead,* Elliott encounters the Traynor family, who made their money from automobiles, but find their business and social position slipping in 1955.

DB And a new Elliott, *Raise the Devil*?

TF Yes, now it's 1962.

DB   You skipped seven years?

TF   Yes, similar to the gap between the first two.

DB   So Elliott and Pidgin must have nearly grown children?

TF   They do, though the kids are only mentioned in passing in the book. *Raise the Devil* starts with an action sequence, which is an unusual thing for my books. Elliott and Paddy go to Las Vegas to rescue a starlet who's run away with a gangster and ended up his prisoner. The starlet is a Marilyn Monroe wannabe and the novel opens as Elliott enters the gangster's hotel suite disguised as a bellhop, carrying a tray of sandwiches. He manages to snatch the starlet away to a waiting plane. But the gangster chases after them, and the whole book rests on the premise that they've raised the devil by kidnapping the starlet. Now they have a psycho mobster haunting the movie set in California where they're filming their low-budget takeoff of *Cleopatra*. Murder ensues.

DB   And here you are writing about Hollywood from the other side of the cultural divide — Indiana, for goodness' sake.

TF   I've been here twenty years, and I've really gotten to know and like the people of Indiana. I've heard writers speak about the Midwest as though they're speaking about this horrible place where the Klan rules and you don't want to go out at night, which is ridiculous. But it is a place where the pace of life matches my own lollygagging internal clock.

DB   The two most recent Keane novels are each remarkable. *The Ordained* and *Orion Rising* strike me as your best. I was especially fascinated by Brother Dennis's pondering in *The Ordained*, his musing about whether life is "meaningless wandering" or "perfect design" strikes at the core of your work. And the two characters, Emmet Haas, who has spent a lifetime waiting for the Jesus who does not come, and Steve Fallon, the corrupt ATF agent, seem to be two versions of what you call "soul death."

TF   In some way they have each surrendered to a totally materialistic view of the world. Haas measures his life not by what he's achieved as a patriarch of the town, but by what he has to show for it. He doesn't have a retirement plan.

DB He's a victim of despair.

TF That type of character pops up more than once in the Keane series. He feigns belief but has no center. I read your interview with Frederick Buechner, and his take on Graham Greene got me thinking about whether or not people like Owen, whose faith is weak, can nonetheless be a force for good. Haas, whose faith is dead, has become a force for evil.

DB One of your characters talks about "learning to live with a limp." Is that it, this attempt to find a way to bumble through despite ourselves? Is that Owen's story?

TF He's trying to get across the void of doubt. That is exactly the way I often think of him. He refuses to take a leap of faith to get across that void. He thinks he can climb down one side, walk across the bottom, and climb up again. Whether or not he'll make it is still an open question.

DB But we like him because he's still fighting. He's kept himself alive in a way that Haas has not?

TF Yes.

DB I like your disputation on literary theory via Professor Corbett in *Orion Rising,* his sense that we've lost something in our contemporary approaches to story.

TF I noticed that Doris Betts touched on that in her interview with you. These new theories and their proponents aren't really on the side of the storytellers. They have another agenda altogether. Yes, I think we've lost a lot if we lose a more traditional view of literature.

I also am fearful that our storytellers have gone off in a direction that society as a whole doesn't buy. Our mythmakers don't really believe in our myths anymore, so they're undercutting them. Some of our problems as a society come from the fact that the people who should be reinforcing our core beliefs have abandoned them.

I enjoy considering issues like that in my books. More than that, I like to have two opposing viewpoints presented that Keane can bounce between. So for example, he runs up against literary deconstruction, the idea that texts are meaningless, in *Orion Rising* and its antithesis, the idea that human DNA is a text that contains all truth.

You may remember that Owen doesn't like the scientist's view either, the one who explains the human genome project to him. Her belief that we'll eventually understand everything via DNA isn't any more appealing to him than the idea that nothing is knowable.

DB So he's trapped between those positions?

TF Yes, between a too literal idea of knowing and the possibility that nothing is knowable. It was fun in that book to have him exposed to those extreme points of view and not be able to latch on to either one.

DB And ultimately he prefers the truth over relationships. Is that why he remains solitary?

TF I think so. As you pointed out earlier, fictional detectives tend not to marry, but they can have significant others. My editor wants to see Owen get into a relationship. Part of the appeal of the mystery series is usually the extended family that travels from book to book.

DB Like Nero Wolfe and Archie and Saul Panzer in the Rex Stout series?

TF Sure, a lot of them now have a small town of ongoing characters. Keane only has Harry and a couple others. Marilyn Tucci, for example, who was Keane's romantic interest in several of the books but who's pretty hard on him. He's just too unsettled to ever consider a conventional relationship. He's put something above that. There's always going to be some truth he's going after, and it will be somewhere between the extremes of nihilistic doubt and scientific certainty. Keane's road is the truth of the human heart, even if he doesn't recognize that.

DB As we discussed earlier, because *Orion Rising* solves this huge mystery in Keane's past, the Cleveland Circle business of 1969, I thought the book had a finished feel. What can you do with Keane now? Can he still be searching?

TF I mentioned a Keane short story I've written since *Orion Rising*, "Main Line Lazarus." The one that goes back to just after *Deadstick*. That was a safe way of using Keane without disturbing the ending of *Orion Rising*. I may do more of that because a Canadian editor has asked for a 25,000-word story, a novella, featuring Keane. He wants a mystery that takes place at Christmas time for a Christmas anthology coming out in 2001. He's asked four mystery writers to each write a story for it. I don't have a really clear vision of Keane's story, but I know that Christmas can't just be peripheral to the story. I'm thinking of going back in time again. He mentions in *Live to Regret* that he once ran afoul of a company that offered psychological counseling for employees of big corporations. I'm thinking of placing him in that period of his life and maybe having him working a crisis hotline on Christmas Eve. He'll be the only one who's working it because he doesn't have family. As his boss leaves the office, he'll make a joke about someone with a pregnant wife who's looking for a room calling on the hotline. Then the boss will leave and the phone will ring. That's all I have so far.

DB   What about sales and reviews on these last two Keane novels?

TF   Well I've kind of plateaued in sales, and I've been lucky with the reviews, except that I don't get many.

DB   You need some lucky publicity, maybe Oprah?

TF   I've had three books reviewed in the *New York Times* and those have been my best sellers. So it does make a difference.

DB   Are you recognized as a local writer?

TF   That's been slow to come given my New Jersey background. A writing center in Indianapolis received a grant to do a book on Indiana writers a few years back. I was excluded because their rule was you had to have been born in Indiana or have lived here twenty-five years. So I was just a few years short. But Rex Stout, who was born here but only lived in Indiana a few months, was included. Indiana is a funny state. Hoosiers have a low self-esteem in some respects, but they're very loyal to someone like David Letterman or John Mellencamp.

DB   Is this writing center a source of support?

TF   Very much so. Years ago, when I was still working for the Indianapolis Power & Light Company, the director of the center was asked to write a piece for the *Indianapolis Star* on local writers. He mentioned several I expected to see and he mentioned me. People at work started asking me why I'd never talked about my writing career. But

I'd only published a couple short stories at that point. I remember the newspaper piece said that "every Faherty story is a mystery whether it is a mystery story or not." The writing center director, who is also a very talented writing teacher, had recognized that the framework of the mystery genre as natural to my storytelling. And that was an important insight for me.

DB   I get the feeling that you're a very disciplined writer, not likely to get obsessed with a character and not inclined toward "spontaneous overflow."

TF   I don't overflow very often. Some days I struggle to get my thousand words. But I have that blue-collar background, the feeling that I have to keep at it day in and day out. If I had a time clock on the way down to my basement office, I'd punch it every day. I want it to be a job. I know good writers who do the all-nighter thing. I could never do that. Not even in college.

DB   Is the work of being a writer similar to Owen's detective work? Both pursuing truth? Both trying to track down God?

TF   Right. Writing estranges you from people, often. It isolates you. Owen's work has a similar effect. I find many parallels between Owen's job and mine. I'm trying to write a dialogue conveying information to the reader and Owen wants to talk about something else. I'm constantly dragging him back. Then Owen has that same problem. He wants to get a bit of information out of somebody and the character wants to talk about something else. Owen has to drag them back to the point.

DB   Is writing more like the ministry than it's like accounting or law?

TF   I think so. If you know all the answers, I don't think you'll be drawn to write.

DB   And when you introduce yourself to readers on your website, you want them to know what?

TF   That I'm a storyteller. I know I say "novelist" to people because I'm as vain as the next guy and it has a more pretentious sound. But storytelling is what I really set out to do. And the mystery is the kind of story I love. I want my books to be good stories and good mysteries. I've read too many bad mysteries with a cover blurb that says, "elevates the genre." I never want to be accused of elevating the genre. I love the genre. I want to write with the kind of enthusiasm you have when something interesting happens to you and you're bursting to get home to tell your spouse. That's the impulse that I hope drives all of my stories.

I'm a little like Owen in that my humor tends to be self-deprecating. I undersell my work. I'm a bad promoter. But you've got to be tremendously egotistical to go into this business in the first place. Why should I have the audacity to think that something I write is going to be worth reading? My really egotistical dream is that the Keane stories will someday be read as a serial novel, as one huge book that will make some kind of final, thematic sense. Remember, I was an English major.

Leaving the business world to stay home and write books has been a major adjustment. Coming from my background, the feeling of being "unemployed" initially frightened me. As I think I said earlier, I thought it would be a year or two at most and I'd know if I could make a go of it. And here I am ten years later still wondering.

But I've gotten my opportunity. And I'm grateful for that.

ERNEST GAINES

A Lesson for Living

1933 — Born in Pointe Coupee Parish, Louisiana
1964 — *Catherine Carmier*
1967 — *Of Love and Dust*
1968 — *Bloodline*
1971 — *The Autobiography of Miss Jane Pittman*
       A Long Day in November
1978 — *In My Father's House*
1983 — *A Gathering of Old Men*
1993 — *A Lesson Before Dying*

Lives in Lafayette, Louisiana

Ernest Gaines has won all sorts of book awards and medals; his books have been made into successful television series, stage plays, and movies. He's even been on Oprah's show. He seems, however, unimpressed by the hoopla. He speaks with humility about all that his characters have taught him over the course of a career that spans six novels and two short story collections since 1964. The 1971 novel, *The Autobiography of Miss Jane Pittman,* and the subsequent televised miniseries starring Cicely Tyson put Gaines on the map as it were. Later successes like *A Gathering of Old Men* and *A Lesson Before Dying* confirmed the accolades Gaines earned in the 1970s. Rejecting the idea that African American literature has to go back continually

to Harlem or Chicago, Gaines has plumbed the realities of many generations of horror and wonder in the rural landscapes of Louisiana. Saying that he is writing so that young people of the South will "know their neighborhood," Gaines accepts the title "regionalist." But he is also quick to point out that Faulkner and Joyce were also regionalists. Eschewing labels, critics, and self-promotion, Gaines has steadily labored at the writing and rewriting since those years in 1950s San Francisco where he discovered the public library and the work of writers like Tolstoy and Turgenev. Translating the struggle he found in those stories of Russian peasants into a sense of the historical struggle he was born into in the Pointe Coupee Parish of Louisiana in the 1930s, Gaines's stories are about standing up, learning to endure — a universal theme. In more recent years, he has moved back to the Louisiana that he has spent a lifetime remembering. He and his wife, Dianne, have restored the schoolhouse/church, the place of many of Gaines's childhood memories. We spoke in October of 2001 in an airport lounge in Columbus, Ohio, where Gaines had traveled for a speech at Ohio Dominican College.

DB So how do you handle this celebrity business?

EG My wife usually travels with me. She keeps things in check. We handle it pretty well. Someone asked Wallace Stegner, after he had won the Pulitzer Prize, how he felt about it. He said, "Well, I'll go out and get a bourbon."

DB So you try not to be too caught up in it?

EG I do, but they usually catch me up in it. If the interviewer has read the books, that's one thing. But if a newspaper reporter or a radio show host just wants to chat — I don't believe in that kind of junk.

DB What about the "Oprah" appearance?

EG Of course it elevated *A Lesson Before Dying* to the top of the bestseller lists. We were six weeks at number one of the *New York Times* list. Everyone sees "Oprah." I don't know if everyone saw "Oprah" on that particular day, but I've met a thousand people who said, "I saw you on 'Oprah.'" All different ages, races, ethnic backgrounds. I don't know how some of those people have free time to watch "Oprah." She was a wonderful person to work with. We were together for about eleven hours there on the plantation where I grew up. She came to Louisiana. Usually she would have the writer come to her studio in Chicago, but she wanted to get down to Louisiana to try some of the food down there. Although she is from Mississippi, I don't think she'd been in that part of the country. I took her to a restaurant, and she liked the food, liked the piece of sugar cane we shared. We had dinner in the big house, the same house where the plantation owners lived and where my maternal grandmother worked for many years. I had worked in that yard myself, more than fifty years ago.

DB How has your world changed since September 11?

EG I've just gone on with my work. I had to speak in Washington, D.C., that following week. That was a long limousine ride from New Orleans.

DB Will this historical moment change what writers write about?

EG I don't think it's going to change what I write about. It is still about love and hate, the young and the old, race, and the rest. And for me it all still goes back to Louisiana.

DB Will a good book make any difference?

EG Well, I'm working on something I call "a thing." I don't know where it's going. My latest novel, *A Lesson Before Dying,* was published eight years ago, and I've been trying to figure something to write about ever since. Just in the past few months a subject has started to come together. After *A Lesson Before Dying* became popular, my agent wanted me to get something out right away, because my name was hot. But I'm not controlled by the market. I have to keep my own pace, my own subjects.

DB What is your new book shaping up to be?

EG I read a part of it at MLA in December. A chapter of it was published in *Callaloo* magazine. They printed chapter three — "The Man Who Whipped Children." I will probably change it many, many, many times. I have no idea how many times it's going to change. Chapter three is probably one of the toughest chapters to write. Maybe that's the reason I wanted it published. No, I think chapter four is going to be the toughest chapter in this particular book. By the time I get to chapter twenty, maybe I will have changed chapter three and chapter four and chapter everything else. I hope I don't have to change the first chapter.

DB   It sounds like whatever chapter you're writing now is the toughest one.

EG   Yeah. Well, chapter four is a transitional chapter. I have a murder, and the police come on the scene to ask a few questions. Then you really have to get down to work. What happened, and why did it happen? You can always write that first chapter and maybe you can write the second one, but when you start getting around to the third and fourth chapters, you have to really start thinking. It's just like Beethoven's Fifth Symphony. "Buh, buh, buh, bum," is okay. Then he has to start working.

DB   And you try to keep the chapters to a certain length and pace.

EG   I usually do. In *A Lesson Before Dying* I was able to hold to around ten or eleven pages.

DB   Does Dianne, your wife, read your work?

EG   No. She'll hear the stories when I read them in public, but I never ask her for an opinion. I wouldn't do that, though I think she'd be pleased. She may be too critical. You can fight your agent or your editor a couple of thousand miles away, but you don't want to be sleeping with someone and fighting with her. I avoid that.

DB   And this all started for you on the plantation in the 1930s and 1940s where you wrote letters for neighbors?

EG   Yes, I wrote letters for the old people.

DB   And your first performances were in church?

EG   I tried to put on a little play. I had to be producer, director, and actor. I even had to pull the curtain. I think I was thirteen or fourteen.

DB   Your church background comes up in each of your stories. There's "Determination Sunday," for example.

EG   That was the day that the people would get up and sing and the meeting would be about three hours. Third Sunday of every month. They would sing and talk of their plans for heaven. Each person had his own particular song. You could identify people by their songs. If you were not in the church, even from a distance, you could tell who was testifying.

DB   It was a way of saying, "I'm still carrying the cross."

EG   Oh, yes.

DB   And this was a Baptist church?

EG   Yes, I was baptized as a Baptist, baptized in the same river that I write about, the same river where we'd fish and wash our clothes. We washed our souls in that same river. My wife and I just bought a piece of property on that same plantation recently. We have a pier on the river about maybe 300 yards from where I was actually baptized, when I was twelve years old. White folks were baptized there too. We were all baptized there, because we all lived on that same plantation. But my stepfather was Catholic, and I went to little Catholic schools during my last three years in Louisiana.

DB   Do you feel indebtedness to this religious background? Is it gratitude, ambivalence, or connection that you feel?

EG   Certainly there is ambivalence, but I would not be the person I am today if I had not had that background. The old people had such strong beliefs and they tried to guide me. The Civil Rights movement really began in those churches, but I was gone by then. Of course I read about it out in San Francisco and saw it on the news. That little church was my school as well. The building is still there, though it is about to fall over. My wife and I are arranging to move it to our property this spring. We want to restore it. No one looks after it. So we want to move it to our six acres, repair it, and keep it up.

DB   Do you frequently get invited to speak at churches or church-related institutions?

EG   Yes, but I usually talk only about my writing. I don't ever get into any kind of religious discussion. I avoid it. Religion and politics I avoid. Religion, politics, and family problems, I stay out of those areas.

DB   But it seems to be the case that people pick up on spiritual matters as they read your books.

EG   Yes. I may not be a particularly religious person, but my characters usually are. One character may have a strongly religious position while another pushes the other way. These arguments make a book.

DB You have many endearing characters, usually the older women who live in the stream of faith. The ministers and the professionals, however, are often treated with considerable satire.

EG I was educated in the 1950s in San Francisco, and I was reading books like *Fathers and Sons* by Turgenev, and Dostoevsky's *Crime and Punishment,* and Joyce's *Portrait of the Artist as a Young Man.* And those books began to make me aware of myself and what was really going on. I began to ask myself about these folks who claim to be Christians. I'm not talking about the old people on the plantation; their faith was real enough. But those folks on television and those who fought against anti-lynching laws made me question the whole business. Many of the younger people at the time developed the same attitude.

DB So you give us Reverend Jameson, say, in *A Gathering of Old Men,* who seems, as part of the religious hierarchy, to recommend accepting injustice. He's the only one who didn't have a gun, the only one who won't stand up to the sheriff.

EG He knew what the result would be. He was trying to save the people from the suffering. But it was time for these old men to stand up. They had to do something big in their lives. They were pushed beyond where they have ever been pushed: they were pushed to the extreme. He just couldn't get there with them.

DB What about Phillip Martin, the minister from *In My Father's House?*

EG Phillip has felt that everything has been solved for him when he became a Christian. When his son comes back, he finds that he's still weak. He had this great strength to lead the people to vote, to be a spokesman for Christianity, but when that son shows up, the program collapses.

DB So the past does matter. Despite his conversion to Christianity, he still has to stand up to his guilt?

EG People ask me about Grant Wiggins at the end of *A Lesson Before Dying.* "What's going to happen to him?" They want to know. I'm not sure what comes next, but Grant will be okay. So will the Reverend Martin.

DB They've both had to carry the load of representing the community, being "the one"?

EG People in those little communities years ago did not vote, so they chose somebody to look up to, someone to lead them. When I was a child, I was always the one to write letters for the old people.

DB And you felt the pressure of representing the community?

EG Yes. I wanted to play baseball and cowboys like the others, but I felt I had to do these things for these people and my Aunt Augusteen, who raised me, insisted that I do those things. I would have done anything in the world to keep from hurting her.

DB Was it a burden?

EG It's like a big rock on my shoulder. My agent told me I ought to be happy to have this weight, because so many writers don't have anything. I told her I'd be glad to share it with them. It's too big for me to carry alone. I've been chipping and chipping away at that huge load for forty-five years now. Each little book, each story, is another little chip gone.

DB Your books also speak powerfully to the issue of displacement. Each of your books, in one way or another, notes the difficulty of leaving and the terror of staying. So many characters, like Grant in *A Lesson Before Dying,* get caught between two worlds.

EG I was finally able to come back when I was fifty, about eighteen years ago. I'd written *The Autobiography of Miss Jane Pittman* and *In My Father's House.* I'd just finished *A Gathering of Old Men.* If I'd tried to come back when I was thirty-five or forty, I'd have been just like Grant Wiggins. All kinds of things kept pulling me back, all my stories went back there to the plantation, but I couldn't have accepted conditions in the South. I had a connection. I had a real close connection to the South and to the memory of my aunt. When I left, I left because I had to, because there was no high school nearby for me to go to, and there was definitely no library for me to go to. I didn't have any relatives in the cities with whom I could live while I studied. I had to leave, but I left something I loved. I left my aunt, and my brothers, sisters, and friends. Those times were mean in many ways. I left some good things, and I missed them. But I was able to come back. So many

Southern writers, like Richard Wright, say, "That's it. Forget it. I will never go back there again." They took everything with them. I have brothers who I don't think will ever come back here to live.

DB How would your life have been different if you hadn't gone to San Francisco?

EG I probably wouldn't have lived. I think I went to San Francisco precisely at the right time. I was fifteen years old and I'd learned a lot in those fifteen years about the South, small towns, plantation life, and work in the fields. I went to the swamps when I was eleven or twelve. I was in the fields at that age. I worked with a handsaw. I knew about hard work. I'd washed dishes. I knew those small towns. I knew what segregation was. I'd felt racism. I knew how to throw trees; I cut them down with my uncle. I traveled with one of my aunts across the parishes. She sold cosmetics. I began to know the people there, in the little towns. I rode in the back of the bus many times. Had I left Louisiana at age ten, I never would have experienced all these things. I could never have written about the things I've been able to write about. If I stayed in Louisiana another five or six years, I probably would have been destroyed. So many of my playmates died in their twenties or thirties. Very few of them got to be fifty. I would not have been able to do the kind of thing that was inside of me. Something inside of me made me want to do something else. But Louisiana at that time was a place of great limitation. There was no high school in the parish where I lived. And no library. I had this brain and I wanted to do things. I'd put on that little play, remember. I wanted to learn more about those kinds of things. There was no place for me. I would have been destroyed or gone mad. I had to go away to understand, to interpret.

DB In San Francisco you discovered?

EG Good teachers and advisors and agents.

DB And the library?

EG Yes. Of course I could not enter a library here in Louisiana. When I went to California in 1948, I used to hang around with my friends on the street corner after the school day. My stepfather ordered me off the streets, so I ended up in the library. I saw books for the first time. I never saw so many books. I just started reading. I found myself trying to find something about rural life, because I grew up on a plantation. But I came up empty. I found lots of books, but none by or about blacks. So, there was nothing about me in those books. Then I found the Russians and read anything that had peasantry in it, anything that dealt with the people, the people who worked the earth. I was about sixteen years old. I thought I knew what I was doing. I was looking for *me* in those books, and it was when I did not find me there (or find my brothers and my aunts and my uncles and the people I knew) that I tried to write about my own place.

DB   Your Aunt Augusteen was somehow at the center of that, too?

EG   Oh yeah, Auntie has always been in the middle, always will be, I guess. It was she who raised me and my other brothers and other siblings.

DB   You say that you sometimes tried to write about San Francisco subjects, and those stories had "no soul."

EG   There was no root there. I was writing about things I didn't know enough about. But when I came to the peculiar subject of the South, what my people have lived, the flavor of things here, the particular parish of my youth, I felt so close to the earth and my ancestry. I could dig deeper inside of me, and hear not only my voice, but their voices. This is what I mean by the sounds of the singing and the sounds of the church and the praying and all those things that would come through when I wrote about my own area in the South but that didn't happen when I tried to write about San Francisco or my military experience.

DB   Do you think it's true for many writers that it's the childhood that nourishes?

EG   Well, someone has said that at fifteen years old you've just about experienced everything that you're going to write about anyway. I still write about things that impressed me at that age, but I've learned to look at it from a perspective of an adult. I tried to write a novel when I was sixteen years old, and I didn't know anything about it. Now, I think I do know.

DB   And the sounds and the smells and the "earthy" part of it goes all the way back to your childhood?

EG   Yes. But remember I was always coming back to Louisiana from

San Francisco. I would come back every two years. I had to go back to the well every so often to smell the earth again and listen to the songs again and visit the boys and listen to the church songs and be around the people who were devout and be around those who were not. I was constantly coming back. I continued to grow in my understanding of those first fifteen years in the South.

DB   You've clearly worked hard at the craft, first in San Francisco with Wallace Stegner and since. And the time you take on each book suggests considerable revision. How many edits, for example, did you go through on *A Lesson Before Dying*?

EG   Not so many, actually. I must have written it three times at most. I worked on *In My Father's House* daily for seven years. I worked on *A Lesson Before Dying* for seven years, too, but I was working on it half the year. When I teach, I don't write. When I write, I don't teach. But the slow pace was a good thing in this case because a lot of things happened to me in those years that changed the novel. I don't know if Jefferson's notebook would have occurred to me if I'd written that book in two years. I don't know if the radio would have been there. I don't know what would have happened. At first I thought the story would be set in the 1980s. It would have been a different thing altogether. It was a blessing in disguise that I was delayed during my work in *A Lesson Before Dying*.

DB   So a book evolves slowly for you?

EG   I know where I want to go, and I know what I want to do. It's like a train trip from San Francisco to New York. You have the general plan, but you don't know all that will happen. You may even wind up in Philadelphia. I would write for a time and then put the book down for six months. The first time I put the book down, I was at the chapter where Grant had to go to the jail for his first visit with Jefferson. I'd gone that far and I had no idea in the world what Grant was going to talk about or what he was going to do once he went into Jefferson's cell. For the whole semester I was teaching, I was wondering what's he going to do when he gets there. I'd never gone inside a jail cell and talked to anybody. I just reread everything I had written and got back into that character, and when he got into the jail cell he said, "Jefferson, Aunt Emma couldn't make it this time," or something like that.

And then it went on from there. But I knew from the start that Jefferson was going to be sentenced to death. I did not know that he would actually be executed. While I was still on the book, I met a retired professor who told me about "Gruesome Gerty," the portable electric chair that was in use in those Louisiana parishes in the 1930s and 1940s. I knew that had to come into the novel. I kept a picture of "Gruesome Gerty" on my desk during the last months on the book.

DB   You dedicate *The Autobiography of Miss Jane Pittman* to your Aunt Augusteen. "To the memory of my beloved aunt, Miss Augusteen Jefferson, who did not walk a day in her life but who taught me the importance of standing." Does "standing" mean taking responsibilities?

EG   Right. You've got a responsibility to yourself and to the less fortunate others. I felt responsible for my siblings and for the community. Aunt Augusteen died in 1953, but I'm sure if I had been in the South in the 1950s and 1960s I would have been expected to be the one going to the demonstrations and marches.

DB   Even a character like Marcus in *Love and Dust,* through Jim Kelly, his mentor, is learning that he's going to have to recognize what he's done. He's going to have to stand up.

EG   It's a common theme throughout all of my work. You find it in the *Bloodline* stories: "Three Men," and "The Sky Is Gray."

DB   You seem wary of many of the labels with which critics try to corner you. To say "Ernest Gaines writes about race" or to call you a "Southern writer" isn't quite adequate?

EG   Someone asked me recently if I was limited by writing about the South. Faulkner wrote about the South and won a Nobel Prize. Joyce wrote about Dublin. I think Louisiana is a little bit bigger than Dublin. Balzac wrote about Paris, so why can't I write about Louisiana? Wally Stegner asked me once who I write for, and I said "everybody." I learned from Russian writers of the nineteenth century and French writers and Hemingway and those guys. Then he said, "If I were to put your gun at your head?" I said, "Then I'll come up with something."

DB   That's when you said you were "writing for the young black men of the South."

EG Yes, and the young white youth. If they do not know their neighborhood, they know only half of what's going on.

DB Gordon Thompson says, "Gaines writes about the small minded and misguided only if he can love them." You are startlingly even-handed in your books. In *A Gathering of Old Men,* for example, the reader is all ready to despise the vile character, Fix. And then we meet him as he sits with his granddaughter in his lap. Or there's the kind white woman in "The Sky Is Gray." And there's Candy in *A Gathering of Old Men,* a character we like, but you show her maternalistic streak. You complicate characters like the white jailer, Paul, in *A Lesson Before Dying.* We're all set to see a stereotype and you jar us with a good, white person.

EG Yes, they virtually deleted the Paul character for the movie, but they've given him a prominent role in the play. I saw the production in New Orleans a few weeks ago, and Paul has a significant place. But I don't know where that comes from. When I first went to California, we were living in government project housing, and there were different races there — white, black, Hispanic, Asian, native American — all there together. I met some bastards, but I met some white guys who would just do anything to help; some of them would bend over backwards to help you. So I knew the Pauls; I knew them in San Francisco. I've known Pauls who have come back to Louisiana to teach. Paul has always been popping up in my life. He's always been there. There were times when he could not afford to show his humanity, but he's always been around. That's something.

DB You don't really have heroes and villains. One theme of *In My Father's House* is the difficulty of knowing someone's character. Even the good people have flaws, and the bad folks have their moments of grace.

EG Sure. Someone criticized the ending of *A Gathering of Old Men* because of my treatment of Luke Will. They said I was helping the KKK because of Luke Will's speech asking someone to look after his wife and kids. "Why'd you make him so human at the end?" someone asked. Well, he is human. He just cannot accept certain things. He cannot accept this black man, but he loves his own little child. He's a human being.

DB   Do you know Will Campbell?

EG   I met him just recently. We both received the National Humanities medal from the President at a ceremony in Washington, D.C.

DB   Campbell talks about these same kinds of things, about loving the KKK, about how they, too, are trapped in a system.

EG   I'm not sure about "loving." Luke Will is still a son of a bitch, but I made him a human being.

DB   I wonder how *A Lesson Before Dying* — both the book and the film — is affecting your critical standing. John Lowe says you have been "shockingly underrated." How do you respond to the critical judgments.

EG   I don't worry about them. Somebody asked me what I think of the film versions of my books. I tell them I don't like everything I see in the movies, but I've seen what they've done to the Bible. I've seen what they've done to Shakespeare, to Faulkner, and to Hemingway. And since they didn't tell me how to write my book, I will not tell them how to make their film. That's how I look at critics.

DB   You don't read too much contemporary literature?

EG   I read my friends, but I go back to the masters: Tolstoy, Turgenev, Faulkner, and Hemingway. I don't keep up, really. And I think it's a shame in a way, because so many of my contemporaries do. They always ask me what book have I read lately and what I thought of it and who said what about the book. I always have to say, "Well, I don't know." They must think I'm the most illiterate person in the world. I keep going back to my old books. The other day I picked up Turgenev's *Fathers and Sons*, which I've read maybe twenty times completely through. Now I only read a chapter or two, and then I put it aside and read a chapter or two of something else, like *War and Peace*.

DB   Is this a good time to be a writer?

EG   Well, this has been the only thing in the world I wanted to do since I was a child, so I don't know. Being a writer was not a choice. I still think there's wonderful things to be said.

DB   If *In My Father's House* was the most difficult to write, which was the easiest?

EG *Of Love and Dust.* I wrote it in about eight months. My editor read the first draft and said he liked the first part of the book and second part, but they didn't have anything in common. So he sent me back to the typewriter with instructions to make it a tragedy or a comedy. He thought the Marcus character needed to be more consistently pictured as having to face his actions; he shouldn't have too much fun. After that edit, he said I'd improved it 99 percent. "Now go over it one more time," he said. When I sent it back, it had been about eight months.

DB What about *Catherine Carmier*?

EG That was the book I learned to write on. That's the book that had Turgenev's influence. I had no idea what a young man might do when he comes back to his old place. How does he react? And then I discovered Turgenev's *Fathers and Sons.* Turgenev is writing about much the same thing.

DB So with the world exploding, Bull Connor in the South and S. I. Hayakawa in San Francisco, you were writing novels?

EG Yes, especially at San Francisco State, my friends, black and white, said I should be out there on the line with them. They wanted me to carry their protest signs. I told them that I was writing a book about a little lady born in slavery who lived to be 110. And they said, "Listen Gaines, nobody wants to hear about a little old lady in slavery; we're talking about the changing times." I said, "But I thought she would be important." So I just stuck to that.

DB And all the way back to *Catherine Carmier,* the issue seems to be more than race. Jackson Bradley, in that first novel, longs for a place beyond race. His restlessness strikes me as fundamentally spiritual.

EG He wants something to believe in, yes. Like many of my characters, he's looking for something; and I think it's God as much as anything else. He is like Grant Wiggins in *Lesson Before Dying* or the young man in "The Sky Is Gray." He's after something to believe in. They all feel this, but they can no longer accept much of their pasts. Their education means a certain lostness. Grant Wiggins, remember, unlike Reverend Ambrose, hasn't the strength to go to Jefferson's execution. Ambrose can go. Grant cannot. When I was writing the book, a friend of mine, a lawyer, had a client on death row. He asked me if I would like to go to visit the prisoner. I couldn't do it. I just don't want to look in a guy's face who knows he's going to die in an hour. Maybe that's why Grant doesn't do it in the end.

DB   *A Lesson Before Dying* can be seen as a debate between Ambrose and Wiggins over Jefferson — a battle for Jefferson's soul. And you leave it an open question at the end. Ambrose goes to the execution. But the camera goes back to Wiggins. You often do that. You mute the dramatic possibilities.

EG   Yeah, I think everything should be that way. The big battles are off stage. In *Love and Dust*, Marcus has already done the killing. In *The Autobiography of Miss Jane Pittman*, the war has already been fought. In *In My Father's House*, the deed has already been done. The big thing is the revealing of character. What's going on inside this character? What happens after the tragedy? That's where you get at human nature. And the characters drive the story. I still wake up sometimes at night and wonder what Grant is up to now.

DB   *The Autobiography of Miss Jane Pittman* was the first big hit for you. Was that because of the film?

EG   Oh yes, I think so. The book came out in 1971 and the film in 1974. The book sold more copies during the three months after the film than it had up until that time.

DB   Now with the explosion of sales for *A Lesson Before Dying* and "Oprah" and all, maybe they won't put something about Miss Jane on your tombstone. But lots of people thought she was a real person?

EG   Oh man, I lived with that for a long time. I'm still living with that. I was at a university recently where this old man got up with a Bible that had red rubber bands around it. It was an old leather-bound Bible. He said it was a Bible Miss Jane had left for the folks. My completely fictional character had suddenly left a Bible!

DB   Is Hemingway a big influence on the plain style of that novel?

EG   Maybe it's Hemingway, but I find that in jazz, in spirituals, in the Baptist churches, and in the language of my people. But I have been influenced by Hemingway, definitely so, just as he was influenced by Gertrude Stein and others.

DB   You have the marvelous sounds of the South in phrases like "root hog or die." And great stories of the folkways. I'd never heard of smoking children, for example. Have you seen that done?

EG   Sure. Our neighbor would tie his children up in croaker sacks and tie the sacks to the tree limbs. We kept moss in the yards and we'd put leaves over the moss and set fire to them to keep the mosquitoes away. (We sat on the porches; we had no screens or anything.) So the smoke was a way to punish those children.

DB   There's considerable humor in your books. I remember when Mary tells Miss Jane Pittman that the Lord will take care of her at the demonstrations, and Jane jokes that the Lord may be taking care of somebody else. Does that emerge just from remembering the voices, paying attention to the past?

EG   I think so. I have a brother who is very funny. He can talk about the most serious things and make you laugh. It is part of my inheritance. I saw the Ken Burns show on PBS the other night, the Mark Twain biography. That reminded me of a fellow I knew who was a writer for the *Sacramento Bee*. You know Mark Twain once was a newspaperman in Sacramento. And the guy said that whenever they needed some money at the *Bee* they would always get an old desk and sell it as "Mark Twain's desk." He said they did that about three or four times. Lots of Mark Twain desks drifting around. I thought of that. Great story. But I don't know who could be funnier than African Americans or Jews. Their humor is linked to their sorrow.

DB   Why was *In My Father's House* so difficult to write?

EG   I didn't know what point of view to use. I tried to tell it via Chippo Simon, but he didn't know enough about Robert X in San Francisco. And Chippo didn't understand the anger and frustration the young teachers felt. I tried to tell it from multiple points of view. That didn't work. And I couldn't figure out exactly what Robert X, the abandoned son, would actually try to do to his father, Phillip Martin. I had trouble with point of view and theme. So I just went over and over and over and over trying to get it together.

DB   One of the remarkable things about that book is the suggestion that one of the legacies of slavery, particularly for the black man, is paralysis.

EG Yes, being unable to act at the time when one must act. Phillip Martin could not move when his young family left him. He cannot act to save his family. And twenty years later, when Robert X shows up, Phillip literally falls to the floor. He's paralyzed.

DB In a letter to Walker Percy, Shelby Foote said, "I seriously think that no good practicing Christian can be a great artist." Can a believer write a good book?

EG I don't know if he can. I think he has to have doubts. I think the writer must feel that nothing is absolute, nothing is perfect. And he questions, questions, questions. Two and two is four, I suppose, but we don't live by figures like that. I feel that you can't really believe in any one thing to the point that you can look at all aspects of the world through one keyhole. I don't care what that one thing is. You cannot see the entire world if you believe in one thing that strongly. You have to have some doubts. Mark Twain says that novels should neither preach nor teach but in the end do both, and I think that's what I try to do in my writing. I do not believe in standing on a soapbox. I don't know if I could tell anybody how to live. I don't know how to live. I just try to get something going, something comic, something tragic. And then I try to write it well enough so that anybody could pick it up and say, "Oh yes, this could be me."

DB *A Lesson Before Dying* is consistent with all of your books in showing a certain doubt about institutional religion. Jefferson is executed two weeks after Easter. You note that the people will have forgotten by then. But Ambrose, the representative of the church, is there at the end. Do you mean to approve of him?

EG I do. I do approve of him being there. I think he has tremendous strength. He shows something, faith, and that was impossible for Grant Wiggins. Grant is still asking questions. Ambrose must be there for the people.

DB Despite the burden, you still take considerable joy in this writing business, don't you?

EG Yes, yes. It's the only thing. It's my life.

PHILIP GULLEY

Mrs. Gulley's Husband

1961 — Born in Danville, Indiana
1997 — *Front Porch Tales*
1999 — *For Everything a Season*
2001 — *Hometown Tales*
2002 — *Home to Harmony*
        Just Shy of Harmony
        Signs and Wonders
2003 — *Christmas in Harmony*
        If Grace Is True
2004 — *Life Goes On*
        If God Is Love
2005 — *A Change of Heart*
        The Christmas Scrapbook
2006 — *Almost Friends*

Lives in Danville, Indiana

M ild mannered and full of laughter, Philip Gulley would seem to be the sort of fellow who would tinker in the garage with you or maybe join you for a ballgame. He is good company. But he has a "Jesus is a Liberal" bumper sticker on his truck. And he has managed to stir up a good bit of controversy with such books as *If God Is Love* and *If Grace Is True*. His best-selling series, the Harmony novels,

seemed to promise small town virtue and happy endings along the lines of Jan Karon's Mitford series or Ann Ross's Miss Julia stories. But Phil Gulley brings readers up short in the middle of the laughter. Something, we suspect, is afoot here.

A Quaker minister, Gulley has incurred the wrath of some of his denomination's guardians of orthodoxy. They fear his softness on hell, his penchant for speaking of grace, his challenge to the ways the church often does business, and his attitude toward Scripture. They'd like him to surrender his ordination papers. The theological hullabaloo has reached into his professional life as well, motivating a move from his early publisher, Multnomah, to his current posting at Harper.

Through it all, Gulley has pressed on with the work of pastoring and writing. With his wife, Joan, and their two boys, Sam and Spencer, he lives the small town life in Danville, Indiana. Danville is famous for its Mayberry Café and the police car from the television series. You can see the car parked just north of the picturesque town square off State Highway 36. With the popularity of the Harmony books, enthusiastic readers are showing up in Danville. Gulley has had to take his name out of the phone book. But in Danville, where his wife is a well-known secretary in the public schools, he is simply Mrs. Gulley's husband, and grateful to be so.

In August of 2006, we spoke of the controversies and the comforts, reactions to books past and ideas about the ones to come, in Gulley's study and at that café on the square.

DB   You're touring with *Almost Friends*, doing readings, finishing a new book?

PG   Yes, the book is called *Porch Talk*. It's a collection of essays. I always thought that my essays should focus on some religious topic, but I recently decided that that makes no sense. So this book features a variety of essays covering a wide range of material, and I've been having a lot of fun with it.

DB And you're still working on *If the Church Were Christian*?

PG Yes, with Jim Mulholland. We work on that every Thursday. That is an undertaking, writing with a co-author. We write well together, but it's kind of tedious.

DB How does this work?

PG We outline it together. One of us will take the lead on a certain chapter, and then we work it together on Thursday. We probably write about three pages a week.

DB Some writers have noted the problem of dual authorship. I find myself wondering which of you went to El Paso as a child, and which one has the gay brother.

PG We tried the "Phil says" and "Jim says" thing, and it interrupted the flow of the book. We do have different styles, and we're trying to write of theological issues in a very accessible way.

DB One of the most interesting things about your career is watching for how critics and publishers have tried to define you. They say you are like Garrison Keillor, Jan Karon, Wendell Berry, Henry David Thoreau, Gail Godwin, Christopher Guest, James Herriot, and more. Do any of these comparisons work? Do you say to yourself, "Yeah, I can see that."

PG I'm flattered by all the comparisons. They give the reader an idea, a toehold into what I might be like. But it's funny. Garrison Keillor is so good, and I'm not there. I'm just not there. I haven't been writing as long as he has. I read his stuff; I'm not as smart as he is, as conversant on so many things as he is.

DB But the Keillor comparison makes more sense than the others?

PG Probably, because we write about small towns.

DB The comparison to Jan Karon is the one that comes up often. I've written introductions to some of her books, and I like her, but I am wary of that comparison.

PG I think when you read Jan Karon you can sense pretty quickly that she is not a minister. She certainly has done a wonderful job in creating a place that people want to return to, and that's a gift. But it's clear when she writes about Father Tim that that is such an idealized vision. I mean the guy stops, what, every five minutes to pray?

DB And he even has a dog who responds to Scripture.

PG Most pastors I know aren't like that guy.

DB In addition, though, what one quickly picks up in your books is a theological difference.

PG Yes, my books are darker, I suppose.

DB Your comment about Keillor suggests that you see your career as developing? Do you look back at the first book and sort of shake your head and say, "What was I thinking?"

PG Oh sure, just like I do my first sermon. I wouldn't preach my first sermon again. I had a publisher come to me recently and ask for copies of old sermons for a collection they wanted to do. I told them that I wouldn't give them copies of last Sunday's sermon, let alone my first one from twenty-two years ago.

DB So we shouldn't expect a sermon collection any time soon.

PG I doubt it; my theology changes too quickly.

DB Do you know Clyde Edgerton's work?

PG Yes.

DB You may know that he had to leave the college where he was teaching when he published his first novel, *Raney.* So he wrote a sequel, *Killer-Diller,* in anger. Somehow the controversy defined his career early on. Does that sound familiar?

PG Oh sure, I got booted out by Multnomah. Things were clipping along well. I had just come out with the first book in the Harmony series, and right out of the gate, it had sold 80,000 copies. It was just going gangbusters. Then I told them I had a book on grace. "Not only will we not publish that," they said, "but if you publish it with anyone else, you'll be done here." I responded, "Well, there is so much hatefulness in religion today, I feel this is a book that needs to be written, and I'm going to go ahead and do it. You do what you must. I won't sue you for violating our contract." I was angry and disappointed. I think that showed in the later Harmony books.

DB What year was that?

PG 2001.

DB So the book was *Life Goes On*?

PG Yes, it had just been written, and they were getting ready to release it. Then they stopped. *Signs and Wonders* was next, and boy do I really go after Dale Hinshaw, my fundamentalist character, in *Signs and Wonders.* Dale began to symbolize everything that I think is wrong in American religion these days: hardness, narrowness, jingoism, the exclusivism, the nationalism.

PG   I really had fun writing those books, but boy, did I get mail.

DB   You got mail from readers who were offended now by these characters who had been merely funny and harmless in the early books?

PG   Yes, and that is one thing that I have noticed among all fundamentalists — Islamic, Christian, or Jewish — they have no sense of humor, no ability to wink and just take the joke in stride. They can't admit, "Yes, we can be like that." I got one of those letters yesterday. In my latest book, I talk about a snake-handling Pentecostal. And I got this angry letter from a woman in Tulsa: "I take offense to something you wrote in the newest book. I am an Apostolic Pentecostal and I am extremely offended that you're referring to Pentecostals as snake-handling Pentecostals. Perhaps you should refer to the Pentecostals as people who've actually read their Bibles and know the truth of salvation." Is that a Dale Hinshaw comment or what?

DB   You get some readers who've felt betrayed?

PG   Sure, they don't want me to have a point. Look at Keillor — my gosh!

DB   He gets a lot of mail about his politics.

PG   But he says things that need to be said.

DB   I remember your story about being fired three weeks into your first pastorate because you didn't believe in hell. Then you got another pastorate where you worked for four years. Then you did believe in hell.

PG   Sure. That's sort of a joke that drives some people crazy.

DB   Somehow this is related to matters of style as well. Your style is sort of disarming: very inviting, very readable. How intentional is that? How studied is that?

PG   It's very intentional. My general approach to writing is the E. B. White style; every word should count. So I don't rely too heavily on adjectives. Every cloud doesn't need to be white and fluffy. And I think some of that too is probably the Quaker approach. Pastors are a relatively new phenomenon in our history. Quakers don't like adornment. There is the emphasis on simplicity.

DB It seems as if your whole career has been vying against pretense. And readers come along seduced by the simple style, only to be caught up short by the thematic zingers.

PG I've been a Quaker for thirty years. We try to keep pretense and power at bay. Part of the problem with institutional religion is that we create a power class. As soon as I get a big head and think, "Well, I'm the pastor," boy, some feisty lady slaps me down. Quakerism keeps me from being my worst self.

DB You have a fondness for the Church but also a suspicion of it?

PG Sure. I think we ought to approach all religious institutions with a healthy dose of skepticism. They too easily lend themselves to destructive practices. I mean we're handling dynamite.

DB Tolstoy says that "Sustained joy doesn't make much of a story." I teach Hemingway, Fitzgerald, Flannery O'Connor, and Kafka. The canonical ones are all pretty dark. The story has to bite and sting. In literature classes, we have a sense that to be literary it has to be pessimistic. Sin makes the story. And you come along writing about mostly good people. Sam is a good person. He does some pretty stupid things, but he's a good person. Taken together, the Harmony novels suggest that all things work together for good. There is a sense that things are going to be okay. These are books about joy and they sell.

PG Sin does make the story, but it's not one you'd want to read all the time. I've been thinking that my books may be too sweet. So I plan to end the series in a cataclysmic, *Left Behind* kind of way. Honestly, I don't know where my series will end. I think I may be done with Harmony. I may revisit it occasionally. But the idea of cranking out one a year doesn't much appeal to me anymore. Or I may let them age a few years, and then join up again three of four years down the road. In *Almost Friends* I introduce a woman minister named Krista, and I really had fun writing her character.

DB And it's a very different book in some ways.

PG   Yes, it's probably a more serious book. And it's probably more relevant because I address the issue of homosexuality. It's just what the Episcopal Church is going through now. And the response to the book has been interesting. Some people sent me letters: "Finally you're writing about something of substance." Others write to say, "I used to enjoy your books, but I will never read them again." That is why you should only write for yourself, because you can't please people.

DB   Sam comes off as envious in this book. He has some really ugly moments.

PG   Right.

DB   And he is offstage for a good bit with Krista Riley moving to the front of the stage.

PG   I think that reflects a real issue for men. I think we do a good job of hiding it. Maybe I'm revealing something about myself here; but when our sense of being able to provide for our family is threatened, we turn into monsters. We have the potential to do ugly things in order to preserve our livelihood. And that certainly was true of Sam; he was all for this woman until he found out people liked her.

DB   It is true that you got a D in college English?

PG   True story. It was dreadful. I had a very rigorous teacher who would count off the letter grade for each sentence fragment. By the time you're in college you should know how to write in complete sentences, but I must have been gone that day. I've always written conversationally. When we speak conversationally, we speak in fragments. I couldn't seem to break that habit in my prose. I just couldn't do it, so I ended up despising the idea of writing. Then I go to pastor this little Quaker meeting in Indianapolis, and they wanted me to write a newsletter. I told them that I didn't like writing. And they said, "Well, go take a writing class." I had just graduated from seminary and I was tired of taking classes, but I drove over to Earlham School of Religion and I met Tom Mullen. In our first class he asked about our history with writing. I warned him about my sentence fragments. He said, "Who cares about that? Why does that matter? Use sentence fragments if you want." The scales fell. I just started writing, and I loved it. And Tom would pound on my papers. But I always remember he'd tell me something nice about them. He'd point out what worked and what didn't. He was a sandwich sort of grader, putting the praise and the criticism together. It was just a marvelous thing. I took every class he taught.

DB And seminary?

PG I did my Quaker Studies at the Earlham School of Religion, but I did the rest of my work at Christian Theological Seminary, the old Butler School of Religion.

DB Other influences?

PG Oh, E. B. White essays. How timeless those are.

DB Did you go to movies as a child?

PG Not a lot. We had the Royal. It has been here since 1927. But I'll tell you what it was for me. I've always been attracted to old people. Then I joined a religion that is full of old people. And I think that's probably why I became a Quaker, because there were the people whose yards I mowed and whose papers I delivered. Many of them were Quakers. I loved sitting and listening to their stories. They'd tell me their stories. People often tell me that I'm too young to write about the people I have in the Harmony novels. Well, I didn't grow up in my era. I grew up in the '30s. I grew up in their era, because I listened to their stories.

DB That's another comparison to Edgerton. He didn't have any siblings, so he felt like he grew up with his aunts and uncles.

PG My wife grew up that way too. Her parents were elderly when she was born. Her father was fifty-five and her mother was forty-three. All of her siblings were away at college when she came along, so she grew up going to funerals and hanging around old people. I knew immediately when I married her that we would get along very well.

DB Is it true that your name was almost Festus?

PG Well, that might be a stretch. My folks were watching "Gunsmoke" when I was born, and my dad did make my mom wait until it was over.

DB How does your life story play in your books? Highway 36 is in there. The Dairy Queen is in there.

PG   Harmony is Danville of the 1960s and '70s.

DB   What is this Mayberry thing they have going on here in Danville?

PG   Oh, that's huge. That is the second most visited Mayberry site in the nation after Andy Griffith's birthplace. People come from all over; busses pull up and disgorge at Danville's courthouse. The Mayberry Café is our tourism center.

DB   Quakerism is a little hard to categorize. There are Quaker Universalists and Quaker Fundamentalists and everything in between.

PG   We cover the gamut, the whole theological spectrum.

DB   In *Life Goes On,* Sam says that he longs to "generally alarm people with his broadmindedness." You seem to be the sort of guy that, coming upon a hornet's nest, goes to poking.

PG   That's born out of my own experience. I've learned a lot from people who poke hornet's nests.

DB   But you've stopped writing about your own children?

PG   Yes. Their friends' parents read my stuff and I don't want them to say to their children, "Listen to this story." I don't want my kids to be teased.

DB   So many of your books are dedicated to the boys and Joan?

PG   Right.

DB   Have the various controversies put stress on them? Or do you try to save them from that?

PG   More my wife than my children. We don't much mention it around the kids and don't see any need to. They know. You know, kids come up to them in school and say "My dad says your dad's a kook." They know that not everyone appreciates my efforts.

DB   Surely some of these firings must have created a strain?

PG   The fear of not being able to provide for my family is always there. But the fact of the matter is that 80 percent of my books sold in CBA book stores before Multnomah lifted their hand of blessing from my work. When they dropped me, my books were immediately pulled from CBA bookshelves. All of them.

DB   So Multnomah basically suppressed their own books.

PG   Right. They pulled them from the Family Bookstores. Boom, no more Phil Gulley. You can't go in today and buy a Phil Gulley book in those places. You might order them if there is a sympathetic manager. I think Cokesbury is the only CBA store that handles my books even now.

DB   So Harper SanFrancisco really has been a salvation of sorts?

PG   I was damaged goods. A writer who has just lost 80 percent of his market poses a problem. They had a lot to overcome, and they've done a wonderful job.

DB   Does the CBA thing bother you?

PG   Sure. The CBA is really suffering. And it's a concern of mine — you can't walk into a Family bookstore and buy a John Spong book. You can't buy a Dominic Crossan book. But you can buy *Left Behind*. You can buy books which suggest God is going to intervene and murder billions of people. But you can't buy a book in which God's love for all humanity is asserted. It's terrible!

DB   The Harper website refers to you, and I like this phrase, as "warm, down-home style." Here again there's the reinforcement of the Karon comparison. The more I read, even in the Harmony series, the more I have a sense of satire, or maybe gentle satire, but satire nonetheless. For example, in *The Christmas Scrapbook*, the narrator tells us that Sam was not a very good liar, "a serious detriment for a minister, who must often fudge things." Is there a way in which your writing is subversive? One critic even refers to you as "lampooning."

PG   That's probably true. You have to do that with religious institutions. Somebody has to be a court jester.

DB   With satire comes hyperbole. You draw it large. Then the problem becomes one of making fun of people. Southern writers fight this battle when they write about their regions. How do you keep from being mean-spirited?

PG   I've had a lot edited out. I've always had very good editors who say "You need to think about this." The barb has become too personal. You really shouldn't refer to John Hagee as "a moron." Stuff like that.

DB   In the last two books you talk about Spong, Borg, Pagels, Buechner, Nouwen, and Merton. Obviously those are the theological voices you've found most useful, at least of late.

PG Oh, yes.

DB Was there a time when you read Barth and Tillich and Niebuhr — the traditional list?

PG Sure, in seminary. You can't go through seminary without reading them. And they were helpful, particularly Barth. But they were also, it seemed to me, though it didn't seem to me then, dealing with angels on a pin. And they were assuming a lot. The first assumption was that they were writing in a Christian culture, and I'm not sure we can make that assumption any longer. You can't just assume that, just because you are talking about God, people are going to stop and listen. They're not. They don't care. So I've really come to appreciate Spong — I think he has a lot to offer.

DB Were there life experiences that pushed you from that first list to the second?

PG Preaching the first list and having people say, "Huh? How do you pray to the ground of all being?" We talk sometimes about what prayer is, for example. We wonder if prayer is going to move a theistic God to intervene in history. It's clear that, if God does that, he does it poorly, and probably doesn't do it at all. So let's talk about that. I found that in Spong and it is so liberating. And noticing the numbers of younger people leaving church. I left the first list out of issues of relevancy. Make it relevant and people show up. Consultants talk about having the right music to keep our youth. Screw the music — it's not the music. It's not bad music that's keeping people from coming to church, it's a worldview that no longer makes any sense.

DB What, then, is the role of a church?

PG I think we're moving away from a worship-centered community where we have to orient ourselves with proper reverence to a God who will either bless us or curse us depending on our sincerity or fervency. That makes no sense. It does make sense, I think, to gather in community. Rather than focusing on what we don't understand or pretending to have the truth, I emphasize community. We are here to care for one another.

DB So it is possible for a church to begin with the proposition that "we don't know"? People will respond to that?

PG I think so. People really want community. That's part of what my new book, *Porch Talk,* is about. I've been contemplating how architectural styles affect community. I grew up in a house with a huge front porch and every house in my neighborhood had one. Everybody was oriented toward their neighbors. Television and different architecture has killed all that. That's what church should be doing now. We've killed community; it no longer comes naturally to us. Maybe the church can fill that void.

DB Do you read contemporary novelists?

PG Oh, sure. I read widely. I like anything by David McCullough. I like James Lee Burke. He's good with words. He uses more adjectives than I do. I mostly just read what grabs me. Stephen King says that, for every hour a writer spends writing, he ought to spend an hour reading. And I try to do that. I try to read at least four hours a day and write about four hours a day.

DB Is there an obvious connection between being a pastor and being a writer? Frederick Buechner says that ordination is a bad career move for a writer.

PG Being Quaker helps. I'm not so sure I could pull it off if I were a Methodist or a Baptist. There is a curiosity about Quakers. People who might be put off by a book by a pastor might be intrigued with the Quaker dimension. We're peculiar, you know.

DB In a *Publishers Weekly* interview in 2002, you say you've "never been able to sustain 100% faith." In other places you talk about beginning with "I don't know." Clearly doubt is important?

PG Really important. When I was growing up Catholic, I was taught that doubt was a sin, so I wanted to try it, of course. I found just the opposite: that doubt is a gateway.

DB What did Multnomah say of the second Harmony novel where Sam loses his faith?

PG It was interesting, because I had a real struggle with my editor. They wanted Sam to have a religious experience that would clarify his conviction that Jesus was the Son of God. They wanted me to write in an altar call at the end of this novel to which Sam would respond and be saved. I said absolutely not; I'm not going to do it. It isn't consistent with Sam, and Quakers don't have altar calls. At least in my books they don't. They finally agreed, but I sensed that that was about the furthest I would be able to stretch the series.

DB   So there were already stresses and strains before the breakup?

PG   Yes. I had wanted to introduce a gay character, which I did in the next book — Harvey Muldock's son, Jamie. But it was clear at Multnomah that if I had a gay character I had to get him saved. He had to repent, find a beautiful woman, marry her, and be saved out of that wicked lifestyle. I said I think people are born that way, and it's time the church starts treating them decently. That clearly wasn't going to fly.

DB   After the first book, readers think that Harmony is a perfect place, and then, boom, in the second book the main character loses his faith.

PG   I don't know any pastor who hasn't experienced that, if they're honest. I know pastors who swear they've never experienced that, but everyone knows they're lying. I don't know of any thoughtful Christian who hasn't doubted, questioned, and wondered.

DB   What about television or movie interest in the Harmony series?

PG   Something rises up every now and then. Michael Landon, Jr., contacted my publishers not long ago and wanted to make a movie of a Harmony novel. I don't know where that is and really don't care. Well, it's not that I don't care. I care if it's done poorly. I think it would be hard to take Harmony to film. It might kill it.

DB   So you are not interested in Harmony game boards and coffee cups?

PG   You pointed out that there is kind of a sarcasm and a shadow in Harmony. The people who sell tea cups and dish towels don't care for the shadow.

DB   Where does the humor come from in your books?

PG   My parents are hysterical. My mother is so sarcastic, so cynical. She's a wonderful mother and she's also very sensitive and caring, but her sense of humor is wicked. It's so fun to spend time with her. My dad's the same way. So we grew up that way — making fun of one another is just splendid.

DB And you still do it.

PG Oh, absolutely. We get together often with all my siblings — most of them live very close to here. My brother lives four doors down, my sister lives six doors down, and my parents live about four blocks away. We get together often and sit around making fun of one another.

DB How much of the humor in your books depends on the reader being able to say, "Yes, I know these people." Do you get a more enthusiastic response from people who have grown up in the sort of religious environments that your books feature?

PG Oh, sure. I get letters. People say, "We have a Dale Hinshaw in our church." They tell me they know what I mean. I got a letter from Fern yesterday. I have met five Dale Hinshaws, one of whom called me last year. The phone rang at about midnight. "This is Dale Hinshaw," he said, and I thought it was a friend of mine playing a joke. I said, "Man you woke me up. Why don't you call tomorrow morning?" "Well, I've been wanting to talk with you for a while," he said. I was thinking, "This doesn't sound like anybody I know." It turns out that he had phoned my brother, because I'm unlisted. My brother, as a prank, had given him my number. So the guy calls from California.

DB And his real name is Dale Hinshaw?

PG Yes. He had read the Harmony series and just loved Dale Hinshaw. He said that, compared to him, Dale was a true man of God. He was, like Dale, just sick about what was happening in the church. He was an angry Episcopalian, angry about Gene Robinson. "We need a few more Dale Hinshaws," he said. Everybody I've met named Dale Hinshaw has been that way.

DB Complete with Scripture Eggs?

PG Absolutely.

DB I heard about a writer who had set out to be a satirist. Every time he dreamed up some ludicrous scheme or target, it turned out that someone had actually done them. When I met Dale Hinshaw, I thought about people I've known or read about in the *Wittenberg Door*.

PG I make it a point to never have Dale do something I haven't read about. People send me their church newsletters.

DB   Are you like Sam when it comes to television?

PG   We don't even have a television. My son has a television that he plays his games on. We limit the games, too, because children should be either reading, outside playing, or helping out somewhere. I don't miss television. I used to be addicted to it. I lived by myself for five years, and I would come home every day and watch television. My wife grew up so far away from any city that, though they had a TV, it never worked. In the first year of our marriage, she got rid of our TV.

DB   Your children are okay with that?

PG   They're okay with it. They seem bored by television. They'll go to somebody's house and come home and say, "They're so boring; all they want to do is watch TV." They don't understand why people would want to do that. They like to fish and play sports. But we really try to discourage the organized sports stuff. That's more about adults than it is about the kids. Our kids do the neighborhood sports, sandlot sports as we used to call them. But the problem with television is overload. It makes me nervous. It isn't about religion for us. We didn't abandon television out of any sense of religion; we just don't like the constant bombardment.

DB   I wonder if you get any responses to your words on the September 11 tragedy in *If God Is Love*. You said that we should absorb the pain, talk about it, and think about forgiveness.

PG   The people who'd be upset about that don't read my books. They don't read books called *If God Is Love*. But the eye for an eye, a tooth for a tooth thing is just killing us.

DB   Let's talk about Scripture. You quote biblical texts with great dexterity. But a lot of your development as a writer and as a theological thinker obviously relates to a changing attitude towards the Bible. Would you agree that current controversies in the church have everything to do with how we read the Bible?

PG   Absolutely. I think it's a dangerous thing to pick up a book and say this is the Word of God. Because, boy, if it is then you better be doing it. But much in the Bible is, in my opinion, immoral and causes as much evil as it does graciousness. It is the unfolding story of our sense of God, and some parts are beautiful and some parts are ugly. We need to read the Bible with eyes wide open.

DB So we're looking for principles?

PG When I read the Bible I look for insight. I don't always find it. I look for understanding. I want to understand why people are the way they are and how and why they make the choices they do. If I were looking for moral guidance, I probably wouldn't go to Scripture. I would probably go get a good book on ethics and read it. I don't know. I used to preach from the Bible. I no longer do.

DB I was going to ask what role the Scripture plays in your Quaker meeting.

PG Increasingly less. That has been painful for some who want me to stand up and read from the text every Sunday. I don't always feel led to do that. I tell them that not all the truth in the world is found in the Bible. But we have open worship and others may certainly read the Bible. I never say don't; I just say I'm not always going to.

DB There are no particular sacraments in Quaker practice?

PG We say there aren't any sacraments but what is regular silence if not a kind of sacrament?

DB So when you gather, what happens? Is there music?

PG We have music, but not all Quakers do. We might sing. We always open with silence, and then we come out of the silence with a song. That's followed by a general time of sharing. What do we need to know about one another? What do we need to be attentive to here? Then, after more silence, I speak, generally for ten minutes or so. Then we have maybe twenty minutes of silence before a closing song. We talk less than most programmed meetings do.

DB You talk a lot about money, and power, possessions. In the first book, the Peacocks win the million-dollar lottery and it takes them the whole book to decide to take it. I like the line where you say, "Christians started out to do good but settled for doing well."

PG Right.

DB You have a good bit to say about the twisting nature of greed. Do you see that as one of the pulses informing all of your writing?

PG Oh, yes, and largely because it is something that I wrestled with. I can be very greedy. I can be overly concerned about my economic well-being. That came out in Sam's strong reaction to money and security. That's my demon. Some pastors are attracted to their secretaries; I've never had that temptation. Mine is "Am I going to make it? Will I be able to take care of my family?" It's ridiculous, I know. It makes no sense. I've done well, but the fear is always there.

DB   The greed problem certainly informs contemporary American Christianity. You can't move anywhere around this country without noticing all of our impressive buildings. And every church, it seems like, has a building project going.

PG   That's going to be one of the chapters in *If the Church Were Christian*. One chapter is entitled "We'd Care More about People than Buildings." I'm wrestling with that right now in my own meeting. Our meeting house was built in 1879. We are out of space. Everything about that building is inadequate. So we hired an architect to design what we thought would be a modest, but enduring structure that would last 125 years. He came back with a 1.5 million dollar estimate. So now I'm reading a book called *When Not to Build*. Many in my meeting are thinking, whoa, that's crazy.

DB   There's also a good bit in your books about rootlessness. You are preoccupied with community. There's Heather, the waitress, who goes away to the city, breaking the hearts of all the men at the restaurant. But then she comes back.

PG   Right. I see that here in Danville. I see people leave; they can't wait to leave and they have big dreams. Then they return, sadder and wiser, as we say.

DB   How important is it to stay close to home?

PG   Well, you're talking to a man who moved back! I would think it would depend on what that home was like. If it was a place that brought you joy and a sense of belonging and a caring community, then staying attached to that is probably important. If it stifled you and degraded you and diminished you, then I think you need to move.

DB   In your case, obviously, the rootedness has contributed to the foundation from which you're able to operate.

PG This town has been wonderful to me. I was born here and moved away. The day after I moved away, I knew it was a mistake, but it took me twenty years to figure out a way to get back.

DB What about your wife? Has she felt at home here too?

PG Yeah, it's a wonderful community.

DB Is there a way in which the underlying thesis of the Harmony series is that ordinary people are really extraordinary?

PG Sure. That's been my experience.

DB Ordinary folks, like Miriam, who on the surface would appear to be one thing, turns really out to be heroic?

PG I find that to be true. A man in my church died last week after a three-year battle with pancreatic cancer. We talk about firefighters and policemen and soldiers as brave. I never saw a braver man than this man was while going through pancreatic cancer. He carried his children and wife through that process with him. The way he cared for them and was always so sensitive about what they were feeling, was so courageous. It was beautiful. This man ran a fruit stand and worked construction, and yet faced this period with such moral eloquence. I don't need to go to Iraq to find a hero.

DB And you want to tell that story.

PG Absolutely.

DB There are also characters like Uly Grant and Ralph Hodges who illustrate this notion of possibility. You seem to believe people can change.

PG Yes, if they know they need to. The only people who can't are those who are convinced they mustn't. Dale Hinshaws never change, because they say, "Why would I?" To change would be a sin.

DB Even with Dale Hinshaw's heart attack, and his wife leaving him, he stays the same.

PG He thinks he's just as he should be. He's just what God wants him to be, he thinks.

DB Nothing ever gets his attention?

PG We know people like that. Then there are other people who say, "Boy, this isn't working out, I have some real issues here that I need to deal with," and they change.

DB   I sometimes wonder if as a culture we really believe that anymore.

PG   Oh, clearly we don't.

DB   I wonder if this isn't the central thing that churches have to offer. We believe that people can change.

PG   That's why I believe that church ought to be about community. Because I think community is where people change. People get to know you and teach you. You listen to them and they have marvelous things to say that change you.

DB   One of the things about Quakerism that's attractive is the silence business. At least I wonder about that. Sam says something about the Quaker superintendent who still believes in words; Sam's not sure he believes in words anymore. Is there a limit to what words can accomplish? Sam says he's preached around 700 sermons, and in *For Everything a Season,* you refer to the cheapening of language. All of our religious words, like "community" and "grace" have become so shelf worn. You're trying to write in an age where language has deteriorated. Is that a problem?

PG   Yes. I think it is a problem, which is why I think silence helps. It provides a frame. I'm writing an essay about that right now. I refer to silence as the bracketing of words, the parenthesis we need more of.

DB   It makes us see the words better, hear the words better?

PG   Yes. That's especially necessary right now in religion. Religion has found its voice too much. We need to be quiet.

DB   The church has certainly found its voice in our time. From Dobson to Falwell and the others we've heard a steady stream about the dangers of the world. The most resonant thing for me in your books is this teaching about the world. You talk a lot about this in the nonfiction. From the flannel boards on, I learned to be not conformed to this world, but to be transformed. You talk about the misleading cafeteria trays in junior high school that suggest that everything is tidy. What's the problem with us against them? What's the problem with the world versus the church sort of theology?

PG   First, it creates an enemy that needn't be. And it suggests that somehow God isn't concerned with the world. The God I would like to believe in is one that's deeply concerned about the world. Isolation is never a proper response to injustice, pain, and human suffering. You can't box yourself off from that. I think that whole concept of chosenness is really wrong. Quakers did it for a long time. It's bad. I think it's antithetical to what Jesus was about.

DB Among these old religious words, what about the word "Providence"? You've had your own stories of magic. You were discovered by Paul Harvey Jr., for example?

PG I have a man in my meeting who is an atheist, but he is very bright and I love him. We meet regularly to eat, and I asked him if he believes in a theistic God. He said no. "If you had to believe in God what title would use for him?" I asked. "Providence," he said. I'm still big on circumstance. As nice as my life has been and as blessed as I've been by meeting significant people, I'd be reluctant to say that God did that, because then the next question would be, "Why didn't God do this for that little boy who just lost his parents to AIDS in Africa?" So I'd be reluctant to say that God did that.

DB We're too quick to play the Providence card?

PG I think so. I'm profoundly grateful for the breaks, the opportunities, I've had in my life, and I intend to use that for good. But I don't want to say, "God did that for me, and boy, maybe if you were a little more holy, God would do it for you too." I think there's real danger in that.

DB The Mighty Men of God in your books: are they the Promise Keepers?

PG Yes, though that might be a little too generous.

DB Through them, and through the character Jimmy, in *Signs and Wonders*, you get to this issue of homosexuality, surely one of the two or three major issues dividing the church these days. Where's this going — what's your best guess?

PG I'm encouraged because we're learning more about the causes of homosexuality. Polls seem to indicate that young people don't have the fear of it that older people do, so that's encouraging. I think ultimately we will see a change on the issue, but I don't think that's going to happen really soon.

DB Do you think the Episcopalians or the Presbyterians are going to survive without splitting over this?

PG Probably not, and I don't think they should. What would be required for them to stay together? It would require those people who are progressive to say to those people who refuse to change, "You're right. We will institutionalize your bias." And I don't think we ought to do that. I think we ought to say, "You're wrong. We're not going to do that. We'd prefer to stay in community with you, but we're not going to do that at the expense of being hateful to an entire group of people." Some of these calls for Christian unity really concern me because it seems it's always at the expense of someone, that it's more important to be together than it is to be kind to a certain group of people. I think that being kind to certain groups of people is the point, is the gospel.

DB Graham Greene's whiskey priest says that "hatred is only a failure of imagination." You have a lot of that sense in your books. Sam says, "Every saint has a past, and every sinner has a future." The more we know, the more we learn to forgive.

PG Yes. Maybe even Dale Hinshaw, eventually.

DB Is the desire to be liked another of your demons?

PG Sure. I think that's a common human experience; we want to be liked as opposed to hated. But the down side of that is that sometimes we compromise who we are and what needs to be said.

DB And that is particularly important if you're a minister?

PG I was fired from my first church within three weeks and that had a tremendous impact on me. For the following years of my ministry, I was very cautious; I had learned not to say what I thought so people would like me. I wanted to keep my job.

DB I think that's one of the most remarkable things about your story, that despite that tangled history, you've returned to truth-telling.

PG That's what I love about writing. Writing gave me a rope to tie around myself in case I got nudged from the cliff. My Meeting can fire me, but that won't have any economic impact on me; I'll still be able to support my family. Writing has been tremendously liberating.

DB   It strikes me as a problem in American Christianity that we hire people to tell us the truth.

PG   It's a terrible way to do religion. The alternative way is to just hire rich pastors, but then that, too, has its problems.

DB   Wouldn't a rich pastor be an oxymoron?

PG   Oh, yeah.

DB   Do you have a Thoreauvian streak? What about the Wal-Mart invasions into small towns like yours? Do you worry about that?

PG   I do worry about it, and my gut hunch is that the economies that serve people well tend to be local economies. I'm not an economist, and I'm sure there are people out there who'll tell me I'm crazy, but it seems to me that the Wal-Martization of America isn't good. Dollar General is in every small town now, and something is lost there.

DB   Would you talk about that sort of thing in a sermon?

PG   I haven't but I might. I do talk about our wanting to have a deal at the expense of other people. Americans want to have the lowest price on everything, but that means that a kid in India is making two dollars a week. Folks, let's think about that. It comes up. But I wouldn't say that Wal-Mart is all evil. I talked to a poor lady the other day and she said, "Thank God for Wal-Mart: I'm not sure my kids could go back to school if we didn't have a Wal-Mart." I'm sitting there thinking, "Now Phil, remember that. You can go to L. L. Bean and buy your kids clothes. Not everybody can. So you need to stop being hateful and stop disparaging these places."

DB   It is such a conundrum, yes. For all our talk about the world, social justice is seldom on the agenda. But you speak of these issues, and you don't strike me as pessimistic.

PG   It is Wisconsin that does it, you know. As long as Wisconsin keeps sending Russ Feingolds to Washington, D.C., I'll be optimistic. There's someone out there who understands what America could be, what America was, and what it could be.

DB   So the world's not going to hell in a hand basket, as several of your characters think?

PG   No, although I think we've taken a decidedly downward turn with the Bush administration. I'm leery of any government which is belligerent and believes that it has a destiny which no other country shares. But there are a lot of thoughtful people out there. It bothers me that Rupert Murdoch isn't one of them, although he owns the company that I write for. There's great irony that the man who publishes John Spong also brought us *The Sun* and Fox Network. And there's the fable of America. I read Howard Zinn's wonderful book, *A People's History of the United States,* and realized that this idealized America doesn't exist. But the fable is so powerful now.

DB   The "city on a hill" and "manifest destiny" is still our rhetoric?

PG   Sure is. And that's really dangerous, because China wants to do that now too. About the only thing that might save us from war with them is our economic bondage to them. It would be economically devastating to them and to us. But it's clear that there's a real ideological clash there.

DB   Critics have been pretty kind to you.

PG   I expect that to change any day!

DB   Do you read all the critics? Do you read all the book reviews? Do they influence you?

PG   If Harper sends them to me, I read them, but I don't go in search of them.

DB   I take it that you don't start a book with a thesis. Where do you start?

PG   With a character. When I introduced a woman minister in my recent book, I knew that someone would resent having a woman minister.

DB   Particularly an unmarried woman minister.

PG   Yes. It has been my experience that the people who are most resistant to women in ministry are women. Guys seem to be intrigued with it. So that's where *Almost Friends* began. I got an email yesterday from a woman who really went after me. "We do not have women ministers; we follow the Bible," she said. That always mystifies me; why would someone support the putting down of their own gender? But that's the power of religion; it makes us hate ourselves.

DB   How does a book develop? Do the characters dictate? Do you wake up in the morning wondering what Sam is going to do today?

PG   Sometimes I do.

DB   Do you outline?

PG   No. I just got a review from a Quaker magazine on *Almost Friends*. It was clear that the reviewer attributed a sophistication of thought to me that simply isn't there and a development of the characters that wasn't present. She said something like, "Gulley has masterfully permitted each character to voice a segment within Quakerism." I certainly wasn't intending to do that. That never even occurred to me. So suddenly I was some genius who thought this all out. Actually, I was just writing down what I heard people say. You know what happens to me when I write a novel? I tend to say things in the novel that I'm too chicken to say from the pulpit. So I can have Sam do things and say things that I might be reluctant to do or say. Because Sam can't be fired.

DB   So fiction gives you some freedom?

PG   And if Sam is fired, if they do come after Sam, that's just another book to write, that's just another dilemma.

DB   In your first books, *Front Porch Tales* and *For Everything a Season,* you seem to have discovered yourself as a writer. You developed a remarkable talent for the vignette: for the newspaper piece, the column, the 1,000-word essay. And so much of that early work is based on paying attention.

PG   I was so lucky. A lot of people are out there observing, writing, and reflecting, I was one of the lucky ones. Other people thought that what I was observing and writing about might be worth reading.

DB   Do you write about the small town because we're having a crisis with the disappearance of such places?

PG   I think the crisis is the disappearance of community. The reasons are structural, the way we have built neighborhoods, and social, having to do with television.

DB   And churches abdicating their roles?

PG   Right. And the way we shop. The lady at Wal-Mart isn't going to ask you how your mother is doing. My mother fell and broke her arm last week. I went into a hardware store here, and the first thing they said was, "How's your mother?" I drive ten miles up the road to Wal-

Mart, because the local hardware store doesn't sell bicycle tubes, and they don't know that my mother just broke her arm.

DB   I thought often of Will Campbell as I read your books.

PG   I love Will Campbell. I would love to meet anyone who refers to television evangelists as "Electronic Soul-Molesters."

DB   He is a kind of spiritual renegade. There are ways in which you've increasingly gone in that direction.

PG   I love how they tried to defrock him, but they couldn't get to him. When my book *If Grace Is True* came out, about a half dozen fundamentalist pastors came after me. They said, "Gulley doesn't believe what's in *Faith and Practice,* so we need to boot him out." I said, "Hold on a minute." I had told the meeting in 1994 that I didn't believe everything in *Faith and Practice,* and I made them write it down. They ordained me anyway. "So how can you now say that that matters, when in 1994 you said it didn't matter?" I asked them. That saved my bacon, that and the inefficiency of Quaker business. We don't vote. So all it took was a dozen people standing up and saying "You can't defrock him; we believe that he is being led by God." And that was enough. If there had been a straight up and down vote three years ago when that book came out, I would probably have been defrocked. But it's that Quaker inefficiency and the fact that I've never lied about who I was.

DB   But you do tinker with the facts, even in the non-fiction?

PG   We attribute an accuracy to memory that simply isn't there. All memory is an embellishment. We simply don't remember well. Memory is so colored by circumstance and bias and what we wanted to do as opposed to what we did. Truth and memory don't match. I'm arguing with Harper right now about my new book, *Porch Talk.* I want the subtitle to be *True Stories and a Few Bald Lies.* Watch out for fact checkers. When *Front Porch Tales* came out, *Reader's Digest* called and wanted to print three of the stories. So they called up all of the people that I had written about and gave me grief because I had referred to a ten-acre plot of land that was actually only eight acres. Then they proceeded to rewrite the stories and kill them. They called me a couple years ago and wanted to do something again. I declined. Their facts suck the life out of things.

DB With your last two books, you've been dismissed as "an example of the revisionist evangelical agenda" and then praised for giving "the best contemporary exposition of Universalism." Do your friends warn you about going too far? Do you get caught up in the swirl of that back and forth? Or have you ignored the swirl of controversy.

PG I guess that early firing inoculated me a bit. I survived that, and, if Harper fires me, I won't like it, but I can survive it. If my church fires me, I'll be all right. Sometimes it is fun to be the target of vicious evangelicals.

DB Some of your detractors say that you believe in some sort of purgatory.

PG I do believe that we need to learn that we are undeveloped. We need to aspire to something more perfect.

DB Even old Scratch?

PG I'm not inclined to believe in a devil. Evil seems so real that we tend to personify it. But I'd like to think that, if there were a Satan, he would ultimately be restored. That is, if we believe in a God who is ultimately good and anxious to restore.

DB What role does evangelism play in all this?

PG I believe in it. I don't like what happens under that name today, but I think that there is much good news and that we ought to speak it. But it ought to be good news. Starting with the premise that "you're going to hell; you're a sinner." That is not good news. It is a terrible thing to tell someone that they're evil, that they were born that way and there's nothing they can do about it. It hasn't helped anyone.

DB Is there a capital "T" truth?

PG If there is, it ought to be love. Everything else seems to be small "t" truths. So many of our truths are really about power. "Here is the truth. I know it, and therefore I have power. If you listen to me, you will give me power," we imply. We never say that's what so much religion is about. It's about amassing power.

DB What's ahead for you now?

PG I really miss the essay. I think the next several books from Harper are going to be essays. I don't have to write now for money.

So I don't have to do anything and I can follow Garrison Keillor's advice about doing what you're enthusiastic about. I'm enthusiastic about pastoring this little Quaker community. I love doing that. And I love writing a book every year. And playing with my boys.

RON HANSEN

Participating in the Divine

Lives in Santa Clara, California

Ron Hansen is all over the lot. He writes novels, essays, screenplays, short stories, children's books, and reviews. He teaches at Santa Clara University. He makes speeches. His readers are often sur-

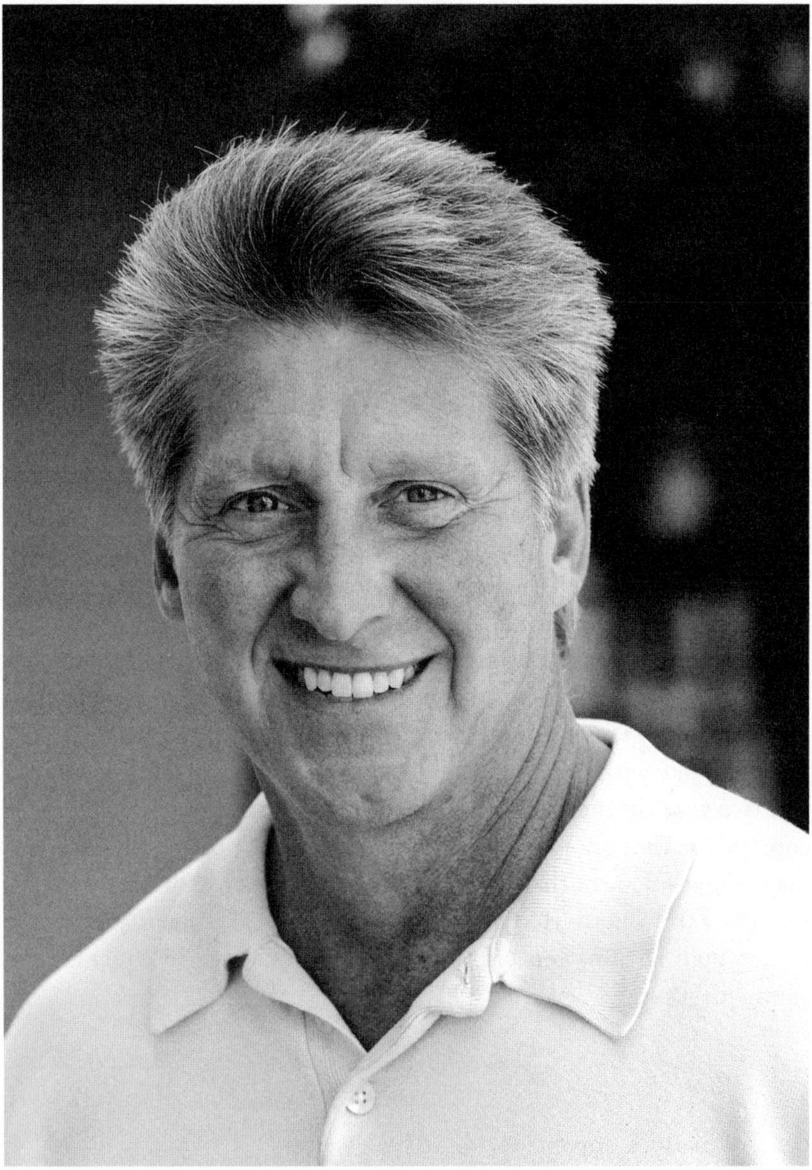

Photograph by Charles Barry

prised that the same Ron Hansen who wrote *Mariette in Ecstasy* in 1991 also wrote, in 1983, *The Assassination of Jesse James by the Coward Robert Ford*. He ranges from the controversial story, *Hitler's Niece* in 1999, to the romantic comedy, *Isn't It Romantic?*, in 2003. His 1996 novel, *Atticus,* is a masterpiece of one sort; *Nebraska* is a masterpiece of another sort. The key word from phase to phase in his career seems to be "surprise." He likes to experiment with different genres, various kinds of stories and narrative styles. Such eclecticism makes him difficult to categorize, and I'm guessing that he takes considerable pleasure in the dilemma critics face when they approach his many offerings.

In a collection of essays published in 2001, *A Stay Against Confusion,* Hansen speaks complexly of the attempt to write from a position of faith. A practicing Catholic, Hansen believes that "faith-inspired fiction squarely faces the imponderables of life." To be truthful, he says, religious fiction must include irreligion. Like any artist worth the trouble, Hansen deals in the fearfulness and joy of day-to-day life, but his eyes seem always to be focused on how we encounter God himself in the mundane. He writes of miracle without much regard for markets or literary fashion. And it has worked.

I spoke with Ron Hansen in October of 2004, an interview that was two years in the arranging. We talked of his books and his remote control, his thoughts about his teachers and the publishing industry, his feelings about faith and the church, and his sense of where his career goes from here. He still follows his instincts, tries to figure out what's pulling him, and offers his readers a chance to consider the same question.

DB   Why does anyone decide to be a writer?

RH   It happens because of a peculiar attentiveness to language and the joy found in shaping it. My earliest memory is of being in a high chair and being spoon fed. The food was green, so it might have been spinach or something, and my sister, who's seven years older than me and famously intolerant of vegetables, was at the kitchen table with my mother. She said, "Mom, does he actually like that?" And my mom said, "He seems to eat almost everything." Wondering why I remembered that primal scene, I learned from a psychiatrist friend that the differentiation between a mother and child occurs when the child starts to learn language. I realize now that in that moment when I couldn't really talk at all, I understood every word they said, and knew that pretty soon I would be able to talk myself. And in an inchoate way I was aware of the insight of Genesis and the Gospel According to John, "in the beginning was the Word" — to speak something is to bring it into being.

Also, I was a twin. I grew up playing with my brother Rob with whom I had a secret language. I don't think we even knew it was a secret language, only that we had identified wooden blocks and toys by certain names only we could understand. My mother would listen in on our play and have no idea what we were babbling about. But when we were four or five, hearing our expression for railroad train, a kind of onomatopoeia like "horhound," she asked us about the word. I think we were imitating the sound of a wailing noise. But when she implied that we were doing something different with language, I got gunshy and we stopped talking that way, whereas I know some twins keep their secret language for their entire lives. But the combination of these experiences attuned me to words. Also my dad, who was an electrical engineer, was proud of his wide vocabulary, and he would employ some arcane or polysyllabic word at the dinner table and ask us if we knew what it meant. He was very particular about definitions. If I said, "I fell on the cement," he would correct me. "No, you fell on the concrete; the cement is what holds the concrete together," he'd say. He knew that Radar stands for "Radio Detection And Ranging." He was aware of the solunar table, the chemical elements, how air conditioners worked, and loved repeating anecdotes from each day at his job at the Omaha Public Power District. An interest in storytelling followed from all that.

DB   Did your brother develop the same way?

RH   Though he has written some fiction, Rob generally practices his storytelling need in acting. This whole writing and imagining things just crept up on me. When I was in grade school, a teacher once assigned an essay, and I had the temerity to ask if I could write a short story instead. Happily, she liked it. Even in high school, writing stories was really important to me, important in ways that writing poems or non-fiction never was. I worked on the literary magazine, but never had any stories published there. I wasn't that good, or my subjects were too shocking. But without any evidence I was confident I would be a wonderful writer some day. And being a writer was the most high-faluting thing I could imagine doing. In college I was in a group meeting, and we were asked what we wanted to do with our lives. A friend said he wanted to be a writer, and I thought, "How can he be brave enough to say that?" I was too in awe of the profession to speak my desire so boldly.

DB That story the teacher allowed you to write was on a religious topic, right?

RH Yes. It's very much like Hemingway's little play, "Today Is Friday." My story took the centurion's view of the Crucifixion as recorded in Mark.

DB It seems like your love for story connected early on to your parents' conversion to Catholicism.

RH My mother converted to Catholicism when she was a girl in an orphanage run by kind Dominican nuns. My father converted at age twenty in order to marry her. They were both dedicated to their faith and infused the family with a joy in church-going. And it was in church as a little boy that I first noticed I was hearing the same stories over and over again and noted too how the grown-ups paid such rapt attention to those stories.

DB And the Mass is a kind of narrative.

RH Right. Liturgy as drama. That's one of the things that I wrote about in *A Stay Against Confusion*. One of the things that's interesting about the old Catholic churches was the stunning visual material that was chockablock in them. There were narratives all over the place, in the paintings, statues, stations of the Cross, and the rest. And the liturgy seemed a theater combining a synagogue service that Jesus would have grown up with and a reenactment of the Last Supper. Mass increased my reverence for narrative. Story wasn't just revered or sanctified; it was understood that it was an element that ought to be incorporated fully into your life.

DB   Some writers claim that too much alignment with the church is bad for their professional lives. Frederick Buechner says that "ordination is a terrible career move for a writer." You seem to argue the opposite. Why is that?

RH   It could partly be the times, I suppose. A religious writer in these supposedly post-Christian days is an exotic, an exemplar of a contrarian strategy, and in some ways such writers may be interesting because of their heterodoxy. While there are probably some people who don't read my books simply because they're so overtly concerned with religious matters, I probably wasn't going to snag those readers, anyway. I realize that there's branding and pigeonholing that goes on, and that's a shame.

DB   So the assumption is that a believer writes a book, and we already know what that book will be about?

RH   Right. The prejudice is that the book will be a stagey, out-of-touch, doctrinaire tool for proselytizing. I wonder how true that assumption is? A person of faith may in fact have more freedom to write about a sinful world than others do simply because he accepts the fact of his imperfections and, confident in the love and forgiveness of God, has made a thorough and honest inventory of his faults and misdeeds. A faith that has settled into a person is not restrictive but liberating. It's the new converts, the neophytes, who sometimes go too far in condemning others or insisting on perfect orthodoxy. People who grow up with a religious faith and are settled into it realize that there's more openness and pliability and solace in it than it might appear to those on the outside looking in.

DB   You have noted the influence of Graham Greene on your work. Some of his critics shouted about didacticism, especially over *The Power and the Glory* and the Catholic novels.

RH   I like *The Heart of the Matter* and *The End of the Affair* very much. In fact, I think there's a falling off in the quality of his writing after the so-called Catholic novels.

DB His specificity offends, perhaps, but surely you thought about this as you wrote *Atticus*. You must have considered James Joyce's line about "saying the unsayable with cunning."

RH I didn't think of it in terms of some sort of strategy. I just thought about that character, Atticus. He was based on my grandfather, Frank Salvador, who was not particularly religious but exhibited the noblest qualities of a Christian. And there are, of course, a lot of ranchers exactly like him. I wanted to be authentic to that kind of character. I knew he would have religious belief like mine, and that his faith would seep into everything he did. But other than urging his wild son's former girlfriend to live according to biblical values, he portrays godliness rather than speaks about it.

DB What about the whole business of celebrity? People coming up to you with books to sign, invitations to speak, and interview requests — how do you deal with that side of this writing business?

RH It's a different aspect of the job. Another kind of performance.

DB Do you grow impatient with it?

RH No. What's not to like with adulation? You feel not just loved but fully understood. When you're writing your pages, you never imagine who your readers are going to be, and then you actually see them at a bookstore or a festival or a writing conference, and you find you've touched a person whom you could not have anticipated even picking up the book.

DB I remember your talking about dropping in on John Gardner. You were just going to go up and knock on his door and thank him for his books. Do people just show up at your door that way now?

RH No. I guess I'm hard to find. That visitation of Gardner probably would have worked out. This was outside Carbondale, Illinois, in the seventies. Reading him, I presumed he was a deep, brooding, professorial type, which is why I didn't barge in on him. But in fact John Gardner was a hale and welcoming farm boy. I'm sure he would have used an admiring stranger's visit as an excuse for a big party. But he wasn't exactly a celebrity. Whereas John Irving is. I once went to a

Manhattan gym with him, and a woman on the elevator glanced up at him and asked, "Aren't you John Irving?" And he hesitated for the longest time before he would say a cautious yes. I couldn't understand his hesitation until I realized that he was outed, that he didn't want to have come to this gym and worry about being chatted up or ogled.

DB I think John Grisham actually had to move because of that. People were getting married in his front yard. And Garrison Keillor is sort of frightened of being accosted by some wacko fan.

RH He's pretty obvious, too, the world's tallest comedian and all. And when Tiger Woods bought a yacht, he named it "Privacy."

DB Celebrity or not, you've set a high standard for yourself. Leo Tolstoy of all people. In your introduction to "Master and Man," you choose a remarkable mentor. You say, "Tolstoy annihilated a great deal of fiction for me." You say, "everything I'd been reading up till then seemed petty and unimportant." Later in your career, you talk about writing as prayer, writing which produces spiritual growth. This is a vision of the profession that we may be losing now.

RH In his book *Spiritual Exercises,* Ignatius of Loyola formulates a way of meditating on Gospel passages in which he asks the exercitant to visualize a fishing boat on the Sea of Galilee, for instance, and apply all your senses to it, to hear the waves splashing, smell the fish in their nets, taste the water, everything. In finding that place, making it real for yourself, the sayings and wonders of Christ will have far greater impact. And though you begin with Scripture, the meditation ought to expand beyond it to include your own problems and questions, all the humdrum details of your life. The Gospel stories become personal for you; become places you can return to for consolation or advice. The same thing happens in fiction. You begin with some subject or situation that you have a need to explore, and gradually the joys or sorrows that you're having in life start entering into the fiction, and you solve problems for yourself through your characters. Writing, or reading for that matter, is a way of having God speak to you through a familiar language.

DB So one subject you started with in *Atticus* must have been children? Or parenting?

RH I was mostly thinking about myself as a son. I was thinking of how rotten I was, or could have been if I fell into addictions, and of how I have strayed from God and came back and strayed and came back.

DB So you're not the loving father; you're the prodigal son?

RH Scott is actually who I could have been, if I didn't have some breaks or the proper dose of discipline.

DB And all this fiction writing started as a textbook salesman with Random House in Illinois?

RH My success with fiction writing, yeah. I'd been writing for a long time, but I first discovered how to write a novel that would sell with *Desperadoes*.

DB And you were traveling then, book satchel in hand, to college campuses?

RH Yes. And at every campus I'd go to the college library to see if they had anything on the Dalton gang or railroads in old Oklahoma.

DB You decided to write on the Daltons and later on Jesse James as a way into the market. You chose the Western as a way in?

RH It was a genre that had fallen into disrepute but had all the ingredients to reach a wide audience. And partly because I grew up pretty close to the region where the Daltons and the James brothers did, I felt there was something I knew about these outlaws that others didn't know. And their stories fascinated me. I was in that do-or-die phase in a writer's career. I felt I had to get a book sold pretty soon or I'd be wilting on the vine, and a literary approach to historical criminals seemed eminently marketable.

DB You say that the church is "the source of your vocation." In the narrative of the Mass, you discovered something of your gift for story. And that informs the early books. But you were surprised that people didn't pick up on the religious motifs in those first books?

RH Yes.

DB Even though you're writing about the Daltons and Jesse James, you're writing about sin and grace and redemption and forgiveness, and nobody noticed.

RH I presumed it would be more evident to others. The religious message was deliberately subterranean, but I thought more people would notice that there was something strange going on here, something that they didn't expect from a Western, sentiments that Louis L'Amour or Jack Schaeffer would not have articulated. And when readers didn't notice, I decided to become more overt about it.

DB   And that happens with *Mariette in Ecstasy*?

RH   Yes. In my earlier fiction, I was looking at the flip-side of the coin, the dark side, and essentially saying, "This is not a good way to live your life." Later on, I concentrated on admirable but still distressed characters, and trying to point out how you can live in the light, and so I worked with Mariette Baptiste and Atticus Cody. I wrote *Hitler's Niece* about Geli Raubal, a lovely young woman, who gets seduced and trapped and finally murdered by a man of sheer evil. *Isn't It Romantic?* is a screwball comedy, a romp, sort of an antidote to the darkness of *Hitler's Niece*.

DB   Do you think of yourself as a progressive Catholic?

RH   There's no denying it, though I'm more at ease saying I'm simply a practicing Catholic, "progressive" being too much a catchall. But I think the church will evolve eventually. We have to. The problem is that the Roman Catholic Church is so large and has been around for so long that it moves very slowly.

DB   Sometimes you speak of the church in ways that sound like you'd like to see things shaken up. Other times you sound suspicious of change. You spoof, "roll-your-own liturgies," for example. There's a tension in you about preserving traditions and the need for change. But you still regard yourself a Catholic. There's still a hole in the day if you don't go to mass, right?

RH   Absolutely. My problem with some contemporary practice is that a lot of thought went into developing the beauty and language of our liturgies, and often those who are extemporizing don't do nearly as good a job of it. I think the proper words and gestures matter.

DB   Protestants, too, are experimenting with worship styles.

RH   I once attended one of those new Protestant rock and roll services that was meant for college kids. I was not a fan. There seemed to be so little thoughtfulness in it, just lots of noise and slogans and repetition. But I sound like an old fogey, and the kids seemed energized. I guess I just wasn't the audience.

DB   How did your recent health problems influence your attitude toward the writing?

RH   In the open heart surgery where my faulty aortic valve was replaced, I felt a calm in accepting whatever God's will for me was going to be. Ignatius of Loyola suggests the correct Christian stance ought to be that of no preference for either riches or poverty, honors or disparagement, illness or health, a long life or a short one. We ought to seek only that which best honors and serves the Lord. We may feel pain or sorrow over any of those conditions, but it is a wonderfully liberating concept. The surgery I had succeeds 90 percent of the time, but of the 10 percent chance of failure, I managed to think, "Well, so what if I die?"

DB   Your wife probably wasn't feeling that.

RH   Right. In some ways a serious illness is far more difficult for the spouse who has to watch and wait. I wasn't a stoic, I was just aware that the ability to write, the opportunity to write, was a gift to me, one given by God, and he has the rights to it.

DB   Who do you think your audience is right now?

RH   I can't figure that out. It's all over the map. It's impossible to predict. Old people, young people. And it's different for different books. There was a Jewish book group that really liked *Mariette in Ecstasy* and they showed up at a reading. They were interested in this cloistered Catholic world in the same way I might be interested in an Orthodox yeshiva. I don't have as many young readers as someone like David James Duncan. I have older folks.

DB   Do your publishers try to push you toward one niche or another?

RH   No. I never sell a book in advance. I always give them a completed manuscript, so they have the freedom to say yes or no.

DB   A risk for you?

RH   Yes, but it feels like there's more integrity that way. I can do exactly the kind of book I want to do and not have to worry about somebody looking over my shoulder.

DB   So no editor reads your work in progress?

RH No. I show it to my wife and my friend Jim Shepard. And generally that's it.

DB Walker Percy says a writer is like a canary that's taken down into the coal mine. When the canary starts to fuss and carry on, "maybe it's time to go to the surface and think things over," he says. His notion turns the writer into an analyst of culture. You pay attention to language, but you also pay attention to the world we live in. I thought of this especially with *Isn't It Romantic?* where you might even be labeled a satirist. And *Atticus* has a good bit of what might be called social analysis.

RH True enough. I make a lot of opinionated judgments about things and can be rather tactless in my remarks. But I've tried to learn to hold my tongue. My wife, Bo, likes to turn on the television, just to see how long it takes to get a rise out of me. I'm exactly the opposite of the channel surfers that men are supposed to be. I find all of it interesting, any channel. I'll watch a cooking show, I'll watch Korean television. Bo is always surprised at where I'll stop. "You're already interested, aren't you?" she'll say. I never know what I'll need in some future fiction, so I stay aware of a lot of different things.

DB Henry James says that the artist is "someone on whom nothing is lost." You're always paying attention. And there's the research? How do you find out so much about this monastery or that nunnery or Mexico or Hitler and the rest? The research must be overwhelming?

RH I do immerse myself in it. But I hardly notice the process. I accrue the history over many years and finally a subject presents itself.

DB You say you just read the stuff and see what sticks.

RH Yes. I think it was Guy Davenport who said "memory is a very good editor." The good stuff will be there when you need it.

DB What about the blurring of the lines between history and imagination? Tony Earley tells a story in *Somehow Form a Family: Stories That Are Mostly True* about the night that Neil Armstrong walked on the moon. He says he was a child then and walked out in the front yard and looked up at the full moon. He wrote about this in an essay for *Harper's*. The fact-checker at *Harper's* looked it up and figured out that there wasn't a full moon that night. There was a waxing crescent or whatever. Tony Earley talks about this now and says it doesn't matter. He says memory and imagination are the same thing. You write about Jesse James, and the Daltons, and other historical figures. How much does it matter if the facts are right?

RH Apparently it matters a lot more to me than maybe it does to Tony Earley. I go to great effort to get it as factually correct as I can. Sometimes this causes me to write a narrative that isn't as dramatically powerful, because I know something didn't happen the way I wish it did. Especially now, where so few people have any knowledge of history, I think it is incumbent on the writer to actually get the facts right. A lot of people thought I made up more of *Hitler's Niece* than I did. According to memoirs of Hitler's friends and O.S.S. reports, virtually everything in my novel actually happened, even the truly bizarre.

DB So did Mark Twain actually meet Jesse James as you say in the Jesse novel?

RH I finished that novel in 1983, so I don't remember much about it. But if I wrote it that way, it's probably true.

DB It works wonderfully in the narrative because it tells you a lot about Jesse James. He wanted to be like Mark Twain — recognized when he walked through hotel lobbies.

RH Yes, fame was important to Jesse James then, and he has become the Elvis Presley of outlaws since. Some people still can't believe he died as he did. But he was doomed. Jesse James was just a charming psychopath who managed to live a regular life on occasion. He wasn't considered a hero in his own time except by one crank newspaper journalist, John Newman Edwards, who made a myth of the outlaw for his own political and economic purposes. There were dime novels written about Jesse James while he was still alive, but they had no more more to do with his real life than the weird stories in supermarket tabloids.

DB Somehow, via imagination, you create a mythology that's truer than the facts?

RH You remember the movie *The Man Who Shot Liberty Valance*? At the very end of it the journalist says, "When history becomes legend, print the legend." I think that's what fiction writers are supposed to do. The facts are your foundation, but you're after an emotional or psychological truth.

DB I remember the line in "My Communist" where the spy is ill and he asks the priest, "Why aren't you praying?" The priest says, "Well, how do you know I'm not?" You must have paused over that line. You are pushing the envelope of didacticism there. You must be aware of that tension in your own work. Readers know you're a Catholic, a serious, practicing, faithful person, so they have certain expectations and suspicions. Maybe they're on the lookout for a message, some gladly, some not. You have that dilemma at the end of *Atticus,* too. Several reviewers picked up on the fact that you bring the prodigal son right to the page at the end.

RH It was one of my final choices in *Atticus* to go overtly to the parable in Luke. Most of the fiction readers I know would have noted the metaphorical connection, but there are others who don't know the Gospels. I thought it would be unfair to exclude them from that connection. I just decided to be blatant about it.

DB Your way of saying, "In case you haven't noticed, there's something interesting going on here"?

RH Exactly. Yes.

DB Do you think much about the idea of Christian fiction, the Christian Booksellers' sort, and secular fiction, the American Booksellers' variety?

RH No. *The Christian Century* has given me wonderful reviews, and I do get invited to venues where the majority of the audience may have read Rick Warren or the *Left Behind* series. And I'm pleased they read me as well. But my own tastes in fiction tend toward the American Booksellers' version of good literature.

DB Flannery O'Connor, speaking to a group of Southern Baptists, said that the Baptists had more in common with the Pope than their northern counterparts — liberals, I think she meant. Is the divide today between those who believe in a sacred something and those who don't?

RH Yes. In the nineteenth century the divide had to do with denominationalism. Now, the divide has to do with theism versus atheism. In our increasingly secular world, if you believe in God, if you worship and serve him, a Christian is kindred with Jews, Muslims, a host of people.

DB How does that influence your sales?

RH I've noticed that I get a lot of fan letters from people of different religions, or different denominations of Christianity. And they indicate how happy they are to have somebody writing seriously about religious faith. I think even fifty years ago that probably would not have happened.

DB But you're not content to make religious people merely your audience?

RH No. I don't want to simply preach to the choir.

DB I heard recently of a survey in which people were asked if they had ever experienced a miracle, a supernatural event. Roughly half the people said yes. But when asked where they would talk about such an experience, they spoke of the therapist's office, the bar, and the hardware store. The church came in fifth.

RH The church doesn't give them the opportunity. You come in and listen but rarely get to tell your own story. I remember once at somebody's party we got on the subject of miracles or supernatural events in our lives. Whether religious or irreligious, everyone had some anecdote to tell. How often do those in ministry even ask what the Spirit is doing or has done in our lives? At the party I referred to, one guy talked about being forced as a kid to go to church on a Sunday morning before he went to a Red Sox baseball game. It was the final game for some retiring player, and this guy prayed, "Oh God, I never pray to you but since I went to church today you owe me one, so could you let him hit a home run?" And the player did, just as if the kid had ordered a bag of peanuts from a vendor. So I said to the guy, "Did you continue going to church?" He said he didn't; he never thought of it; he wasn't religious. And I said, "What must God think of you? You're an ingrate!"

DB So how does a novelist write about miracles? Shelby Foote and

Walker Percy used to debate whether believers could write novels at all. "No practicing Catholic could write a good novel," Foote says. Novels are based in this world and feature questions, not answers. No miracles allowed. John Gardner was another who was nervous about any sense of the doctrinaire. You refer to books that "sermonize." So how do you manage this line between the secular and the sacred?

RH I think it's odd that folks like Foote talk about religious belief as a hindrance, but they don't talk about political belief or other advocacies. Some people are doctrinaire about feminism or vegetarianism, and it doesn't come up as objectionable. It's only when you start talking about faith that people get edgy.

DB Are the challenges any different for a Catholic writer like yourself or Jon Hassler or Tim Gautreaux and Protestant writers like Fred Buechner, John Updike, and Doris Betts?

RH A lot of friends of mine who grew up in fundamentalist traditions feel that they have to leave their faith before they can write. In some ways they felt shackled by their religious backgrounds. I never felt that. And Updike and Buechner and Betts come from a mainstream Protestantism that hasn't seemed to cramp them. A good many of my writer friends find their faith to be a great resource, but the lapsed Catholic, the lapsed Baptist, the cultural but non-religious Jew are probably the majority at universities and on the book scene.

DB The lens through which you look at literature in your book *A Stay Against Confusion: Essays on Faith and Fiction* is a sacramentalist lens?

RH Yes, ceremonies of graced moments — external signs of an internal grace.

DB The Reformed view speaks about literature that moves one not simply to meditation but to action. Do you see those views as necessarily opposed?

RH No, I don't. I think that the fact that these feelings we have are given an external manifestation, or a sign, means that our faith has to be shown naturally in our activities in the world. And as the Epistle of James points out, faith without works is nothing. I was once in a panel discussion about Catholicism — I hate panel discussions — and

I was trying to define the difference between a Catholic imagination, a Protestant imagination, and a Jewish imagination. One woman there thought that I was impugning all these different traditions. I was talking about the dialogical imagination versus the analogical imagination. I wasn't saying one was better than the other; I was just identifying their differences. I think it was perfectly legitimate. She thought I was being unecumenical in some way, but you have to recognize and appreciate the differences in order to be able to fully communicate your own perspective.

DB There's a long strain of American writers — from Emily Dickinson, who says "We believe and disbelieve a hundred times an hour," to Melville, who "could neither believe nor be comfortable in his unbelief," according to his friend Hawthorne. Do you resonate with this strain?

RH Periodically. About once a week, I find myself thinking, "What if I'm mistaken about all of this?" But, as *A Streetcar Named Desire* has it, "Sometimes there's God so quickly."

DB Does that find its way into the writing?

RH The doubt doesn't, no. I think I write out of faith because writing for me is a form of prayer. And I don't feel there is much profit in skepticism and doubt. To be skeptical and mistrusting is the easiest thing in the world. But so much negativity is hard on you. You can wear yourself out in going through an investigation of your faith all the time. And I've had enough positive experiences, near miraculous experiences, that I know something's up. I don't have to figure out the God question anew. The religion I was given solves a lot of the questions for me. If there are theological gaps to my understanding, I'm not going to worry about them; I would be kidding myself if I thought I got it right and Thomas Aquinas or Paul Tillich or Karl Rahner didn't.

DB You have a *gift* of faith?

RH It seems like a lot of people are trying to get ABCDEFG, the full sequence, and I'm content with the jot and tittle of A, C, and G. All the mysteries don't have to be solved for me.

DB "Lord, I believe, help thou mine unbelief" is the best we can do.

RH Yes, exactly. There's a poem by John Berryman — one of his "Eleven Addresses to the Lord." He records something like a wise man saying that even to say God exists is in some way untrue. We're too limited in our intelligence and God is so much bigger than our imaginations. You read memoirs of people who flail about for years trying to figure out whether God exists. Reason just gets in the way.

DB But some floundering finds its way into your books?

RH Sure.

DB You have to be true to that truth as well?

RH Yes, I have to record longing, lostness, and the rest.

DB You say, "Great art teaches us what Christ taught: there is something going on here that matters." So art is the sharpening of the hearing, sharpening of the sight. It's learning to pay attention, or it's helping readers pay attention. John Gardner says you have to do all this and also love your characters and your readers. Now you've written about Jesse James and Adolf Hitler. Is all this too much to ask?

RH Well, there has to be somebody you're rooting for, I think. Maybe it's even the finer person that character could have been that you're rooting for. In *Hitler's Niece,* I really liked Geli Raubal. She was my resource in dealing with the evil that was surrounding her. With Jesse James there were lots of things I found affecting or admirable in him. But I still recognized that he was a bloodthirsty psychopath in spite of his being a good family man.

DB Janet Burroway says that *Atticus* "may end up giving didacticism a good name." Are you reclaiming some territory that recent writing has tended to abandon?

RH Sure. Oliver Goldsmith always began each story with a sentence which was basically the theme. This is what you're supposed to get out of it, he seemed to say. I liked that, because as a reader you would wonder how he would get back to this theme, and eventually he did. The pleasure was in watching the balls he'd thrown up fall back into his hands.

DB But it must drive you crazy at some level. Isn't the shorthand a diminishment? *Atticus* equals prodigal son? Ron Hansen in five lines. Jesse James equals "the wages of sin." Doesn't that annoy you?

RH   The fiction writer over time is aware of so many other things going on in the narrative; you just hope that readers are picking up on some of them. Why do I name one character Renata, for example? Why is this church near the *jardin* described in this particular way? There's that guy in *Atticus* whose name, in Mayan, means "he who sees in the middle of things." Why are these colors chosen? Why is this one scene located where it is? Writers think about all these things during the long haul of creating a novel, and we hope the readers will catch at least some of them, so we try to be accessible, and that may make us seem didactic.

DB   Besides the Catholicism and being a twin, you also write about a sense of place. In *Nebraska,* you talk about "thereness."

RH   That's in *Atticus,* too. It is a realization that you've found where you want to be. I have that feeling about California. I went there first when I was about two years old. I don't remember much about it. Then I went again when I was about twelve or thirteen. And I thought, why would anybody want to live in any place other than California? I was always seeking a way to get back.

DB   Yet in your latest novel and in that collection of short stories you go back to Nebraska?

RH   Nebraska is the country of my imagination. Even when I was living and writing about a convent in upstate New York, in a sense I was writing about Nebraska. An awful lot was determined by my upbringing there. In some ways it's kind of a nightmare country for me. But I think even other Nebraskans who have stayed there would recognize why I say that.

DB   Didn't you and your brother think about writing a book together about growing up as twins?

RH   Yes. I don't know if we'll do it. My brother was writing his memories and got about twelve pages into it when he lost the file because his computer died. The pages I saw were great, memories that were totally separate from my own. But he hasn't shown much inclination to go back to that material, so the project is on hold.

DB   And he trained for the priesthood?

RH   Yes, in the Society of Jesus, but he left formation after nine years. He's married now, with two children. I just saw a *TIME* cover story about a gene for religiousness. Scientists are saying that maybe there's actually a gene that makes people religious or irreligious. I'd have to say my family has it. I have a cousin who was a Presbyterian minister, another cousin who is an American Baptist missionary. My sister was a Dominican nun, my brother was a Jesuit, my great-grandfather was a Bishop in the Mormon church.

DB   Wasn't your father's move to Catholicism a dramatic thing for the extended family?

RH   Two of his older sisters didn't talk to him for years. But by the time I was growing up, their differences had been settled.

DB   You say that writing a book is like telling a joke.

RH   In that you have to know pretty much what the punchline or ending's going to be. And know various stops along the way.

DB   So your characters don't take over your life?

RH   No. That doesn't happen to me. It's more like writing a letter. You know there are some things you want to say, but you don't know exactly how the words are going to come out.

DB   If you hadn't been a writer, what would you have been?

RH   A priest, an English professor, possibly a lawyer, although when I was a kid I liked the idea of being a magazine illustrator. A friend's father did that and it seemed wonderful, especially since I liked sketching and painting portraits.

DB   Do you still paint?

RH   No. It was feeding from the same engine that powers my writing. And you have to keep up with art or you lose your hand, your skills get atrophied. Were I to pick up a paint brush again I would have had to relearn the craft.

DB   What about the books that never make it to print? Do you have fits and starts and discarded manuscripts?

RH   Every once in a while I look through my files and discover some story I'd given up on. On occasion I haul it out and finish it off. I had one story that I worked on for ten years. Finally I got it into a shape where I could actually sell it. A lot of times I'll start something and have no idea what's wrong with it. I just put it away and eventually something else happens that helps me figure it out. "My Communist" was a good story when I heard elements of it, but I didn't know how to turn it into a narrative or finish it until I read a letter about his missionary duties in Alaska from a Polish priest. Once I encountered that broken English, and got his voice, I had the story. There are those who have never had an unpublished thought, but I certainly have. I depend on my editor and my friends to say "maybe this is not worthy of you."

DB The word that reappears in reviews of your work is "surprise." You've done Westerns and a farce, and a detective story and a historical novel. Where does such range come from?

RH I'm simply interested in lots of different things.

DB And you don't want to run the same track twice?

RH That's part of it, too. I try to keep from being bored. I couldn't handle the same material book after book in the same way as some mystery writers, for example, do.

DB The danger with the range is that it may obscure the connectedness. Wouldn't you say that there is, from beginning to end, something holding all that work together?

RH Yes. I'm probably not the person to say. Maybe a psychoanalyst could say just what. The simple answer is that virtually everyone I concentrate on is an outlaw or outsider. I write of characters with abiding desires who are out of the mainstream, and are confused by how other people react to things. Atticus Cody was a perfectly normal guy but was out of his element in Mexico. Geli Raubal was a lovely girl but a waif thrust into the limelight and seduced by a seemingly loving uncle who turned out to be a monster. Another type of alienation. My characters are on quests and often feel they're heading into some strange and dangerous frontier that they don't understand. That's even true of my screwball comedy *Isn't It Romantic?* A French couple winds up in a Nebraska town named Seldom and odd hijinks ensue. A lot of my characters are guilty of reckless ambition or are caught up in the pursuit of fame.

DB And there you verge toward spiritual themes. Salvation and redemption and the like are floating around in that water, too.

RH   Yes. And questions like the one Bob Ford faced: "Are you going to be Judas or are you going to be Barabbas?"

DB   And you aim at parable?

RH   At their core, parables are stories about ordinary people, but metaphorical stories that somehow communicate something deeper and open-ended. All fictional narratives aspire to that.

DB   Something is left unsaid?

RH   Right. And listeners puzzle about the meaning. The message gets bigger and bigger the more one thinks about it. A parable has to be unsettling; things get turned on their heads. I think that's true of good fiction, as well. That's the greatest argument against didacticism. There you're dealing with the familiar and heading towards the familiar and often-stated. Good fiction starts with the familiar but shapes it or corrupts it in some way.

DB   So, even though you are a person of faith, you're still writing about questions. You're still trying to pull things inside out. Still creating puzzlement?

RH   Absolutely.

DB   Do people tell you that your books have saved their lives?

RH   One woman wrote that she'd read *Mariette in Ecstasy* while her husband was dying of cancer. She said it was a wonderful solace for her. That's gratifying. Every once in a while people come up and say they've read one of my books over and over again. And often what they're reacting to in the book is what they've made up, not what I've intended. That's great. Their own story is getting told.

DB   You've had the opportunity to work with John Irving and John Gardner, but your first readers now are Jim Shepard and your wife?

RH   Right.

DB   Other influences?

RH   A really early influence was Edgar Allan Poe. I loved the horror, and the stories were stunning when I was reading them, wide-eyed, in grade school. John Updike's fiction began to be a passion for me in high school. William H. Gass is really important to me, just on the level of his glorious sentences. I have quoted or stolen from Shakespeare in every novel I've written. And I like a lot of poets: Galway

Kinnell, Elizabeth Bishop, Paul Mariani, Sylvia Plath. And Dylan Thomas and Gerard Manley Hopkins, of course.

DB   But you don't yourself write poetry?

RH   I've committed a poem, on occasion, but I'm not very good. Michael Ondaatje is really good, and manages to write fantastic fiction as well. That's rare.

DB   Do you have a fellowship community?

RH   Yes. Tobias Wolff is a good friend who's close by. John L'Heureux. A lot of the Stanford people I knew decades ago remain dinner and party friends, and the Jesuit faculty at Santa Clara are a great community. I can always find someone there who'll know the answer to my questions. If I have a question about Latin, I know who to approach, and if I have a question about Poland I know just who to ask. I just write an email about food in Germany, say, and the answer comes within hours. It's fabulous.

DB   What about your books being made into movies?

RH   *Mariette in Ecstasy* was made but never released. The production company went bankrupt. *Atticus* was a Hallmark Hall of Fame production called *Missing Pieces* that played on CBS and starred James Coburn. Warner Brothers is scheduled to begin filming *The Assassination of Jesse James by the Coward Robert Ford* in August, with Brad Pitt in the lead. And *Desperadoes* is moving ahead to become a movie, too. A director is interested in *Isn't It Romantic?* But I'm a little out of the loop about the vagaries of these productions.

DB   When you sell the option on the book rights, you're done? They don't have to consult you at all?

RH   No.

DB   You ran into controversy with *Hitler's Niece*, probably for the first time in your career. Tough?

RH   It was very strange, because at the same time my book came out there was a book about Mao Tse-Tung and a book about Stalin. Both were novelizations of historical figures. No reviewer said, "How dare you?" about those books. It was as if I had violated some canon of taste. There were a number of wonderful reviews for my novel, but it just takes a few prominent, negative ones to earn you the seemingly permanent tag of "controversial." My sin was that I portrayed Adolf Hitler as a twisted and evil personality but never forgot he was also a human being. Some reviewers seemed to think appreciating my accurate portrayal of him was equivalent to approving the Holocaust.

DB   You do that with Jesse James and Bob Ford and Emmet Dalton. You show that these are complete human beings. That is the mastery of those novels. But with Hitler, that's forbidden territory?

RH   Cynthia Ozick, whose fiction I like a great deal, says she even dislikes those baby pictures of Hitler where he looked so cute, because she wants to think of him only as a monster.

DB   But he was a baby. How do you get around that?

RH   Exactly. That's what's interesting about him. But he's beyond objectivity somehow. Nobody would have condemned a nonfiction account of what I wrote, but the novel in doing what novels are supposed to do created quite a stir. I got some really nasty letters and some strange people haunted my book signings. The furor, such as it was, has died down, and now I frequently get letters from readers saying how good *Hitler's Niece* is.

DB   You followed *Hitler's Niece* with *Isn't It Romantic?* I wondered about the proximity. The controversial and serious big book followed by the smaller, lighter book.

RH   Writing *Hitler's Niece* was a gloomy business. I wanted to do something airy. It was fun for me to write *Isn't It Romantic?* Jim Shepard and I wrote a first draft of it as a screenplay in 1990 and it went nowhere, but it formed a rough blueprint. I took the script out of the drawer right after I finished work on the galleys of *A Stay Against Confusion.* I changed a good deal about the script and added a hundred pages of characterization, jokes, and shenanigans to have it function as an honest to goodness screwball comedy.

DB   Does writing a book always affect you emotionally? You descended into a dark world in *Hitler's Niece.* Does that take a toll?

RH   You know Haley Joel Osment — the child actor in *The Sixth Sense?* He said when he read the script for *The Sixth Sense* he was really scared, and he didn't know how he was going to handle making the movie. But when he went to the set, he saw these actors with gruesome makeup drinking coffee. They were throwing frisbees back and forth, and he realized it wasn't scary at all. Even when he was in the scene, he was aware of the distance from reality. Ideally, the same thing is true when you're writing fiction. You recognize the ghoulish or darker aspects, but you're so aware of the artificiality. You're thinking about the perfect metaphor, or whether or not you just committed the sin of a comma splice. Those practical matters are constantly keeping the horror at bay. Although I did watch a lot of Hitler documentaries on the Arts and Entertainment Network while I was writing, I never had a nightmare about him. But of course dreams are about unfinished business, and I was finishing him each day.

DB Why didn't reviewers pick up on the religious elements in your early novels?

RH I don't know. Especially in *The Assassination of Jesse James by the Coward Robert Ford*, I thought it would be clear that Bob Ford, in his later life, was a version of both Judas and Barabbas. But nobody got it.

DB The first two books reminded me of Russell Banks's book *Cloudsplitter*. He does with John Brown what you do with Emmet Dalton. The tale is told by the survivor. You give yourself a little distance that way, but you also get the sense of nostalgia. You say, "The past is closer to Emmet than the sweating glass in his hand." It's a book about the past that is not celebrating it, but simply examining it. Is there a nostalgic impulse in a lot of your work?

RH Yes. Growing up in Nebraska, I felt the past impinging on the present more than it does in other places where there's been so much tearing down and rebuilding. I only had to walk a half block to be in fields or corn and sunflowers with railroad tracks and empty boxcars and all that guns and hardware stuff. As a kid I could go instantly into the nineteenth century. I could ride my bike to Devil's Slide, a cave near the Missouri River where Jesse James supposedly hung out.

DB So legend is not that far away?

RH Seemingly. Writing is partly made up of nostalgia, but it's a job of acquainting readers with fresh information, as well as remembering things for yourself.

DB What about the criminal as celebrity? Is that part of what fascinates you?

RH I am always curious about who becomes a celebrity in the United States. There's Scott Peterson on every channel. There's Courtney Love. Paris Hilton. Donald Trump. Sometimes we celebrate actors who really can't act, and singers who have terrible voices. Fame just falls on them.

DB We are fixated on the bad seed?

RH Yes. But Jesse James's own explanation for his crimes is that they were a continuing counterinsurgency against the North after the Civil War. But villains, of course, invent rationalizations for everything.

DB Where did you find that word "honyock"?

RH My brother-in-law calls my niece that. I don't know where it comes from.

DB But you obviously do a lot of research. You have to be a student of language and linguistics. You have one "He was half-a-bubble off level" in one of the Westerns. Did you somehow research the origin of that saying?

RH I consult Eric Partridge all the time, and see when slang words and phrases were first recorded. Sometimes I'm really disappointed, because I had a great phrase I can't use. "World War II usage" must be the most common phrase in Partridge, but the carpenter's level has been around for a long time. The letters I get about historical accuracy are always from horse fanciers or gun fanciers. I had Bob Ford in one scene shooting a gun without a bullet in it. A few readers called me on that, saying that would ruin the gun's hammer; he'd never do that. But they failed to see that it was at a theatrical and irresistible moment. Bob Ford didn't care about gun handling right then. Another time I said that Jesse James and Charley Ford traveled an extraordinary number of miles on horseback in one day. A stable owner wrote me about the impossibility, but I got the information directly from Charley Ford's account in a newspaper — he too was amazed they'd ridden that far — and the reporter made no incredulous comment about it. My homework helps in replying to those skeptical letters.

DB Is *The Assassination of Jesse James* Jesse's book or Bob Ford's book?

RH I modeled it on the architecture of Shakespeare's *Julius Caesar,* only two thirds of which is actually about Julius Caesar. The rest is about Mark Antony. The same thing is true in the chapter structure of my book.

DB You became more and more fascinated with the Judas figure?

RH Right. When John Lennon was killed, I was in the midst of writing that book, and the Hinkley assassination attempt on President Reagan followed. So I got really interested in assassinations and those who commit them.

DB There's also the fascinating business of Bob Ford wanting to *be* Jesse James.

RH Yes. He has to kill Jesse to supersede him.

DB This also gets at your twin subject in some odd way, too.

RH I know.

DB Are those first two books Westerns or comedies?

RH I think they're funnier than other people think they are. I even think there are a lot of funny moments in *Hitler's Niece.* But readers aren't really looking for humor in those books. In *Isn't It Romantic?* I go after more slapstick and broad comedy, so you can't miss it.

DB Are Jesse James and Bob Ford sinned against as much as sinning? Or, do you just want to give them a complicated human dimension?

RH The latter. Remember the scene at the end where Bob Ford rejects a young woman who wants to work as a prostitute for him? That was actually in the Creede, Colorado, historical accounts. Right after he was killed, there were newspaper stories about him. They interviewed anybody that had talked to him in the last few days, and that's where that story came from. That story fascinated me because it was so atypical of our interpretation of what "the dirty little coward" was like.

DB It's perfect for adding complexity to his character.

RH Right. One of the things that always bothered me about the Jesse James films was that they just left out Bob Ford. He was merely the weasel who came in and killed Jesse. Nobody wanted to wonder why. And Jesse James actually killed people in the same way that Bob Ford killed him. It was like something from *The Sopranos*. Jesse was cutting down his enemies right and left.

DB   The genesis of the Jesse James book was the ballad?

RH   Sure, the song became wildly popular in 1882. I became fascinated with the song while researching the Daltons, who were so influenced by the James Gang that I started reading a lot about Jesse. Then I realized that nobody had ever gotten the story right. Solving questions about his killing was what got me going.

DB   The genesis of *Atticus* is interesting, too.

RH   Something happens to you and then something else happens and gradually these things accumulate, and then they somehow start to compact together and you realize they're all part of the same thing. That's how a story begins. *Atticus* began really from a talk with John Gardner. This was the last dinner party I had with him before his motorcycle accident and he was talking, of all things, about death. A woman there told a story about her grandmother's death. She said that when the grandmother died a picture fell off the wall and crashed on the floor. The first page I wrote about Atticus Cody was of him getting up in the middle of the night and looking out at the icicles hanging from the kitchen gutters and suddenly a milk pitcher crashed to the floor. I was just noodling around with images, but the novel began to take shape then, and my memories of Mexico tumbled together with the intimations of a death. We often get signs, and we don't know what to make of them. Only in retrospect can we put all of the elements together.

DB   You say a novelist has to discover what's pulling him?

RH   Yes. It's similar in most of the things I write. I have stories that I have somehow latched onto without understanding why.

DB   You discover the why as you write?

RH   Exactly.

DB   Where did *The Shadowmaker* start? I thought it was going to be "The Man That Corrupted Hadleyburg," but it veers into another direction.

RH It began with a line in John Cheever's *Falconer.* Cheever was one of my fiction teachers at Iowa. He has a character who asks another guy if he likes his own shadow. "I've never liked mine," he says. I thought that was such a funny thing to say. Also, there was a poem by Robert Louis Stevenson about a shadow and how it changes shape through the day. I thought that was fascinating. I began to think, "What if shadows didn't work to expectations?" I guess I was in some Jungian place, but I wasn't really trying to explore that. I just played with the idea. Also, I'd spent some time babysitting, so I'd read a lot of children's books. I always wanted to write one. So I decided I would do this shadow thing.

DB You seem to share Sherwood Anderson's assumption that everybody's life is interesting, and everybody's got a story to tell.

RH Sure. Sherwood Anderson was strolling down the main street of a little Ohio town and seeing all the people, a brave enterprise especially as he looked for the oddities, the strange person. There's something Gothic, misshapen, and grotesque in many of his stories. Likewise, many of my stories are based on real events that are in some ways outlandish. "Wickedness," for example, is based on the true stories of the victims and survivors of the awful blizzard of 1888. I change all the names, of course, and I fabricate whenever it suits me, but I often turn to real events and real people and look at the world with reverence, which means that the most obscene or unattractive person is also an important subject.

DB You say all your stories are experimental?

RH Well, I try different things. In "The Killers" I wanted to interpret in my own way Hemingway's famous short story and also deal with the idea of celebrity, people grasping for fame in whatever way they can. It's sort of a prelude to *Jesse James,* because Rex kills Max in order to become Max.

DB Is there going to be another story collection?

RH I hope so. I've got seven stories finished now and several more in mind.

DB Is the genre still healthy?

RH No. The publishers want novels. About a year ago my editor called and wanted to know what I was doing, and I said "I'm writing some stories right now." She called again a few months later, and I said I was working on a novel, and she said, "Well, at least you're not writing short stories." Short stories have moved into the territory of poetry. Subcultural. My friend Jim Shepard just published a book of stories, *Love and Hydrogen,* that I think is wonderful. It came out simultaneously with his novel, *Project X,* but most of the reviews paid attention to the novel and not to the stories. I thought the stories were extraordinary.

DB   In "The Boogeyman" you write a bit about Vietnam. Why have you written so little about that?

RH   I have an unpublished novel manuscript, *The Escort,* that handled much of that subject for me.

DB   John Gardner says that "good writers are androgynous." Your story "Sleepless" cuts across all sorts of lines. You not only write about a woman, but you write about a woman who's a psychic. And you do so with great compassion.

RH   When I was a textbook salesman from Random House in Illinois and Indiana I was on the road a lot and used to listen to nighttime radio. Weird stuff where I could find it. There was a woman psychic on one radio station, and she would give responses to callers' questions based on the timbre of their voices and whatever else she could pick up. Some of the things that are in "Sleepless" are just what I listened to as I was getting to the next college town. But getting to your point, good fiction writing is dependent on developing empathy for whichever characters are your subjects. Walking a mile or more in their shoes. Male writers enter women's bodies and minds, female writers enter men's. That's the androgyny John was talking about.

DB   One thing I love in that story is when she describes looking at the word "dear." The psychic sees the word "read." She has "the truly seeing eye."

RH   Right. And that's what writers do, of course. Almost every writer I know resonates with the idea that what they're trying to do is get order out of chaos. They're seeing some anagram of a word or situation, and trying to puzzle it out. Trying to get the misunderstood understood, and the complicated simplified.

DB In the last *Nebraska* story you say, "Everybody here is famous."

RH Yes. Everybody in the world matters. Everybody here is extraordinary.

DB Where did HarperCollins get the cover for *Mariette in Ecstasy*?

RH I suggested they base it on Bernini's sculpture of Saint Teresa of Avila.

DB What about the historical sources for that book?

RH Well, Saint Teresa of Avila had a number of ecstasies throughout her life. But at one point they just stopped. For seventeen years she had no recognition of the existence of God at all, but she just kept loving and serving him without complaint. And she founded one convent after another in Spain, according to a strict interpretation of the Carmelite rule.

DB That's where you get the notion that God "keeps his deepest silences for those that he loves the most"?

RH Right, yes. Part of the gift of the desert experience is that God is saying "Okay, you understand a version of me, but here's the real me." And then you just see this blank page, this void, which is indicating to you that you simply cannot grasp the vastness, the hiddenness, the mystery of God. Mariette was also based on Therese of Lisieux, a late nineteenth-century French Carmelite. She had a wonderfully childlike sense of God. She used to describe it as similar to her father standing at the top of a flight of stairs with his little girl on the bottom step, and she can't crawl up, so she just holds out her hands and her father comes down and picks her up and carries her to the top of the stairs. Ultimately, I think all of us realize that's who God is. But it's in the nature of novels to have problems, so I decided to give my nun the stigmata. I looked into the biographies and medical reports on Anne Catherine Emmerich, Therese Neumann, Padre Pio, and a number of others who had the stigmata. Particularly important was Gemma Galgani, a gorgeous young woman in Lucca, Italy, who had the stigmata and wrote many letters to her priest confessor about her sufferings. I chose aspects of all those various mystics in order to create my own.

DB The question of credibility is in the middle of things here. It seemed to me that there were at least three possibilities: she was a con artist, she was a self-deluded hysteric, she was the real deal. And you kept all that in tension?

RH I wrote from the perspective that she's the real thing, but left room for the obvious questions. In all the accounts I read about the stigmatics, there was always the question whether they could have done this to themselves, through physical injury or neurosis. In Therese Neumann's case, the investigators in Germany asked, "Why is it that she always gets the stigmata in private and not when witnesses are around?" Things like that. So I had to honor the history of this strange affliction. The doubts had to be there. Mariette Baptiste is, after all, the daughter of a physician, so she may have some medical legerdemain going on. The sisters feel she's capable of pulling the wool over everyone's eyes.

DB You insist on these complications in all your books. Your Atticus is more complicated than Harper Lee's?

RH I may be branded a heretic for saying so, but, as much as I love it, Harper Lee's celebrated novel is more of a young adult book, which is why so many read it in high school. The questions it raises are such obvious and handily discussed ones, and you know exactly whom you're supposed to root for and whom to despise.

DB When you write a book that so clearly alludes to some other source, as with *Atticus* and the parable of the prodigal son, you face the problem of formula. You already know the end of the joke. How do you handle that problem?

RH I simply tried to imagine, "What if my son actually was killed in Mexico, or committed suicide in Mexico? How would I react, and what sort of things would happen to me?" I'm trying to be authentic to the experience of a person who was there and in pursuit of a mystery.

DB It comes back to being truthful to the story.

RH Right. I enjoy reading Raymond Chandler, but there's always a cartoonish aspect to his mysteries. You don't quite believe in his characters. His sardonic humor and irony continually come into play. I was trying to resist doing that. I wanted real people, credible characters. I repeatedly tried to track everything they did or said, asking, "If that person knows what she knows, or what he knows, would they answer the question in this way?"

DB I wonder if *Atticus* is really about shame? Atticus isn't just looking for Scott. He's also looking for himself.

RH I hadn't thought of that, but you're right. Atticus is wondering about how he lost track of Scott. One of the most touching scenes for me is when Atticus pages through Scott's address book. He realizes that he doesn't recognize most of the names there. I think every parent realizes that at some point. I can never remember all the faces and names of my stepchildren's friends. I always feel embarrassed about that and fake it. "How ya doin'?" And the same probably is true for Atticus and Scott.

DB When you were doing the research on the Hitler book, were there moments when you thought, "This reminds me of the way things are now"?

RH There's some element of warning there, yes. People can be very susceptible to charismatic figures. To that extent, the book is political, I guess. There's always a sense of conspiracy and ill-dealings in governance, but it seems party divisions are becoming greater these days. Real hatred is becoming more prevalent. In Nazi Germany people said, "Well, maybe if we put these unruly people in charge, we wouldn't have so much violence." But it just became uglier. I'm not political because I just don't know very much about it. And there are too many other things I'm interested in to take the time to get fully educated.

DB In *A Stay Against Confusion* you speak of the power of literature. John Gardner says that literature should "ennoble and chasten." You quote that line. Robert Frost says that a good writer is "supernaturally wise." What does Gardner mean? What does Frost really mean when he says that poetry "ends in a clarification of life"? Gardner says "We figure out our lives through fiction." Is all of this too much to take on? Do you feel the weight of that?

RH I remember instances where I was cold in a blizzard and called

upon Tolstoy's story "Master and Man." Once I was in a very dangerous situation, parachuting from a plane, and I thought of Shakespeare's *Julius Caesar.* "It seems to me most strange that men should
fear;/Seeing that death, a necessary end, / Will come when it will
come." I've noticed in my own life that in moments of desperation or
loneliness I've called upon fiction, or poetry, or plays, to simplify my
desperation or to realize that I'm not alone. I think that's what literature does.

DB   Can literature promote virtue?

RH   Certainly. Alexander Solzhenitsyn's fiction is wonderful for
showing how in the worst, most awful sorts of situations, you can
still have integrity and dignity.

DB   How present is that in your mind as you write a book like
Atticus?

RH   Very present. I want to create characters who are larger than
life, but larger in the sense of their souls. And sometimes that soul is
decadent and corrupted and sometimes that soul is really pure —
something you would want to imitate. So the crayolas can get pretty
bright sometimes, but what you're trying to do is highlight those
moments of decision where people actually make the right choice
and perfect themselves, or make the wrong move and bring themselves woe.

DB   Where does taste come into this debate?

RH   There's a kind of fiction, the kind that, unfortunately, some
Christian bookstores prefer, which is evangelization and testimony.
This is how my life was saved, where I found Jesus as my Lord and
Savior. But that's not how Jesus himself would have told the story.

DB   In your latest novel, *Isn't It Romantic?*, you turn to the entertainment. It was time for *dolce,* for sweetness?

RH   I recognized that if Cary Grant could do a tapdance between serious movies and comedies, I could go there, too. A lot of writers seem
to feel straightjacketed into one genre or the other. They're either
comic writers or serious writers, but they don't do both. I'd like to be
ambidextrous.

DB   At one point in your career you were known as a "Western writer." Does that phrase have the same resonance as, say, "Southern writer"?

RH   The West is far more vague. It can mean Wyoming or California, and they have little in common, while Georgia and Alabama probably do. But Wallace Stegner claimed he was never reviewed in the *New York Times* until after the Pulitzer Prize for *Angle of Repose,* so there is a sense of the West as other and segregated in many people's minds.

DB   How about "Christian writer"?

RH   I appreciate that label. I'm proud of it. The Gospels insist we ought to be.

DB   "Catholic novelist" is all right?

RH   Yes. It is more like saying "Nebraska novelist," in some ways, because that's part of my unshakeable identity. It doesn't really categorize the fiction as much as it does the author.

DB   *Isn't It Romantic?* is certainly full of Nebraska and humor. How do you manage to get the laugh without denigrating the people of the region? When Natalie says she loves the place because "no one's trying to be smart here," for example, Dick says that he's not so sure that's a compliment. Neither am I.

RH   The crucial thing was that all the comments were jokes on myself and things that other Nebraskans would recognize and laugh about.

DB   So you're laughing with, not at them?

RH   Absolutely. The book sold well in Nebraska, but a French woman read the novel and said, "This is so mean." But Nebraskans are hollering with laughter when they give readings from it. They recognize the outrageous possibilities all around them. The general reaction has been very positive, though the book stayed under the radar.

DB   How does it feel to revisit one of the old books?

RH   I had to reread *Desperadoes* recently, because of the movie they're trying to make. I was pleased that I wasn't ashamed of myself. It was the first time I'd read it in fifteen, maybe twenty years, and it didn't make me cringe.

DB   Did *Isn't It Romantic?* come more quickly than *Atticus*?

RH   Yes, *Atticus* took three years, and *Isn't It Romantic?* took much less. There was no intention to make these people three dimensional. I just wanted to have them there as their functions. It is a farce, after all.

DB   You still enjoy teaching even though the writing career has bloomed?

RH   I like it. You need an audience, and you need a reason to get out of the house. I do get weary of dealing with some student sentences and misspellings, though. You know how that can be.

DB   And the new book?

RH   I'm writing about Gerard Manley Hopkins's "The Wreck of the *Deutschland*," and telling what actually happened on the shipwreck itself. It's a *Titanic* adventure intercut with Hopkins's discovery of himself as a poet. It is also a gloss on the poem. It's really about the heart of a poet, and considers the five nuns in the poem, their sense of exile, and Hopkins's own sense of exile. He felt shipwrecked in his own life, I think. He was writing the poem at the happiest time of his life, as a theology student in Wales, but he did have a sense of being cut off from his London family. He was a brilliant scholar, and was denied a fellowship at Oxford to continue on for a PhD just because of his religious conversion. In those times, in that particular place, the choice of religion closed off all kinds of opportunities. It brought back the whole specter of the religious wars. He was dealing with that in his own life. And at the same time these nuns were exiled from Germany because Otto von Bismarck created the *Kulturkampf* as a way of ridding himself of his political enemies and in a strategy of divide and conquer that Hitler adopted. He chose the Catholic minority of southern Germany as his enemy, made the schooling occupations of religious orders illegal, and got the whole population to rally around his own prejudice.

DB   What do you figure is pulling you here? Or do you even know completely yet?

RH   At first I thought it was a fascinating story about what actually happened in the shipwreck of the *Deutschland*. The ship did not go under the water; the ship foundered on a sandbar so it became a reef unto itself and the water crashed over it. And because it was the middle of December, some people froze, while others drowned. They were washed off into the sea, and, in that temperature, they didn't live very long. They were marooned in their own way. It was a slow death. Reading about this in the newspaper, and knowing very little about it, Hopkins decided to launch into this dark ode. That was fascinating to me. He was touched in a way that sparked his poetic genius. And it spawned the wonderful sonnets that followed. Had he not done it, he wouldn't have done all the other things.

DB   You're not driven by the market?

RH   John Irving told me that my "editors must just scratch their heads." I don't worry much about sales. A lot of the stuff I've taken on is not smart marketing.

DB   Style and craft matter to you?

RH   Yes, I spend a lot of time revising, editing, and carefully poring over stuff. If there's a sentence I consider really nice, then I have the courage to go on. And if everything is humdrum, I think, What's the point of this?

DB   Do you think God cares about dangling modifiers?

RH   I hope he doesn't. Or split infinitives, either.

SILAS HOUSE

Ruralist

1971 — Born in Lily, Kentucky
2001 — *Clay's Quilt*
2002 — *A Parchment of Leaves*
2004 — *The Coal Tattoo*
2005 — *The Hurting Part* (play)

Lives in Lily, Kentucky

I talked with Silas House on his back porch, which looks out on a yard where his children play surrounded by trees and elbow room. Confessing that he rambles, Silas spoke of his remarkable success with his first three novels: *Clay's Quilt, A Parchment of Leaves,* and *The Coal Tattoo.* We tackled those subjects that so often turn up in Southern literature: place, family, history, and religion. But we paused repeatedly over Silas's thoughts on faith. He was "raised Pentecostal," he says, and he talks of a childhood faith that both haunts and freshens his fiction. An accomplished short-story writer, and a recent entrant in the battle to halt mountaintop mining, Silas's truck sports a bumper sticker that reads, "I've Been to the Mountaintop and it Wasn't There." He has also worked as a creative writing professor, a rural mail-truck driver, and a short-order cook in a fast-food restaurant. "A series of bad jobs can really make a writer," he says. Silas House rides his success with humility and grace. Quietly dedi-

cated to family and friends, he still drives the roads of Laurel County, still loves Loretta Lynn, according to his other bumper sticker, and still supposes there's meaning in the days flying by. An hour with Silas at Cracker Barrel or in his truck or on his porch and you'll have a sense of how humility and integrity join. Silas House believes that writers change people, and that we all have a responsibility to preserve those stories that matter. Thus he listens intently and writes of what he has heard.

DB Let's start with the psychiatrist's couch. I say "Lee Smith" and you think?

SH Mentor. I read *Fair and Tender Ladies* when I was in college, and right around that time I published my first short story. When I read that book, I was absolutely stunned by how amazing it was. I had read *Black Mountain Breakdown* in ninth grade, so I had a history with her work. But I was so amazed by *Fair and Tender Ladies* that I wrote the only fan letter I've ever written. I told Lee how much the book meant to me and included a copy of my short story that had just been published in a small journal, *Appalachian Heritage*. She wrote me back a postcard and said that she really enjoyed the story and wished me the best of luck. I figured that would be the last I ever heard from her. About a year later, my cousin and I went over in the mountains to Hazard to a book signing she was doing. As we stood in line to have our books signed, she asked me my name. She said, "Your name sounds awful familiar; did you send me a story?" I couldn't believe she remembered. I was really embarrassed. Then we got to talking, and she said I had to come down to Hindman School to this workshop. She said it would change everything for me. I immediately started saving up money to go to Hindman. I was newly married, had a new baby, and no money. Lee wasn't there that year, because she only goes every other year. I worked with Sharyn McCrumb and Robert Morgan. Robert Morgan was a huge influence. The next year I went back and worked with Lee. But we were so broke that year that I didn't have enough for tuition and board. So I stayed in a tent. That's become sort of a legend. I was ashamed to tell them that I didn't have enough money, so I just told them I liked to camp. It rained the whole week.

DB   James Still?

SH   I only had a couple conversations with him, but his books, especially his poetry, have been hugely influential. He did say one thing to me that changed my whole life and changed my writing. It was there at Hindman and was the only major conversation we ever had. In a very naïve way, I had asked for advice. He told me to "discover something new every day." That was all he said. He was like that, gruff and of very few words. But that really had a huge impact on me. From there on out I consciously tried to discover something new every day. That not only changed my writing, it changed the whole way I lived. I think that statement had more impact on me than anything else I've ever learned about writing. I did an MFA after my first two books were published, mainly to get my degree so I could teach, and because I felt I had more to learn. But I learned more in that statement than I did in the two years of my MFA.

DB   So the writer is somebody who's paying special attention?

SH   Yes. People always think that writers are smarter than other people. That's the biggest hoax in the world. I just think writers are the ones who are looking in different ways; they're observing what a lot of other people take for granted, and just writing it down.

DB   Widow Combs?

SH   Learning her story made me an activist. It was a major moment in my life. I was doing research on *The Coal Tattoo* and learning about broad form deeds and the way that coal companies stole land. Of course, the government helped them to do that; the government had an equal role in the whole business. I happened upon the story of the Widow Combs. Later, I found a picture of her, a sixty-four-year-old woman, being carried away by two deputies. I don't see how anyone can see it and not be moved by it. It was part of a series of pictures that won the Pulitzer Prize. My family had always taught me to stand up for what I believe in, but to see the Widow Combs standing up against those bulldozers made me realize that I had to not only be a steward of the land but also be brave enough to make some people mad. In 1965 in Knott County, Kentucky, they literally carried her off her place. They were mining the mountain above her on a broad form deed. She owned the land, but they owned the mineral rights; someone had sold them fifty years before. The rocks and slate and the mining debris kept coming down on her home and destroying her land, so she just went down two days before Thanksgiving and lay down in front of the bulldozers. They had to carry her away. What was especially admirable about her was that she remained completely still. She didn't fight; she was just completely still. I put that in *The Coal Tattoo* in the scene where the women face the bulldozers. They're completely still. They're different, though, because eventually they do fight. They use the stillness as much as they can, and then they say, "If we don't fight we're going to lose our land." It was thirty years before broad form deeds were outlawed, but without the Widow Combs they never would've been.

DB   "Pantsie?"

SH   Oh, Lord. I have a first cousin that I was raised with that I call my brother. His name is Terry Dean. I never was able to pronounce pants. I was too country. I'd call them "paints." So he calls me Pantsie.

DB   What about Druther's?

SH   That was my first job. I actually started working there before it was legal for me to work. I was raised with a really strong work ethic. That was in London, Kentucky. Both of my parents had been raised incredibly poor, so even as a child I can remember feeling guilty for having so much more than they had when they were children. I guess we were lower middle class, and by the time I was a teenager we were middle class. I was very aware of that, very aware that I had more than them. And I wanted to make my own money. So about three or four weeks before I turned sixteen, I got a work permit and started at Druther's, which originally was a Burger Queen. I was a fry cook there and later left for a better job at Western Steer Steakhouse. That was out on the interstate in Corbin. I was a plate loader, which was basically a cook's assistant. I did every job there. I was a bus boy, waiter, cashier, and an assistant manager eventually. But I met my wife, Teresa, there. The first time I saw her she was reading *Black Mountain*

Breakdown by Lee Smith, and I thought, "I gotta ask that girl out" because she was reading on her break. Then she insisted that she drive, and she pulled up in this little pickup. She was playing Allison Krauss and I knew that I would marry her. Lee Smith loves that story; we tell her that she's responsible for our union.

DB   Sandra Stidham?

SH   She was my seventh grade teacher, and I still keep in touch with her. When I was in school, the Kentucky education system was in ruins. We didn't have any kind of literature course, for example, until we were seniors in high school. Miss Stidham knew that wasn't right. She knew that we should have some literature, so she just took it upon herself to teach us. She brought in all of her own books, her own personal library. It was an amazing thing to do. She put them all in the back of the room. She had a little notebook, and we could borrow any book we wanted. These were books that our public schools didn't have. They hadn't bought any books since the 1960s. Those books became hugely important to me. I found *Jubilee* by Margaret Walker, *The Outsiders* by S. E. Hinton, which is probably the most influential, integral novel of my generation. *To Kill a Mockingbird* was the major one for me. She made us do book reports. For a while there I bought my own books. The only place you could buy books in that town was at the flea market. So I was getting books that I probably shouldn't have been reading at that time. I read *Mandingo* and was completely shocked by everything in it. I read *Peyton Place* and did my book report on it. That book is pretty racy. After I did my book report, Miss Stidham pulled me aside and said, "I've noticed that you have a really strong understanding of literature for your age." She decided to steer me toward books that were more acceptable than *Peyton Place* and *Mandingo*. That's how I came to *To Kill a Mockingbird*. When I did my book report on it, she saw how affected I was by it. She gave me that book. You hear about teachers having a huge impact, but I don't think that I would've been a writer if she hadn't done that.

DB   She says you were "born to write."

SH   Well, I always wanted to be a writer. But not until I read *To Kill a Mockingbird* did I feel like it was something I could do with my life. My family always ingrained in me that I should do something. I shouldn't just try to make a living and raise my family. You should do that, but you should also try to make a positive impact on the world.

DB That's probably related to your religious heritage?

SH I think that's a big part of it.

DB How do you explain your fascination with books? Where did that come from?

SH I was born that way. I wasn't raised in a house where people were reading a lot. They were obsessed with never falling back into poverty. I wouldn't say they were workaholics, because that has negative connotations, but they worked all the time. My mother worked in the cafeteria at the elementary school; my father was a supervisor at a fiberglass factory. Then they were always working at the house. My father poured concrete on his days off. But it wasn't like I was this child who was left alone, because his parents were working. They made work something that we all did together. I never felt left out or anything. When they read, they read the Bible. But my father had been a big reader as a child. He had been obsessed with James Fenimore Cooper. But nobody in my family sat around and read the way that I do. I think I was just born that way.

DB But you did grow up going to church?

SH Oh, yes.

DB And so the Bible was the King James Version?

SH Oh, yeah.

DB Does that have something to do with your preoccupation with language?

SH I grew up hearing stories. My family was all storytellers. They knew how to tell a story; it was innate. They just knew how to do it without even knowing they did. They knew how to exaggerate. Every time they retold a story, they'd change something. They knew how to pick up small details. I don't think I would've been a writer without the church. You know, there are all these little factors that make you into a writer. One of them was Miss Stidham and *To Kill a Mockingbird*. Another was having a family of storytellers. And a major one was growing up in a family that went to church. People would stand up and give their testimonies. Poetry would just fall out of their mouths, pure poetry. They weren't saying anything for their own glory. They were just putting words together in a beautiful way to articulate what they felt. I can remember from a very young age these people standing up and giving testimonies. I was always struck by how everybody had a story; everybody in the church had their own particular story. There was this one woman whose husband wasn't saved. Her recurring theme was how hard it was to love this man completely while knowing that he wasn't of the same mind as her. And there was another woman, a widow woman, and a man who'd been healed from cancer. He would tell that story over and over, but you never got tired of it, because he always told it in a different way and there was always the perfect little details. Then there were the sermons, too. It always amazes me how these preachers, none of whom were educated, could tell these brilliant, amazing stories and make these analogies and have these metaphors and similes that were just amazing. I don't know where they came from. They hadn't been to seminary. Some of them hadn't even been to high school. People always ask me if I work hard on my metaphors and similes. I don't. That comes very naturally to me and I think that's from hearing those sermons full of pictures all my life. We went to church three or four nights a week: Sunday school, Sunday night service, Thursday night Bible study, and Tuesday night prayer meeting. We would go to tent revivals and camp meetings. My mother was a singer. She sang all over the place, and so I would go with her. When we went to Mammoth Cave, the whole church went. The whole way there, we were in a van with everybody singing church songs. That's the thing about the Pentecostal faith. It's a culture; it's more than a church, and that's why it's so hard to leave it. I'm always quick to point out to people that, even though I am not a member of the Pentecostal church today, I still identify with the Pentecostals, and I never ever will say anything negative about the Pentecostals.

DB   You see the world through that lens?

SH   Yes. When you're a writer, people assume you're agnostic. They all assume I'm an agnostic or an atheist. They also assume that I could never ever embrace Pentecostalism, that I would be completely against all that. They're wrong. I'm glad I was raised that way, very glad. In my writing, I try to portray Pentecostals as human beings as opposed to the snake-handlers, poison drinkers, and fanatics that the media projects. In *Clay's Quilt*, one of my Pentecostal characters is a fanatic, of course, but the main Pentecostal character, Easter, is a complex human being who thinks deeply about her faith.

DB She even goes through considerable doubt.

SH Definitely.

DB Jack Hoskins?

SH That's my uncle. He was murdered when I was eleven years old and that's another thing that made me a writer. Maybe the major thing. After he was killed the family stopped telling stories about him for a long time. Because they knew that stories about him would always end with everybody breaking down and crying, they stopped. The way he died was so unjust. His murderer went free. It took us years to get over it. I don't mean this in an arrogant way, but I think *Clay's Quilt* enabled them to get over it in a way that they hadn't before. This death was the only time in my childhood that I can remember when my parents didn't pay attention to me. The whole world was revolving around that instead of me. I think that's when my observation skills became the best. I remember the murder, the funeral, and the whole mourning period. My parents thought that I didn't understand, but, of course, I did. I even went to the trial. I heard all the testimony and heard the way that people told the same story from so many different points of view. It really helped me as a writer to understand point of view, the way that people see things differently. But the main thing I learned is that, if stories are not written down, eventually they die. I didn't want that to happen with my uncle. That's when I really started keeping track in a serious way. It also changed our whole family dynamic. It hurt our family in so many, many ways. This is really hard to talk about, but my uncle was actually killed by my fourth cousin. When you're an Appalachian family, you know who your fifth and sixth cousins are. It's like this is part of your immediate family. So it caused a division in the family that has never been healed. I think that's one reason all my books are about families. No matter how mad you get at each other, there's still an unconditional love, this thread of unconditional love that holds you together as an Appalachian family. Family is the only thing that matters, you know. I just saw the movie *Hotel Rwanda*, about the genocide there. I remember a scene where folks are being dragged away, and this man, who has a little bit of a pull with the government, watches. His wife begs him to help their neighbors, but he says, "I am saving up all my favors for when it comes to our family. We have to watch out for our family; that's the only thing we can worry about right now." It's a universal thing. I think the reason it's lasted so much longer in Appalachian families is because they've suffered hardship, real hardship, more recently than most other Americans. And also, being an Appalachian is being a perpetual immigrant in this country. We'll always be treated as immigrants. We have an ethnicity that hasn't become mainstream. Lots of immigrants came here and became American in the way they spoke and ate and the rest. Appalachia is one of the few places in America that has held to a unique ethnicity.

DB   Why is that?

SH   It's in our blood not to let go of things easily. We're Scotch-Irish, Cherokee, African-American, and more.

DB   You are also interested in those people who fled the mountains for Detroit, Toledo, Dayton, and other factory cities, only to feel displacement and homesickness.

SH   I'm writing a play right now, commissioned by the University of Kentucky, called "The Hurting Part." It's all about a family who moved to Dayton. It is about homesickness.

DB   You deal with that in "The Unsent Letter."

SH   Yes, the play is based on that story.

DB   Who has written about the poor white migrations from the South?

SH   Harriet Arnell's *The Dollmaker* would be the major one, I guess.

DB   Joyce Carol Oates has a piece about moving to Detroit.

SH   *The Dollmaker* is one of Oates's favorite books.

DB   We haven't talked about Aunt Sis yet.

SH   Well, I've said I was raised in a Pentecostal home. But my parents were pretty laid back.

DB   Liberal Pentecostals?

SH   Yes, as crazy as that sounds. They gave me the sacred upbringing, and Aunt Sis gave me the profane upbringing. I'm exaggerating only a bit. After going to church three or four times a week, I would stay with Sis for a while. She would sneak me out to a Bob Seger concert. She snuck me into my first bar when I was fifteen. The first cigarette I ever smoked came from her pack. I smoked it in her bathroom. I would sneak over to her house when she got home from work at eleven o'clock on a school night, and she would let me stay up and watch the late show. She let me read her "True Story" magazines. I read one recently that I found in her closet; I couldn't believe how dirty it was. This was in the late 1970s. So she evened out things for me. She took me to see *The Exorcist* when I was four years old. She didn't have very good judgment at all, but she was the quintessential cool aunt. Aunt Sis and my mother were so different, but they had that unconditional love for one another. They had sort of a mother and daughter relationship. It was never a problem for them that Sis was out partying every night, and my mother was at church every night. I think that's amazing that they were able to avoid falling out over that. They accepted each other the way they were.

DB   That must inform your portrait of Easter and Anneth.

SH   Absolutely. The whole book grew out of this huge fight they had one night when Aunt Sis threw a kettle at my mother's head. I thought they'd never speak again. But the next day, it was over. They made up so easily. My mother said, "Sisters don't really make up; they just go back to the way things were." The whole book, *The Coal Tattoo*, came out of that line.

DB   What about your friends from literary climes, people like Michael Chitwood and Ron Rash. Have you found a community there?

SH   It was hard for me initially when I started going to conferences and the like. A lot of readers believe that writers are smarter than other people. They've completely bought into that. There are academics, so many of them, who forget that literature should be about people and not about stylistics. I realized that so many writers and academics were prejudiced toward me just because of the way I spoke. They thought I was ignorant, because of the way I talked, until I'd talked long enough to convince them otherwise. Therefore, you tend to form really strong relationships with those people who don't treat you that way. The first people who really embraced me who were established writers were Michael Chitwood and Ron Rash, who has become known recently as a novelist, but has been known in different circles for a long time as a poet, a great poet. Another was Larry Brown, a major friendship for me. I just worshipped his writing. We were doing a book signing together in Jackson, Mississippi, when I first met him, and I was completely in awe. Afterwards, our publicist took us out to eat. This restaurant had a smoking room, and Larry and I both ended up there. It was the first time I ever met a writer where in the first ten minutes we weren't talking about books. We were talking about fishing and squirrel hunting and knives. He said, "You know it's so good to meet a writer who knows how to smoke a Marlboro, how to fish bluegill, and how to hunt squirrels." Our whole relationship was built on that. My closest friends tend to be like that; they tend to come from backgrounds similar to mine. Pam Duncan is my best friend in the writing world. She's a writer from North Carolina. But at the same time, one of my best friends is also very different from me. She's a writer, Neela Vaswani, raised in New York City. Her father is South Asian Indian, and her mother's Irish. On the surface, people would think, "Why are they such close friends?" But we both relate to being ethnic. People see her face and reach a particular assumption about her, just as people hear my voice and reach a particular assumption about me. So we relate. She's a huge part of my writer's community.

DB What about Algonquin Books?

SH I always dreamed about being with Algonquin. Most of my favorite writers were there: Larry Brown, Kaye Gibbons, Clyde Edgerton. A lot of people will buy an Algonquin book just because it's an Algonquin book. I don't think any other press can say that. They have a history of publishing really great Southern literature. I was really honored when they called and thankful to them for giving me a chance.

DB You've had considerable freedom there?

SH Yes. If I'd been with another publishing house, for example, I think there would have been more pressure with my second book, *A Parchment of Leaves*. *Clay's Quilt* did really well for a first novel, to my surprise, and I think to Algonquin's surprise. The smart commercial thing would've been to write another contemporary book. But I went the opposite way with *Parchment*. I can see all these little things that have fallen into place for me. I feel really blessed. I thought what happens will happen; things will happen when they're supposed to. There for a while I didn't think I would get published. I worked on *Clay's Quilt*, worked on the book and worked on getting it published for almost eight years. I never gave up. I thought it would happen when it was meant to happen.

DB But you've known you were a writer for a long time?

SH Yes, but it's built in intensity.

DB How is it that you came to transfer the power of *To Kill a Mockingbird* into your own life? Why is it that some readers are able to claim a book that way?

SH By the time I read *To Kill a Mockingbird*, it didn't have the impact that it had when it was published. The world had changed. As a child in the late 1970s, I witnessed racism. When I was very small they still had water fountains in Corbin, at the Newberry Department Store, labeled "whites" and "colored." So I was completely aware of racism but on a different level than something that was written in 1963 would've been. The huge impact for me with that book was in the family dynamic. The story features these incredible characters. Reading that book and reading *Black Mountain Breakdown* convinced me that books didn't have to be set in Hollywood or New York. They could be set in small towns and be about rural, working-class people, and still matter. *To Kill a Mockingbird* was about social change, not only in race relations, but in everything. One of my favorite lines in *To Kill a Mockingbird* is, "You never really know a man until you put on his shoes and walk around in them." And my favorite line in that book is, "There's only one kind of folks. Folks." Period. "Folks." That's one thing I'm trying to show in my work. My characters come from a unique place. Someone might be reading about them in Idaho or Oregon or California or India or Australia or wherever. But at the heart of it, we're just people, we're all just people. We all have the same struggles and desires. People tend to think that Appalachians are cartoon characters — the "Dukes of Hazzard" or whatever.

DB You speak often of feeling incredibly blessed by your writing life. You even talk about your books as "gifts." Gifts to you. You say that writing *A Parchment of Leaves* sometimes felt like taking dictation, recording the words of a ghost. In one speech you referred to it as "a supernatural experience." Can you explain that?

SH Well, all my books are supernatural to some degree. But *A Parchment of Leaves* was that way to an eerie degree. I just wanted to write the book, because I knew that my great grandmother was a full-blooded Cherokee and was taught to hide that. So I thought the whole book would be about being Cherokee. But, though that's part of the book, it turned out not to be the major part. There was this woman's voice pushing me. She did a lot of things I didn't want her to do. She ends up killing a man, and she ends up getting raped. I didn't know any of that was going to happen when I started writing the book. The character informed me of all that. The character took control of my life for a while. I write a book in a very methodical way. I believe in method writing. In *A Parchment of Leaves*, Vine is a great gardener. She has a natural ability to make things live. I'd always raised a garden, but when I was writing that book, I raised a huge garden. It took up so much time. That whole book was written in the garden. I don't really know how to articulate it, but it was all completely given to me. There are whole passages in that book, pages and pages, that I read and have absolutely no memory of writing. I'll think, "Man that's good writing." But I don't feel responsible for it, because I don't remember writing it. It was just given to me. A lot of people will laugh at me for saying this, but I do believe that writers are just mediums in a way. The act of imagination is supernatural.

DB So you really think of the characters as taking over?

SH I don't think that I have a book until I feel like my characters are living people, that they exist, and that I carry them with me everywhere I go.

DB You say that "if there's not joy in the writing there won't be joy in the reading."

SH I believe that. I've never forced myself to write. I never sit there and stare at a blank page. Writing is always hard. But when it becomes miserable, I just don't do it. If I'm not enjoying the whole act of writing, I scrap it. I don't use it. There's a really thin line between the writer and the reader, and whatever I'm feeling when I'm writing, the reader will be feeling. That's another level of the supernatural act of writing.

DB No outlines or note cards?

SH No, no. With *Clay's Quilt* I knew I wanted to write a book about a family whose whole dynamic had been changed by murder. With *A Parchment of Leaves* I knew that I wanted to write about a Cherokee woman who marries an Irishman. And with *The Coal Tattoo* I knew I wanted to write about two sisters who are incredibly different yet love each other unconditionally. And that's all I knew. With the new book I'm writing now, I know I want it to be set in the summer of 1976. I want it to be from the point of view of a ten year old whose father is a Vietnam vet. Every writer works in the way that works best for them. When Lee Smith does a book, she has a whole notebook for each character. She knows what their favorite color is and what they eat for breakfast. She has it all written down. I discover these things as I'm writing the book.

DB Does this new book have a title yet?

SH *Their Secret Trees,* but I don't know if that's going to work or not.

DB You not only want to tell a good story, something that taps into the universal hunger for good stories, but you also want those stories to be "shot through with hope." In one speech you change "hope" to "light." How does that work?

SH Serious literary writers, these days, the ones who win all the big awards, tend to be writing doom and gloom. They are so cynical, so devoid of hope, that, reading them, I feel like slitting my wrists. I don't think readers really want that. People want hope. That's really the fundamental thing that we share. It just makes sense to me that every story should get to that. Lots of people think that if you have too much hope, especially at the end of the book, then you come off as sentimental. My reply to that is, "What's wrong with being sentimental?" We're sentimental by nature. We're human beings, and we are sentimental. There's a difference between being sappy and being sentimental. There's a movement in contemporary literature to strip everything of sentimentality or hope or love. When *The Coal Tattoo* came out, I was absolutely ravaged in the Memphis paper. The reviewer just tore me down, because my characters said, "I love you" several times in the book. I'd respond by noting that people actually say those words to each other. That's real life, and that's what I'm supposed to be writing about. If you take the love and the hope out of the book, then you don't have real people — you don't have real characters anymore. And it just becomes this doom and gloom stuff that, frankly, I think is pretentious. Recently, I was at a reading and a writer announced, "I'm going to read this poem about going to church. But I want you all to know that I haven't been to church in ages. I stopped believing in God long before I stopped believing in Santa Claus." She had to make sure that we knew she didn't believe in God, lest we think that she was an ignoramus. That's bothersome to me, very bothersome. Such assumptions have pushed me in the opposite direction.

DB But this is a tricky business. You say you've resisted a sequel to *Clay's Quilt* because you "want those characters to stay happy." You say "nobody really wants to read about happy people." In your speech at Calvin College, you said "nobody really wants to read about saints."

SH Nobody wants to read about happy people but they want to read about people becoming happy.

DB Ann Ross has made a mint out of writing about happy people. Jan Karon and Phil Gulley have explored this territory a bit.

SH It's a fine line. I write about working people, and there are two things that they completely embrace: despair and happiness. They don't do either halfway. When they're sad, man, they're sad all the way. And when they're happy, they're happy all the way. And I must say that I love Ann Ross's books; she knows how to tell a story and her characters might end up being real happy, but they struggle, too. They feel real to me.

DB Do you see a difference between a happy ending and a hopeful ending?

SH I think a hopeful ending is a happy ending, but I'm not sure a happy ending is a hopeful ending. I always want to give the reader some power in my endings. The more interactive you make a book, the more the reader will remember it. If you give readers every single bit of information, they're not going to carry the book with them. If you lead them to where they can come to their own conclusions, then they will. People are all the time asking me about *Clay's Quilt*. They want to know if Cake and Dreama end up together. A lot of people get mad because I didn't tell them. But the majority of the people are really happy that they can come to their own conclusion about that. The major question I get about *A Parchment of Leaves* is about whether Vine ever gets to see her family in North Carolina again. I think it's very clear at the end that she and Saul have rectified their situation, that his love for her has taken over anything that might make him pause. He's going to take her to see her family. If he doesn't, by God, she'll go by herself. She's a strong woman, you know? But the reader has to work that through.

DB So a happy ending might just be too neat where a hopeful ending might indicate a tending toward affirmation?

SH In the end of *A Parchment of Leaves* Vine admits to Saul that she's killed his brother. Then she waits to see what he's going to do. Is he going to go wild, hate her, leave her? Is he going to forgive her? He ends up forgiving her. That's all we know.

DB This actually circles back to the question of how faith circulates in your fiction. You talk about writing as "testimony," a really loaded word, given your Pentecostal background. While at the same time you maintain a loyalty to the notion that your characters are in control of the story. How do you pull that off? You say, "I want my readers to know that God exists and that we ought to be paying attention to him." How do you hold to that purpose and at the same time let your characters lead the way?

SH I'm not sure how credible it is when your mother brags on you, but the most gratifying thing that anybody has ever said to me about my writing was something my mother said after reading *A Parchment of Leaves:* "You know I always thought you would end up being a preacher. Now I think that you are. I think that you are delivering a message to people." My books are not blatantly Christian, but all my books have a message about being the best person that you can be. *A Parchment of Leaves* is definitely my most religious book. The entire message of that book is that forgiveness is the whole thing. When I think of being a good Christian, I think the major thing for me is being able to forgive people. Without forgiveness you can't move on. I think that being a believer has a lot to do with forgiveness and kindness. So that's one thing that I try to do in my books. I show people being actively kind. My books always have believers. And part of my testimony is that, just because you're a believer, that doesn't mean you're ignorant. I teach in an MFA program in Louisville, and, during one of my readings, I said something about having been raised Pentecostal. A woman there later warned one of my friends: "Don't trust him too much," she said, "he's a fundamentalist." Because I made it known that I believed in God and considered myself a Christian, I was automatically a fundamentalist. This took place during the presidential elections. Assumptions were made about my politics and more. You say that the Southern stereotypes are among the last people can still get away with, but I'd say Christian bashing is still pretty much in vogue, too.

DB Jim Wayne Miller says that the most common Appalachian malady is homesickness. That clearly plays in your books. Laurel County is not only the South as a historic region, it is also a mythic ideal.

SH One reason I feel such a strong sense of place is because, when you're from Appalachia, you have to constantly defend where you're from, so that makes you end up loving it even more. That's something I figured out while I was writing *The Coal Tattoo.* I had been asked so many times about my sense of place with the first two books. I always write about things I don't completely understand, and so one thing I was exploring in *The Coal Tattoo* was love for place. Anneth and Easter and the others end up actually fighting for the place they love. My favorite passage in *The Coal Tattoo* is the scene where Easter is sitting on her porch, breaking beans. Her husband is drinking beer. She thinks about all the city people driving by. She knows they would see her and El sitting on the porch and shake their heads over what poor little lives these people lead, how simple their lives are. She knows how wrong they are, how complex her life is. It never bothers me when I go places where people talk about illiteracy and that stuff, because it's just so ridiculous. What really bothers me is the assumption that this place is simple. That makes me defensive. Lives here are as complex, as complicated, as lives in Manhattan.

DB Isn't there a way in which a writer is always an outsider, though, even in his or her own place?

SH I've often felt like a man without a country, because when I was growing up the only other boy that I knew who wanted to be a writer was John Boy Walton. That was it. He was the only person I had to relate to. Thank God for Earl Hammer and "The Waltons." At the same time, lots of people think that, because I was this boy growing up in this really rural place and wearing my writer dream on my sleeve, that people made fun of me. They didn't. I didn't have anybody to relate to, but everybody encouraged me. At the end of my senior year of high school I had to write a senior will. You will people things, good wishes. Every single person willed me a best seller or a Pulitzer Prize or a published novel. At the same time I felt like an outsider because they were playing in the quarry and I was reading books.

DB And the place you're from may not be there anymore. The South is changing. Appalachia is changing.

SH There's definitely a homogenization of the South that can be seen as healthy progress: economic progress, civil rights progress. But sometimes there's something wrong. A culture is dying, too. I have a friend who's from Columbus, Ohio, who says he doesn't have a sense of place. They never talk there about being Midwestern or being

Northern or being anything. When he comes down here, we're always talking about being Southern or being Appalachian. Our whole world revolves around that. I tell him how sad that makes me for him. It's such a huge part of my life, that identification with the people of this place and others like it. I don't consider myself a Southern writer per se or an Appalachian writer per se, but I do think of myself as a rural writer. I've gotten letters from every state in the United States and from foreign countries. They say, "Black Banks reminds me of my place." It's the rural thing they've spotted.

DB Has this identification that Southerners feel about their place increased in the last decade or two? As a child, I don't ever remember seeing Confederate flags, for example. Now you see them all the time. It is as if, because the larger world has identified the Southerners in a certain way, they've sort of adapted that stereotype.

SH When you see something slip away, you get stubborn about it. When I was growing up, I didn't know I was Appalachian. I never heard that world. Now my children have Appalachian week at their elementary school. The school brings in fiddlers and basket makers and chair makers and potters, and they teach them something called "heritage skills." Nobody ever taught us anything like that. It's only because it's started to disappear. That causes people to say, "We've got to hold on to this."

DB I remember an essay you wrote about the company that will retrain accents for eighty dollars. That's amazing. What do you think about "Blue Collar Comedy" and Jeff Foxworthy and the rest? And what does it mean to "talk proud"?

SH To talk proud is to mask your accent and try to be something that you're not. There was this woman in our family who went off to Ohio and worked and then came back. She'd been gone a year or so, and she came back enunciating everything. She spoke clearly but her grammar was awful. She was pronouncing words with a proper Northern accent, but she got her grammar all wrong. She was talking proud, and we laughed. The Foxworthy stuff is harder to explain. A lot of Southern writers would disagree with my opinion, but I think one thing that's really special about Southerners is that we are able to laugh at ourselves. If Jeff Foxworthy wasn't from Georgia, that would be trouble. If he was from Massachusetts or Michigan, then we would be mad about it. *O Brother, Where Art Thou?* is a really good example. That movie is absolutely loaded with Southern stereotypes, but when it played here it was a much bigger hit than it was in New York City. We went in and laughed at all those stereotypes, because it was almost as if it was making fun of the stereotypes and the people who believe such stereotypes. And there's Dollywood. They're making a killing by selling hillbilly lifestyles for forty dollars. But most of the money is staying in the region. In the Smokies you can go to the Cherokee reservation. There's this man who will pose in front of a teepee. You can get your pictures taken with him. Cherokees never lived in teepees, but this Cherokee man is probably a millionaire by now because he is playing off these stereotypes. It is complicated. I'm not going to put Appalachian stuff in my work to sell my books. I don't ever put outhouses in my books. But if a character happens to be barefoot, I'm not going to keep them from being barefoot just because they're Appalachian.

DB You got into the controversy over the "New Beverly Hillbillies," the television series that was eventually scrapped?

SH Yes. All these groups raised money to fight this reality show. They took out ads in the *New York Times*. Now I know people who don't have enough money to heat their homes, to feed their children. There's so much that money could've gone for. You should pick your battles wisely. Why should I be ashamed for somebody from my region to go on a reality show? People who go on reality shows are just asking to be made fun of anyway, no matter where they're from. That's part of the deal. I was saying, "why not?" The producer was from Appalachia, and he wanted to make a show where the city folk were made to look stupid, so why not give him a chance? But a lot of people got mad at me for that. CBS finally gave it up. The protest worked, but it was a stupid thing to protest. There's too many other things. We should be taking out whole page ads about children being murdered. Not a reality show.

DB You've said that you want your books "to give a voice to working people." You want the strong faith of the people of this region to be known. Are you writing to demystify stereotypes?

SH Well, some stereotypes are based in fact, and I can't deny that. Some people within the region were upset by *Clay's Quilt*, because they thought I perpetuated some stereotypes. Like people drinking all the time, and people doing dope, and running the roads. They didn't like the honky-tonks and all that. But that was the world I was part of in my early twenties. It exists. So I wrote about it. On the other hand, people say that I have broken some stereotypes. The best letters are from people saying I made them understand a place they had completely misunderstood. I try to have human beings in my stories. That's what breaks stereotypes, making your characters real. When you read something that's really stereotypical, the reason it's stereotypical is because the characters are one dimensional, you know? You have a stereotype when you have a character whose only purpose is to drink moonshine. I write about the people I grew up around. I think that they're beautiful people. They believe strongly, and they never lay that belief aside. They are vocal about what they believe; they have a strong work ethic. I was on a radio program not long ago, and this woman was interviewing me for a live call-in show. She said I was there to talk about Appalachian stereotypes. She said, "Come on, Silas, we all know that people in Appalachia are lazy." I said, "Well, how do you know that?" She said, "You just drive through there. Look at the trash, and look at how people are living. Everybody's on welfare." She went on and on. I asked her if she'd been to downtown Louisville lately. There are people like that everywhere. Why didn't she notice the people who have nice homes, people who are working for a living, and trying their best to get by in the world? I tried to suggest that this history of poverty is hard to overcome. She believed that Appalachian people are shiftless, because they're all originally from Scotland. It's unbelievable what people will say. Another woman called in to say that Appalachian men beat their wives. It's just unbelievable.

DB Do you write by ear?

SH I never put anything in dialogue unless I've heard it. A little goes a long way. I think that when you put a lot of dialect on the page it becomes "Hee Haw"-ish. I tell my students that dialect should be used like salt — a little bit flavors and too much ruins. I don't like phonetic spellings. That makes the character look ignorant. The main thing I use is syntax. I think Appalachian people have a unique way of putting sentences together. When you see that syntax, then you can hear the accent. People in the South use a lot of similes when they speak. We never say, "The sky is black"; we say, "The sky is black as the ace of spades." I think that Southerners tend to be better story-tellers because of that. I'm thirty-three years old, and I continue to hear new metaphors. Just the other day, my grandmother was talking about her days of living at a boarding house. She was telling us how my grandfather came to court her the first time. "He rode his horse up a mountain that was steep as a calf's face," she said. My aunt was talking about my grandfather, who was in the hospital. The doctor had said my grandfather was about dead, but "didn't act it." My aunt said, "That Johnny Shepherd is tougher than a pine knot." Over and over they talk that way. So I use those similes, and I think that gets a lot of the Appalachian flavor without having to use all that stuff that sounds condescending.

DB You want your readers to be changed by your books?

SH In *A Parchment of Leaves,* I was just thinking about the simple thing that the world could be a better place if I could be kinder to people, if I could be more forgiving. If I could just get one person to leave the book feeling that way, then I've accomplished something. It's like the line in *To Kill a Mockingbird,* "There's only one kind of folks. Folks." After I read that line I was never prejudiced about people again. I saw that people were people, no matter who they were, or what they looked like, or where they were from. I know so many writers from this region who will go out on a book tour with a chip on their shoulders, "Oh god, I have to go through Michigan; every-body's going to be horrible there," they think. When I go on book tour, I don't go with that attitude. I find that 95 percent of the people around me are good people. Because of where I'm from, 5 per-cent are rude. You tend to really remember those 5 percent, but I always try to remind myself of the others who were so welcoming to me.

DB We were talking about Larry Brown a moment ago. Doesn't he say, "You have to lose sentimental feelings about your characters"?

SH Yes, I believe that. I am more sentimental than Larry. He and I talked about that many times. I think you should never get too sentimental about your characters, but you should give the reader the opportunity to. I love my characters. But at the same time I'm completely aware of their faults. If you lose sight of your character's faults, then you've lost your character. Anneth, from *The Coal Tattoo,* is a real person to me. I think about her. Part of the reason I love her is because of her faults. She has made really bad mistakes, and I think the reader relates to her. If I had sentimentalized her too much, then the reader wouldn't have cared for her. I allowed her to make mistakes. Even Easter, who would be most easily sentimentalized, makes mistakes.

DB She backslides?

SH Yes. And she becomes selfish. Nobody wants to read about perfect people. You know, Larry was more gloom and doom than I am, but he does have hope in his books. It's subtle but definitely there. Heartbreak is also all over his books.

DB Ezra Pound says that everybody's didactic. We all know that every writer has an agenda. We also know that writers learn to hide their agendas. How do you get away with what you call "sprinkling spirituality" throughout your books?

SH I guess it's easy for me, because I'm writing about people who are like me. So I think it's very natural to the book that a certain didacticism comes through. My characters are like that.

DB But it's not you, it's them? You're one step removed from the danger of planting your beliefs?

SH Right. For example, Easter thinks about religion in a very different way than I do. She thinks about it more in the way my mother does. I would be closer to the way that Anneth thinks about spirituality. Or Vine. I let their beliefs carry the story.

DB You see a difference between the words "religious" and "spiritual"?

SH I do. Easter is more about religion as an institution, the whole organization of religion. I think it's important to her. The whole act of going to church, the act of having a congregation, matters. Anneth and Vine, on the other hand, find their congregations in the trees. To be honest, I don't care if it's a problem. I'm sure some people have been put off by the spirituality of my books. I don't care; that's just too bad. There's plenty of books that are too secular. Spirituality is a huge part of my life and a huge part of the lives of the people that I write about, I don't worry about it. I want to write about people who are believers, because I don't think there's enough of them in literature, especially contemporary literature. I am writing a book now that is my most secular book. The family in the book doesn't go to church. They operate more on the mindset of being good people, but they're not religious at all. There's nothing overtly religious. But that's just because of the way the characters have come to me for this book.

DB You say, "I was raised Pentecostal." You don't say I was raised *a* "Pentecostal." That distinction seems important. It sounds like it is in your blood — not something you did, but something you were. Yet you must feel ambivalence about some aspects of Pentecostalism. Is there a side of it that you can embrace while another side that seems dangerous? I know you've had your times of rebellion. Is your attitude toward religion a love/hate thing?

SH Well, I never really left my faith. When you're a Pentecostal, you reach an age where you either completely embrace the church or you rebel against it. And I rebelled against it, went wild for a while. I drank and partied and was the opposite of how I'd been raised to be. During that time, I was wild because I knew that the doctrines of the Pentecostal church were too strict. I couldn't accept these man-made laws that had nothing to do with God. Women had to wear dresses; women couldn't cut their hair. If you say the word "shit," you're going to burn in hell forever. If you go to movies, it's a sin. If you go to the carnival, it's a sin.

DB Don't forget dancing.

SH Oh, yes. If you dance, it's a sin. I knew that those things were not right for me. I saw that such rules were keeping a lot of people from worshipping God. I was wild because I thought I was going to hell anyway. I might as well just do it all. Slowly I began to figure out that a cuss word doesn't mean that I'm going straight to hell. If I go to an R-rated movie, it doesn't mean I have back-slid. So I began to see how I could be a Christian but also be of the world. The major thing that you hear over and over in the Pentecostal church is not being of the world.

DB   In the world but not *of* the world.

SH   Worldliness is wrong. That's why I don't go to the Pentecostal church right now. We're still searching for a church that works for us. We've tried several churches, and they're all so boring. When you're raised Pentecostal, you're used to people clapping and dancing and singing these fast songs and hollering. There's nothing organized about it. We've gone to a few churches around here where everything is so organized and ceremonial. They were even more man-made than the Pentecostal variety. I feel at peace in being a Christian and living a Christian life, but at the same time I feel the need for a congregation that I don't have.

DB   You have no formal religious practice?

SH   I come out here on the porch every morning and write. It is six o'clock and the world is coming awake, and I can hear the birds. Everything is just beautiful as the mist is coming over the rise. I'm completely aware of God, and the morning is worship. For me the whole act of writing is worship. So I have a church in a way. When I'm walking in the woods, it's church. But at the same time that sounds really paganistic, New Age, and corny to me.

DB   And individualistic?

SH   Right. So I'm still searching for the right way to have a congregation.

DB   It sounds like you're trying to take the best from what you grew up with and work out your own plan somehow?

SH   Sure. When I was twenty-three or twenty-four, I had started back to church with my parents. I thought I could go to church there, still believe my own way, and have fellowship. They are good people. Then I went to a concert, a Shania Twain concert, embarrassingly enough. There was another church member there. He acted so ashamed. He wouldn't speak to me; he acted like he hadn't seen me. I realized he was doing that because he thought it was wrong for us to be there. I knew that most of the church folk would gasp audibly at the idea of us being at that concert. I haven't been back to that church since, in any kind of serious way, besides Easter and Christmas. I feel really blessed for having been raised Pentecostal, but it's really messed me up in a lot of ways.

DB   And you've found some connection between the church and the honky-tonk?

SH   What really struck me when I first started going to honky-tonks was that it was all about celebration. It was all about celebrating being alive. The whole honky-tonk thing was more about celebrating the self. Whereas church is more about celebrating God.

DB   But the energy was similar?

SH   In the Pentecostal church, very similar. The music is rousing and hypnotic. Music makes you do things. They know what they're doing when they start playing that music for the altar call. It's the same way in a bar. If you want to get people to buy more drinks, you play a drinking song. If you want them out on the dance floor, you play dancing songs. And so it is similar. It feels corny to say such things, but in church, when everybody's clapping and everybody's singing together, you feel very alive. And it is the same way in bars; when you're out there dancing, you feel very alive. You feel very blessed to be alive. Both places can make you happy and thankful. But I guess my major problem with the church overall is that so much of it is man-made. I think that often God must just laugh at some of the things we've come up with in our churches. There's this line in a Woody Allen movie, I think it's in *Hannah and Her Sisters,* something about if Jesus Christ knew all of the atrocities that have been committed in his name, he'd vomit.

DB   You've worked at the promotion side of the writing business — the tours, the signings, and the rest: Don't you resent the time away from the writing that all the promotional work requires?

SH   I realized early on that, if you're a literary writer, you have to be aware of both the art and the business. People still think that you write a book and send it off and that's it. But if you really want your books read, you have to get out there and work. That's the hard part. That's the really hard part. I've benefited a lot from those book tours and they can be fun. I knew that I'd have to go out and make people know about my books. I knew this, because I had read so many great books that nobody'd heard about. I didn't want my book to be a book that nobody's heard about.

DB   Dying in the remainder section?

SH   Yes. Algonquin is a house that really does touring big time. They believe in sending you out on the road. And Algonquin has authors that booksellers and the public come to care about. My wife, Teresa, and I have done a lot of stuff on our own. My wife has a background in public relations, so she knows how to do that stuff. At first I said, "I'll go anywhere! I'll do anything! For free. I'll pay my own way just to get the word out about my books." Then after the third book, I started saying, "I just want to stay home and write a little while." Now I actually get offers to go places.

DB   A lot of writers now seem to be making careers out of being speakers.

SH   I made a living out of that for three years. And I made a really good living at it. It's obscene what people pay for those speeches. I love getting out and meeting people who read my books, and I've done book tours since March 2001. Nonstop, basically. I have a hardback and then, ten months later, I have a paperback. So I love that; it has enabled me to travel to places that I've never been. I'd never traveled anywhere before my book tour. I'd only been on a plane one time, a really short flight, a prop plane to Ann Arbor. Before the tours I'd been to Gatlinburg and Cincinnati and that's about it. So I got to go all over the country and meet amazing people. When I'm sitting there at a bookstore, and this will reveal me as a complete sentimentalist, I always have this overwhelming sense of gratitude to these people. I almost always tear up at some point and think about how they have come to this bookstore after a long day's work. They're tending to their mother and father or whatever. Everybody has some struggle in life. And they have gone out of their way to come to the bookstore, and they've paid twenty-three dollars for my book. And some of them say, "Do you mind signing my book?" Good God, I'm honored to sign your book. It's just so gratifying for people to actually read your books. I've done calls to book clubs. The publicist says that will sell more books. That started the word-of-mouth. Nowadays, the only way literary books become big sellers is through book clubs. But if these people have taken the time to read my book, then the least I can do is come and talk to them. On the one hand I think you've got to do it to sell books, and on the other hand I'm thankful that people are reading my books.

DB Do you still work for NPR?

SH It's incredibly hard to write a really good four-minute short story. And I've not been able to do it in the last year or so.

DB You fish, you squirrel hunt, you hike, and you kayak?

SH Yes, but I consider all of those things writing. One of my neighbors jokes about me walking around in the woods all day. But he doesn't understand. I'm working. I'm working in the woods.

DB You say clogging is the most fun that anybody can have fun legally?

SH We clog right here on the porch. We're always getting together here on this porch.

DB In one of your dedications, you say you hope your girls learn to dance. Do they?

SH Three or four times a week.

DB Do they go to vacation Bible schools around here and to church with their grandparents?

SH They go to church with my parents. I have to re-educate them when they come home. A while back my daughter opened my brother's refrigerator, and there was a beer in there. She said, "Terry's going to go to hell." I had to set her down and explain stuff.

DB Talk about the phrase "Bible cracking" that comes up in *Clay's Quilt*.

SH I got that from a preacher who came through. Most preachers have a well-prepared sermon. He didn't. He would come in and let the

Bible fall open, and stab his finger in there. Whatever verse was there would be the basis for his whole sermon. I thought that was an amazing talent. I've learned that many people do that. They put their fingers on a particular verse and feel that they were meant to read that verse at that time in their lives. It is supposed to be prophetic. In my research for *A Parchment of Leaves,* I read somewhere about how people would get named by just letting the Bible fall open. Whatever name they first encountered, would be the name. I like that whole idea, because it's giving your self up to what's meant.

DB It implies providence, a directing power, although it could be seen as a superstitious act. You weave that in with both possibilities open. Is baptism a big part of the Pentecostal experience?

SH Total immersion.

DB Do contemporary readers understand that?

SH The only thing of the religious experience in *Clay's Quilt* that people have not gotten is backsliding. A lot of people ask me about that. No one in the South ever asks me about it. But I get letters all the time from out West and up North from people who don't understand. They'll know what it is from having read the book, but they'll want to know about the term. They'll say they've never heard of it until they read my book. I just assumed everybody knew what it meant.

DB You have many references to government aid, the anti-poverty programs and so forth that have sprinkled Appalachian history. As with Denise Giardina, you seem dubious about some of the aid programs.

SH It's all bureaucracy that goes nowhere. What tends to happen is that these people come in who don't know how to talk to people from here. "We're going to do it this way," they say, and the native Appalachians are strong-minded people, and they're not going to respond to somebody bursting in and saying, "This is the way we do it." The programs fail miserably. People don't like outsiders coming in. It works if people come in and try to understand the place, but if they act like they're bringing civilization, that's trouble. I'm a real cynic when it comes to the government and politics. I think we live in a great, great country, and we're incredibly lucky to live here, but we've got a long way to go. Everything goes back to big business. All those special-interest groups are sickening. My new book is about cultural divisions. I have a Vietnam veteran and his sister, who was a protester. Her picture ended up in all the history books, so it was a picture that changed the way the nation thought about Vietnam. She comes to live with him, and he hasn't forgiven her. The book is about both sides of the question.

DB *Clay's Quilt* began with a short story about a trip to Myrtle Beach, and you wrote backwards from that scene. You said they're looking for something they'll never be able to find. This gets back to that homesickness question, but there's also an implication of a spiritual vacuum. Even the beautiful mountain place will not ultimately be enough.

SH You can see that in the book I was trying to find my place, my spiritual place.

DB And Clay is trying to solve the mystery of his mother?

SH Yes, but he's also trying to figure out how to worship God in a way that's best for him. In the beginning of the book, Clay leaves the church house, and he sits in the creek. Easter says, "What are you doing?" "I believe in God, I do," he says. "I sure hope so," Easter says. Then he goes through that party period, and then by the end of the book, he's sort of found his place in the world spiritually and romantically.

DB There's a lot of you in that.

SH That book is really autobiographical.

DB Do people confuse you with your characters sometimes?

SH People call me Clay all the time.

DB What is a "conscious heart"?

SH It is a heart that's aware of how our actions impact others. And it's also aware of living in a world that we don't rule, that is ruled by some great forces. But mostly it is a sensitivity to everything.

DB And a sense of guilt?

SH Yes.

DB Isn't Anneth driven by guilt?

SH Yes. Both books probably center there. That runs back to

Pentecostalism, of course. I'd venture to say that the major theme that runs through my books is guilt. Most of my characters are driven by guilt, by feeling bad about something they've done and trying to overcome that.

DB   Clay refers to Alma's music as providing "a moment of complete creation." How does music inform your books?

SH   Music has just been a complete balm. Music has saved me over and over. I was raised in music. My mother was a gospel singer, and every single person in my family does something with music. They brought it into my life. Music is an expression of passion. I write about really passionate people, and so the music comes in naturally.

DB   And you listen to music when you write?

SH   Yes. I need it.

DB   Some of your books could even be thought of as ballads.

SH   I see that. A lot of the ballads were about people who'd come through hardship or been murdered or murdered somebody. There is definitely a ballad element to *A Parchment of Leaves*. But I don't do that consciously. My scenes will often have the rhythm of whatever song is being mentioned in the narrative. In the beginning of *The Coal Tattoo*, for example, "Maybelline" is playing, and the whole rhythm of that fits when it's read aloud. It's very staccato. The scene in *A Parchment of Leaves* where Saul rides into Redbud is completely set to a bluegrass instrumental. When the song changes tempo, then the paragraph changes. I was writing with the rhythm of the music. I think, somehow, that readers get some sense of that rhythm.

DB   At the end of *Clay's Quilt*, Clay realizes that he has "to accept that some things in this life are unbearable and go on." That line feels like a summary. Is that fair?

SH   Learn to accept things, embrace them for what they are, understand that things happen for a reason, and move on. I believe that.

DB   And the second novel, *A Parchment of Leaves*, is dedicated to the women. There's a matriarchal business there. The men are noisy and violent, and it's the women where the faith is. Is that based on your own experience?

SH   Very much so. I was raised around a lot of women. I was very respectful of women. I don't think people teach their sons that anymore. Or their daughters, for that matter. Women don't expect to be respected anymore. It's not that I have a problem with equality or anything; it's just that I think we'd have a better culture when men respect the women. When you've been taught to respect women, you've learned a lot.

DB Were the women the storytellers?

SH Not necessarily. But women were definitely as strong as the men. That's why it bothers me when people assume that men in the South are misogynists. It's not true. Of course, there are lots of misogynists everywhere, but I was raised in a society where women were equals.

DB Even at church?

SH Especially at church. Pentecostals are one of the few denominations that readily accept female preachers. The women more freely doled out wisdom to me as a child than the men did. Men tended to be more quiet about spirituality and emotion. The women demanded respect, and most of the women in my life were raised in tough circumstances, so they had to work hard. I was always conscious of that and wanted my books to be tributes to them and all the things they taught me.

DB In what way is *A Parchment of Leaves* about confession or about being able to give up your secrets? Even Esme finally gives up her secret.

SH Originally that novel was in third person and it didn't work at all, because the whole book is about Vine confessing everything to the reader. The major way that book resonates with readers is in their identification with her. They feel as if she's told them everything. Serena knows a lot, Saul knows a lot, but the reader is the only one who knows everything. And confession is part of the whole kindness thing. Can you really completely love somebody while also knowing all their deepest, darkest secrets? Vine is able to do that — she knows and loves anyway. She doesn't judge people because of their mistakes. She doesn't judge Aidia, who abandons her child. If we were able to live in a society where we were able to tell our secrets without fear, it would be a better place for the world.

DB Several of the religions of this region make a good bit of confession and repentance. If you can air your story, then you can live. I thought you tapped into that marvelously in *A Parchment of Leaves*.

SH I went to my parents' church for Father's Day, and a woman got up and said, "The other day I was cooking. Potatoes were burning, the phone was ringing, and someone came to the door selling Hershey Bars. I took the whole skillet of potatoes and threw them in the sink. Lord God! I was so mad. I was mad at the child at the door, I was mad at whoever was on the phone, and I was mad at the potatoes." She had to stop and breathe for a minute. "Thank God I've got some potatoes to eat, and thank God I've got a front to door to go to," she said. She was talking about how anger got the best of her. She was cleansing herself somehow.

DB Although you didn't get too much into race issues, you do mention Melungeons.

SH We didn't call them Melungeons. Around here they're called the Blue People or the Moon People. There's a family of them in the next county over, Clay County. I first encountered the word in Lee Smith's *Oral History*. A cousin of mine has proven that my great grandmother was a full-blooded Cherokee. I also wonder if there isn't some Mulungeon in our family, because a lot of my cousins have blue gums, blue eyes, and black hair. Race is something I haven't written about much, because I grew up in a world that's 98 percent white. But, it's always been easy for me to relate to ethnic people. I tended to be friends with black people or Middle Easterners when I was working on my MFA, because we were all outsiders. I felt an affinity with other ethnicities.

DB Your second novel, *A Parchment of Leaves,* seems more sophisticated about the role of memory and the power of the past. You register moments that ought to be noticed and use Still's line about paying attention. Were you working through your own heritage in some way?

SH In *A Parchment of Leaves* I dealt so much with memory and the power of the past because I had become a parent. For most of *Clay's Quilt* I wasn't. When you have children, you're always aware of all the little moments. You wonder if you'll remember the way your baby smells. Will I remember the way she sat in my lap? You want to preserve those moments. That happens a lot in *A Parchment of Leaves*. That was my way of preserving the moments. There's a field near here that has all these wildflowers in it, and in *A Parchment of Leaves* I have a scene where Birdie runs out into the wildflowers. It's my favorite passage in the book. That scene is completely based on a moment with my eldest child as she ran through these flowers. I thought I had to remember that moment forever. That novel was a way to preserve those things. I love novels that transport me to a particular time period. One of my favorite novels that does that is *Alias Grace* by Margaret Atwood. It's set around the Civil War period in Canada. With *A Parchment of Leaves* it was a given. It was about my great-grandmother, so I set it around the time that she would have been about eighteen. The book starts in 1914, and I really enjoyed going back to that time. I lived that life. When I was writing that book, I must have driven my wife nuts. For example, we don't know what darkness is; modern people don't. I unplugged all of our outside lights; I unscrewed the bulbs in all of our motion sensor lights. Sometimes I would just walk through the back field at one or two o'clock in the morning in complete blackness to experience darkness the way that Vine did, or the way people of that time period did. I never watched TV. I only listened to the radio, and I wrote a lot of letters. I avoided the Internet. I just lived as much like them as I could. We ate out of the garden. There's a scene where Vine picks blackberries. I've been picking blackberries my whole life, but I went to the bramble down at the edge of the woods in the hottest part of the day, when you wouldn't normally pick blackberries, and I picked them for three hours to get a complete sense of the way she picked them in that scene.

DB   And then you came back and wrote it out?

SH   Yes. I tried to put myself into that time. People say you can't capture a place unless you live there, unless you know it intimately. So how is it that we capture a time period? You just have to do what you can do to understand it. There are all these things that worked out perfectly in that book for the time period. The whole question of civil rights for Native Americans, for example, changed dramatically after World War I. If Vine hadn't killed Aaron, she wouldn't have been able to accuse him of rape. The authorities would have said, "You're Cherokee — there's nothing we can do about it." She couldn't have testified against a white man in court. I tried to make all those things real subtle. The major mistake I made in the book was I didn't mention the influenza epidemic. It would have been a major part of this time period. But it just didn't come up, and there was so much going on already. I also wanted World War I to be this thing in the far background.

DB Did the flu epidemic reach up into these hollers?

SH Yes. It traveled on the train lines; that's how influenza spread to the rural areas.

DB Now you're getting up early to enter the character of a ten year old in the 1970s?

SH Yes, and I have to listen to disco. I'm listening to a lot of one-hit wonders like Disco Duck. Songs a ten year old would have been aware of in 1976. Abba.

DB So do you have to dig this all up on the Internet?

SH Sure. And I have some musicologist friends that help me a lot. The book is set from June until August of 1976, so I've been buying *TV Guide* for that period. I have a *TV Guide* from every week in that period, and that really helps me to know what a ten year old would be watching on TV. I've also got all the *Billboard* magazines from that period, so I know exactly what was on the radio.

DB Are you going to start eating Twinkies?

SH Sure, and lots of cereal.

DB You call *The Coal Tattoo* your first "issue book." There does seem to be more agenda this time, at least in terms of the mining company, "the blot on the landscape." In Whitman's phrase you "vivify the contemporary fact." You shine a light on the social issue. Has the issue-centrism been a problem for reviewers?

SH Not really that I know of. Nobody's commented on that in a negative way. Even though the major issue of the book, the strip mining, takes place in the 1960s, it's still very relevant today. A more subtle issue in the book is the idea of rural people being more simple than other people. I really tried to deconstruct that in this book. These characters have incredibly complex, complicated lives.

DB And finally, it's a story about sisters.

SH Exactly.

DB They can't live together, and can't bear to be apart. Do you have a sister yourself?

SH I have a first cousin whom I think of as a sister. I was raised with her and a half sister. But *The Coal Tattoo* is about being a steward of the land and how that land affects everything. During the writing of the book, I discovered my opportunity to be a social commentator. I hadn't had the opportunity, within Kentucky at least, to voice my opinion about things. My uncle had a coal tattoo, and I thought that was a great metaphor for how the land becomes a part of us.

DB *Publisher's Weekly* said "the tattoo is the indelible imprint the land leaves on the human soul." That's a nice sentence.

SH Yes, it is.

DB Where do you get the names? Anneth and Matracia and the others?

SH They're all names of people I've met. I was a rural mail carrier for seven years. Talk about a wealth of names! Matracia came from a country singer, Matracea Berg, who's a good friend of Lee Smith's. Serena was an older lady on my mail route. I was writing that character and really didn't have a name for her. I think I was calling her Isabel for a while. Then one day I met this older lady, Serena, on the route. I thought, that's how my character will look when she gets old. Then I knew her name.

DB And Dreama?

SH Dreama was a girl I went to high school with. I loved that name. I thought it was perfect for the character. My brother calls me Pantsie, and I call him Cake. He used to have a sweet tooth when we were little. Aidia is named for a Sarah McLachlan song. Melungeons tended to have really different, exotic names so I wanted her to have a completely different name. I know a woman named Easter, and I thought it was the perfect name for that character.

DB   How do you explain Anneth's depression? Or self-destructiveness?

SH   I don't know. In the early manuscripts of the book, Jewel, her murderer's sister, tells Anneth that she's manic-depressive. Now we call it bipolar. Jewel tells her to go to the doctor. I wasn't sure that she was manic-depressive; maybe she lived such a large life that she wore herself out. She'd go into these bouts of blueness. But I cut that scene where Jewel tells her that. I didn't want to diagnose her. I wanted the readers to come to their own conclusions. A lot of people are misdiagnosed as being manic-depressive. They're really just remarkable people. I am very much like Anneth. I have incredibly manic phases where I'm just so happy. I appreciate everything, love everything. Then I'll just go into these bouts of something — I don't like to say "depression." I fear people are overdiagnosed nowadays. I really put a lot of myself into Anneth's bouts of blueness. She would feel a heaviness in the cheeks, and this thing coming at her for no reason. When it hits me, I think about my two healthy, beautiful children. I have no reason to be bereft. My family is healthy and safe, but I feel down.

DB   In which mood do you write better?

SH   I'm depressed if I'm not writing, so I guess I'm always happy when I'm writing. I get really blue sometimes, but it's not like I am manic-depressive. I think "blue" is the best word. When I was a child, people were always talking about "being blue," and people don't talk about that anymore. Now they're manic-depressive and on Zoloft.

DB   Is *The Coal Tattoo* a book about prayer?

SH   I don't know. I would like to think that, but I never thought about it. One of my favorite things in that book is how Anneth accepts herself as a "sinner" but at the same time also accepts herself as a Christian. When she gets married for the first time, for example, she insists on a minister. Matthew is surprised by that, but Anneth says that even sinners have their choices. Later in the book Easter had a period of doubt when Easter says she doesn't believe in God anymore. Anneth says she'll believe enough for both of them. There's a sense of ambivalence about God in the book. The greatest belief comes through doubt or after a period of doubt. That's one thing that has always bothered me about Pentecostal doctrine, that doubt is a rejection of Christ. I remember asking that typical question that kids ask about Adam and Eve and who Cain married. I learned that I was not to question the Bible. That was a refrain that I heard over and over again. You're not to question God.

DB   Have the movie folks shown any interest in your books?

SH   They've shown interest, but it's never panned out.

DB   Do you think about the Hollywood money and all that?

SH   If you thought about that, it would ruin you. There was a really good screen play of *Clay's Quilt,* but the screen writer couldn't get any bites. There was a horrible one that got the interest. The first scene has Clay Sizemore wearing bib overalls. It was awful. I have had inquiries about *A Parchment of Leaves,* and some students at NYU are looking at some of my short stories.

DB   But *Clay's Quilt* is still the best seller of the three?

SH   Yes, it was a big book club book. And it's contemporary. People nowadays like that. *The Coal Tattoo* has been out since September 2004 — not even a year. It's the smallest seller so far, although I think it's my most accessible book.

DB   You have more sales outside the South than within the South. Why is that?

SH   I don't know. I think it's because of the rural thing. I think people really relate to that.

DB   And your relationship with critics and reviewers has been pretty good?

SH   My reviews on *A Parchment of Leaves* were amazing. I feel guilty about that, because it's the book I feel least responsible for. I don't feel like I wrote it. My reviews for *Clay's Quilt* were almost all positive, and the reviews for *The Coal Tattoo* were more positive than negative. I did get more negative reviews on *The Coal Tattoo* than on any other book, however.

DB   Why?

SH   It bothered some people that the sisters loved each other so much. It bothered some of those reviewers. I read reviews with a sense of detachment.

DB You don't trust them too much?

SH That one in Memphis made me mad, but it would've made me mad even if it wasn't about my book. It was all about how sentimentality is bad. It would have angered me if they had been writing that about Tim Gautreaux. It made me mad because it was attacking a particular vein of literature. It didn't really have that much to do with me.

DB When you describe the honky-tonk, you have a strong sense of the interplay of decadence and glamour. There's something very attractive, adventurous, and energetic in that life, an underside. You really get at that in the short story "Coal Smoke."

SH That's my most successful story by far. It's been more accepted nationally because it's so gloomy, I think.

DB But you still have hope for that character, the young woman getting all dressed up to go to the honey-tonk.

SH I think it's really hopeful. Most people don't. I tackle some of that same stuff in "Total Immersion." That story is about a woman known as "the whore of Black Banks." She goes to church and gets saved. She tells everybody. She's been having an affair and she tells the man that they can't have an affair anymore. He just laughs and says, "Yeah, that'll last." She invites people to her baptism, and they all laugh and say, "The church will cave in." It's a story about trying to become a Christian when no one believes it can happen.

DB So you believe that people can change?

SH You have to believe that.

DB What gives you the most pleasure these days? Does the teaching feed the writing?

SH I was a professor for a year at Eastern Kentucky University. It's not been made public yet. I signed on down there because they said they were going to do all these things with the writing program. It was even announced in *USA Today,* but it just didn't work out. So I've left there, and I'm going to be teaching at Lincoln Memorial University. I decided to teach in order to get off the road a little bit. I also hoped to make a difference through teaching. LMU has a mission to serve the youth of the region, and I'm looking forward to that. We're going to start a major literary festival there; we'll probably call it the James Still Literary Festival, because he's a graduate of that school. We hope to establish a good center. I'm really excited about going there.

DB The teaching doesn't distract you from the writing?

SH At Eastern it did distract me. But it wasn't the teaching, it was the other stuff: tenure review, committees, and all that. Being in the classroom and encouraging students, that's a real blessing.

DB Do we have too many writing schools and writing workshops and the like? (I'm thinking of O'Connor's line about how writing programs don't stifle enough writers.)

SH I don't know. I had a really good experience in my MFA program. I was thirty years old when I went in it. People expect too much from MFA programs, too. Nobody can teach you how to write. You can be taught how to be a better writer, but you can't be taught how to write. I think there's some little kernel that you're born with, and then you have to teach yourself. Larry Brown, for instance, taught himself to write. He read good books and learned how to write. He never had any writing classes; I don't think he even had any college. Maybe a couple of courses.

DB Would you want your children to be writers?

SH It's a hard thing to break into, but it's been a good life for me for the past four years. Whatever makes them happy is all I care about.

DB "Daddy" is your most important word, or so Teresa says in an article she wrote about you.

SH That's it.

DB How has your extended family responded to your celebrity?

SH They don't go on about it or anything, but I know they're proud of me. There are a few people in the extended family who are kind of stand-offish. They might wonder if I think I'm smarter than them or something. It goes back to that business of people thinking that writers are smarter than other folks. In any rural place, there's a bit of prejudice about intellectuals. Not that you're treated badly, but people don't know how to act around you.

DB Are there other risks that are involved in being a writer?

SH   You always run the risk of revealing too much about yourself. But I think that's the only way you can be a good writer. I reveal everything about myself. But the nice thing about fiction is that nobody knows, really, what you're revealing. The mountaintop removal thing has caused me some grief within my family. Some people in my family don't understand why I'm speaking out against mountaintop removal. They think I'm speaking out against the coal industry, which has brought my family out of poverty. I'm saying mountaintop removal is the wrong way to mine coal, because it's so irresponsible, wasteful, and mean. They don't realize that, if we didn't have mountaintop removal, there would actually be more coal-mining jobs. Mountaintop removal is mostly about machines. The hardest part of my coming out against mountaintop removal has been knowing that I have cousins who are mad at me. But I'm not going to back down, although I hate to have family mad at me.

DB   Do you still think the best training for a writer is a whole series of bad jobs?

SH   For sure. I tell all my students that.

DB   Do you miss the mail delivery job?

SH   God no; I hated that job! I did that for six and a half years. And it was the best job in the world for that first novel, because I got so much press off it. There was a story about it in *USA Today*. That was the slant. But it became tiresome. I finally decided not to do any more interviews, if all they wanted to talk about was me carrying the mail. I wanted to talk about my books. It felt exploitative to me, so I just stopped doing that. I guess the publicity department really suffered when I quit carrying the mail. They lost their slant.

DB   What's a press kit writer?

SH   When Gillian Welch, or someone, has a new album coming out, her record company will put out a press kit, three months before. It will have an extensive biography and include reviews and articles done on her along with an introduction to the new album. They call me up and ask me to write the biography. I talk about her life, where she's from, and how she got into music. Then I connect her life to the new album. I just did one on Del McCoury, the reigning king of bluegrass. I've written them for Lucinda Williams and Leanne Womack, a mainstream country star. It's like writing a feature for a music magazine.

DB You've become remarkably successful. Is the key to your success somewhere in your underscoring of the family and neighbor connections we are all longing for?

SH My idea of being a successful writer is having one person get some real pleasure from my book. If they were entertained, if they were informed, or if it made a difference in their life, that's success. You hope that a million people will read your book, but my great hope is that one person will be changed by something they found in that book.

DB But you don't have an ideal reader in your mind as you write?

SH I write the books that I want to read. I think all writers do that. Margaret Mitchell wrote *Gone with the Wind* because she was hospitalized for a long time and had read every book that she could find. She'd run out of good books to read, so she wrote one that she wanted to read. Writing is a selfish thing. Every writer I know writes for some self-indulgent reason. Lee Smith says that she writes because she's looking for salvation. I think I'm always writing, often about faith and religion, but always about something I don't understand. I write books in order to understand. I didn't understand why my grandmother hid being a Cherokee. That was the whole impetus for that book. Why did she have to hide that? Why did she feel the need to hide that, even up until the 1950s? *The Coal Tattoo* is about fascination with sibling relationships. I wondered if my cousins, whom I thought of as my brother and sister, loved me as much as I loved them. I tried to understand that better, and I also tried to understand the reason that I loved a place so much. My new book is about trying to understand how we've come to be at such odds with each other. It's sad to me that people hate each other just because one is a Republican and one is a Democrat. That's awful! We make so many assumptions based on someone's politics. After the election, one of my best friends said he couldn't believe so many stupid people went out and voted for George Bush. I said, "Wait a minute, some of those stupid people are my family. They're not stupid; they're just voting for what they believe in. That doesn't mean that they're evil or ignorant; they're just doing what they think is the right thing to do." But he hated them because of who they voted for. I'm an Independent. I think they're all horrible. I think that Clinton was just as bad as Bush. But it bothers me when people decide that someone's a certain way because of their religious bent or their political bent or whatever.

DB You're trying to clarify that question in this new book?

SH Yes, even though I know it is an unanswerable question. In *A Parchment of Leaves*, I really asked an impossible question when I wondered about evil in the world. I wanted to explore this. In the end, I didn't really have an answer, but in a way I did. The answer was that evil doesn't matter as long as there is forgiveness and kindness to counter it.

DB Do you believe that ink always lasts?

SH Yes, I do.

DB Which is to say, there's power in words.

SH Libraries discard books after a certain amount of time, and books go out of print. But somewhere decades and decades down the road, someone will find one of my books. Writers are looking for a little bit of immortality. We at least know that the book is going to last until after we're dead, for a little while anyway.

DB There's a way in which the story doesn't exist fully until it's written?

SH Exactly. You know a thought is different from a thought that's made into a solid sentence.

DB Which actually gets back to the religious idea about the word becoming flesh?

SH All writers believe that. I have several relationships built on letters, on written words. I really like that idea. Larry Brown and I were together maybe ten days total, but once a month he would write me a seven-page letter, and I would write him back. When you have a relationship like that, you know somebody in a deep way, because they pour out things in those letters that they wouldn't say if you saw them every day.

DB   Not email, but real letters?

SH   Real letters. I think epistolary novels are something we're going to see a lot more of, because letter writing is a lost art. That's one reason I loved *Gilead* so much. And *Fair and Tender Ladies, The Color Purple*. A lot of my favorite books are epistolary. I think that's one reason that my books have been read as widely as they have. People are longing for a sense of place. It is in our DNA. People all have a sense of place somewhere in their blood, so they long for that connection to home. People always tend to read about things that they are missing. When things like letter writing get lost, they'll soon get written about. Sorry, I ramble.

JAN KARON

Called to Write

1937 — Born in Lenoir, North Carolina
1994 — *At Home in Mitford*
1995 — *A Light in the Window*
1996 — *These High, Green Hills*
1997 — *Out to Canaan*
1998 — *Miss Fannie's Hat*
1999 — *A New Song*
2000 — *Jeremy: The Tale of an Honest Bunny*
2001 — *A Common Life: The Wedding Story*
        Patches of Godlight: Father Tim's Favorite Quotes
        The Mitford Snowmen
2002 — *In This Mountain*
        Esther's Gift
2004 — *Shepherds Abiding*
2005 — *Light from Heaven*
2006 — *The Mitford Bedside Companion*

Lives in Charlottesville, Virginia

Jan Karon's career seems miraculous from every angle. A late-comer to writing, she built an enormous following in a decade. Since *At Home in Mitford* debuted in 1994, readers have been lining up to purchase sequels, organizing book clubs to discuss the novels, and

Photograph by Mark Tucker

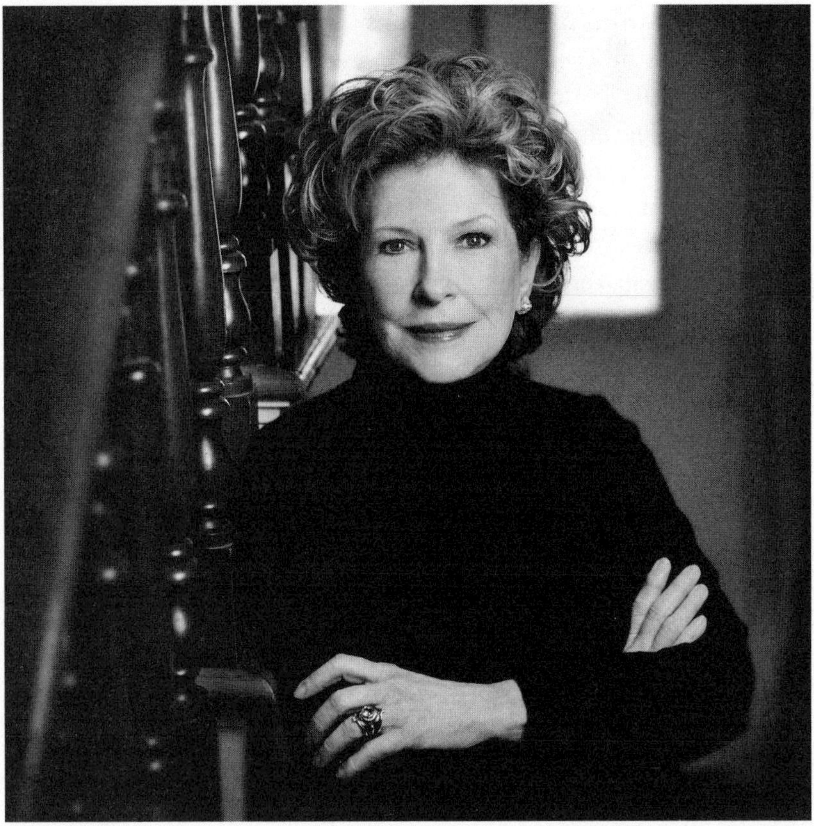

spreading the word about these books that defy categorization. Martha Spaulding in *The Atlantic Monthly* labels the novels "children's books for adults." Michael Pakenham in *The Baltimore Sun* says they are "no more pernicious than sweetened iced tea." Such remarks, of course, reflect generations of literature classes where we've been taught that sin makes the story. A character in John Updike's novel *S.* says that modern novels are those books that "try to make us feel shabby." Having seen enough of such books, Karon decided to write "the book I'd want to read." Does she belong in the popular fiction section, the romance, the religion department? Is a Jan Karon novel beach fare or serious business? Don't answer too quickly.

"Writing about a good man gone wrong is easy," she says. She chooses to write about the "legions of ordinary, good, well-meaning, faithful men out there, some of them even clergymen." Her hope was that her readers would recognize themselves and their neighbors in her novels — and the idea has taken hold. "I'm simply trying to write about a life of faith, which most people have never read about, never seen," she says.

I spoke with Jan Karon at her antebellum home in Charlottesville, Virginia. She had just finished the eighth Mitford novel, and the renovations on the house and grounds were nearing something like completion. (The house, built by slave-labor in 1816, is on the National Historic Register and has required as much attention as Father Tim, Cynthia, and that cast of Mitford characters.)

Getting to Mitford wasn't as easy as I'd hoped. My flight was nine hours late. But it turns out that there is a Mitford, a hard place to get to and an even harder place to stay, perhaps. But definitely worth the trip.

DB   I'm grateful for this chance to talk.

JK   I'm honored to be asked. I must tell you that I don't feel that anybody has yet understood my work. Maybe every author feels that. I think that people are either afraid of it or take it far too lightly. I don't think anyone has really understood that these books are much more than vehicles to get the orange marmalade cake recipe out there. Many of the people that you've interviewed are teachers, academic people. Intellectuals. I have never considered myself intellectual.

DB Reviewers and critics do wax repetitive when they come to Jan Karon. Let's start with a question that I suspect has a not-so-obvious answer: "Who are these 15 million and more readers?" People make guesses about what they think your audience would be, but I've run into college deans and ten-year-old children who read your Mitford books. Garrison Keillor has a little story called "You Changed My Life Mister." Do you get people at book signings who tell you that?

JK Oh, always. I kind of feel like a bartender, you know. As you might expect, it's the women who turn out, but not exclusively. We do have a large male reading audience. I once devoted an entire newsletter to their letters and comments. Not long ago, a Vietnam veteran wrote to tell me that he had suffered for years with nightmares, cold sweats, and depression and that reading my books had been the most comforting thing he had encountered. They were healing to him. I hear from doctors. I hear from lawyers. No Indian chiefs yet. But all kinds of men. Certainly clergymen, too, of course. Most people think my demographic is a fifty-four-year-old woman with a high school education, a grandmother who has never worked. She cooks three meals a day or something. This is wildly inaccurate. The most wonderful thing to me about my reading audience is that it is *all* ages and both sexes.

DB Even children?

JK My reading audience starts at the age of ten. Precisely at the age of ten. Goes all the way up into the nineties. Many families read my books. One of the things that thrills me most is that my books are family reading material, as was Charles Dickens's work. You know, of course, that Dickens published in installments. The father would go to the bookstore with his shilling in hand, and he would take home the latest installment, which everyone was wildly excited about. Nowadays we get excited about the next installment of reality TV, I guess. But then people really were excited about Mister Dickens's new installment. Typically, the father would read over the chapter carefully so as to make sure that there was nothing in it to give the children nightmares. Then the father would read the installment to the family. Now that's what happens with my books, though it is not always the father doing the reading. I got a wonderful letter from a woman in Texas. Her husband is a rancher. Often their power fails. One day they just crawled up on the bed, she and her son and little girl and the father, who couldn't work that day because of the power outage. They just started in on the Mitford books. They've read every single one. I tell you, if it gets any better than that, I don't know what I'll do. I also think it is important to say that I love my readers. I don't really very often write directly to my readers. I never sit down and answer that wonderful fan letter I got last week — this is for you, Sara Maxwell in San Antonio. But I do sit down and write with all the love that God has given me. And I think that's what people feel, see, hear, and read in my books, though they would not be able to articulate it.

DB Your popularity may contribute to this notion that your books are light. After all, we tend to think of the literary as that which "bites and stings," to use Kafka's phrase. Professors talk about *sentance* and *solas*, the two dimensions of literature — the edifying and the pleasure-giving, the wisdom and the comfort. But we push pretty hard on the *sentance* side.

JK "Bite and sting." That's what we've been stuck with for years.

DB The sort of books you're likely to study in a college classroom are the ones that disturb and unsettle. So there's the literary — Ezra Pound says, "a book is a ball of fire you hold in your hand" — over against the popular, what we sometimes call "beach-reading" or "airport reading." Somehow, I don't see you in either camp.

JK No, I'm not. I never really wanted to be in a camp. In fact, I run from being in a camp of any kind. People wanted to put me in the camp of Southern Writer. No way. Then they wanted to put me in the camp of Regional Writer and then Religious Writer. I *refuse* to be in any of those camps. Here's what I am trying to do. When we go to the bookstore or go to the literary reviews, we read about lives of sexual abuse, lives of dysfunction, lives of drugs, lives of crime. I'm trying to just simply write about a life of faith. People don't know what a life of faith is about. They've never read about one. Most people have never seen one. So how can they understand? If you've never made a biscuit, how can you know how to make a biscuit? You go to a book to find out how to make a biscuit. So that's what I wanted to do. I wanted to document what, in my lifetime, I had never before found documented. I wanted to document a life of faith that had nothing to do with that, what was that man's name — the evangelist in the novel?

DB Elmer Gantry?

JK Yes. Since that book in 1927, every clergyman is a low-down, adultering, thieving, corrupt hypocrite. Or they were melancholy and depressed, doing and thinking weird things. I mean, come on. How boring. That makes me mad.

DB There's a whole line of these books, of course. You can go all the way back to Hawthorne and Howells, Frederic and Caldwell, and up to Steinbeck and Updike. The preacher in American writing usually comes off as a horror.

JK Do you understand how easy that is? Writing about a good man gone wrong is easy. There are legions of ordinary, good, well-meaning, truly believing, faithful men out there, even some clergymen. I thought it was time somebody got a chance to see one of these guys. It's not like he's Mister Goody-Two-Shoes. He's not. And while some may label my books as shallow and over-sentimental, I think they also frighten a lot of people, and that's just fine with me.

DB So there is an edge to them?

JK If they really read my books, they will definitely find an edge.

DB And you believe that "a clarification of life," to use Robert Frost's phrase, can occur by reading books like yours?

JK I do. I do. When many people read a book, they expect to find someone who is utterly unlike themselves. That's what they've been served for who knows how long. But when you read a Mitford book, you will find yourself. It's that simple. I guarantee it. You will find your mother, you'll find your father, and you'll find all the people you go to church with or don't go to church with. You will find the people you know and grew up with. Now maybe that sounds boring because, if you already know those people, why would you want to read about them? Because nobody else writes about them. And here they are. What I'm actually doing is documenting a culture that very much exists today and will continue to exist. I want to document this culture because I respect it. I have high regard for ordinary people. They don't have to have three adulterous affairs or go to the south of Italy and do something strange and bizarre in my books. I mean they can just go to the Grill and have a hamburger. Because ordinary life has the most wonderful dramas — little dramas. I love the small human dramas.

DB But there's "bite and sting" in that too, I suspect. I often quote Saul Bellow to my students: "Of all the things one might omit in one's studies, the worst is to omit oneself." Paying attention is at the core of education, certainly, and probably at the core of religious faith as well. By calling us to attention to our own everydayness, you accomplish something important.

JK I grew up in a Scottish-Irish mountain culture. I grew up with the wonderful music of that Scottish-Irish speech ringing in my ears. You know what I mean? You know what I mean. You been from up there. You been up there in them hills and hollers. I seen you in there. I love that. How is anybody in New York ever going to hear that? Or California? Or Illinois. They're going to miss it. But I'm trying to make them hear that speech, enter that world. I try with all my heart to be faithful to that dialect, not because I'm making fun of it, but because I love it. And I think other people love it too.

DB But you don't take easy shots at the backward Southerner, which, at least since Eudora Welty, has been popular fare in Southern fiction.

JK Right. No shots. I love these people.

DB Another line running through the Mitford books has to do with fun. Many of us who grew up in conservative religious environments, who saw life from the beginning as earnest and serious, have become pretty buttoned-up. Particularly early on in your novels, the real

question is whether or not Father Tim is ever going to loosen up a little bit. Is he ever going to be able to express himself and just relax? I
don't know where that comes from for you, or how big a preoccupation that was in your mind.

JK   Definitely a challenge for me. I've always been so responsible I
can hardly stand it. You know I've been just covered up with seriousness and earnestness and wanting to get it right. Father Tim has to
learn to let God get it right. That's why I had to introduce Cynthia. After the second book, since Tim had fought his feelings for so long, we
still didn't know if he was going to marry Cynthia. We had the marriage banns, but we still weren't sure if he'd actually go through with
it. In Boone, North Carolina, a woman came up to me and said, "Ms.
Karon, if you don't let Father Tim marry Cynthia, I'm gonna quit fooling with you." Everybody was thinking, "Let's just get on with it." And
I didn't know whether he was going to marry Cynthia or not. Was he
just going to continue to be a clergyman? Maybe he would just keep
on moving among the people and let us watch how people lived and
how the village shaped lives and so forth? Or was he actually going to
have a real life? And I determined that if I could stand to write these
books, he was going to have to marry Cynthia, because she would
loosen him up. And I have not found anybody to loosen me up. I have
to work on that terrible job myself.

DB   In the first two books, especially, Father Tim can be so enrag-
ing. I found myself writing lines for him. He is so stifled, so inward.
But as we learn more about Tim over the seven books, about his frustration with his father and trying to get it right, we see that even Tim
has a need for grace that he doesn't fully recognize. And that ties to a
related question, the business of striking out toward the dream. Obviously people are fascinated by your personal story, the saga of giving up the big job and the Mercedes for a car with rusty fenders and
starting off on an adventure. Any of us who have ever thought about
quitting our jobs to hike the Appalachian trail or bicycle through
Montana or write a novel, have to sort of pause over that. And Father
Tim is like us, so fearful of change. You have one whole book that's
dedicated to the difference between change and improvement.

What's your advice to people? How do we change? How do we take that kind of risk? How did you take that kind of risk?

JK   It was entirely through prayer. It's just that simple. I did not have the guts to do such a thing. I hardly have the guts to live this life. This is a very hard life. I find it hard. Most earnest religious people do find it hard. But I felt so bad about myself, because here I was in advertising and the first thing I knew I was going to be fifty and then I was going to be sixty, and would I still be in advertising? Would my work still be dumped in the trash can?

DB   You'd been doing this for thirty-two years?

JK   Yes. And somebody would mute my commercial with that remote, a commercial I'd been working on for months, pouring my heart into. I gave advertising everything I had. In the latter part of my career, I was Christian, and I then especially gave it all I had because I realized God had planted me there for a reason. And it all counted for nothing. It never counted for a darn thing. Except, God never wastes anything. He was teaching me a lot about writing novels at that time. He was preparing me for such things as going into a recording studio and recording my own books years later. He didn't waste anything.

DB   You feel called by God to be a writer?

JK   I just couldn't stand any longer to throw my life away. I knew that my life belonged to him, so I prayed for two years in a very concentrated way. Not sort of round robin, as many of us pray, but totally focused. "Lord, if you want me to write books, you're going to have to show me how. I am scared to death. I have a nice home, I have a nice car, I have an income, and I can pay my bills. What are we going to do here? I don't know how to do the writing thing." And at the end of those two years, He did speak to my heart. I can't say how. But He said, "Go, already. Go, get out there, I'm with you, and you're going to be fine." When you put your house on the market and you sell it a day and a half later, you figure this is probably going to work out well. But then you get into living the dream. Having the dream is pretty exciting and it can keep you going for a number of years, but then you have to live it. And then, of course, the economy got very hard, and advertising agencies were not using freelancers. For two and half years, I could hardly make my mortgage payment, and that payment was relatively small. When I turned to God, terrified, He always said, "Don't look back, don't look back, I am with you." And the worst thing that happened was that I sat down to write a book at last, after all those years. I had dreamed of being an author since the age of ten. And it was so bad; it was so bad. I had failed. I did not know how to write a book. Mr. Churchill's line came to me then and has been very important, very core. Just "never, never, never give up." Period. So that's what I've done. I just decided to write a book I wanted to read. I hoped to find a small vein of readers who would share my sense of things. I remember very well visiting a library and opening up a then popular bestseller. On the first page there's shocking language, and then somebody's having sex on the table on the second page. I don't need that. I didn't want it in my life. Yes, people have sex on tables, I suppose, but I don't want to read about it. I had to be careful about which shelves I went to in the library. If I used a shelf where the authors were long dead, I could read those books. If they were living, I couldn't read them. I said, I'm just going to write a book that I want to read. If nobody wants to read it, I can't help it. Lord, if you brought me this far, it's your problem.

DB So when God calls you there's still that desert?

JK Oh yeah. Has to be.

DB But you can understand how people get nervous when writers start saying that God called me to write. What kind of book is somebody going to write who was called by God to write the book? You probably know of the correspondence between Shelby Foote and Walker Percy where Foote argued that a Catholic can't be a good writer. He said a Christian couldn't write a novel because a novel is, by definition, about the questions and not about the answers. If you're going into it as a Christian, then the work is bound to be didactic. It's bound to be so message-ridden that it can't be literature. How do you avoid that problem?

JK I love what Ernest Gaines says about writing a novel as like taking a trip from San Francisco to New York. You have the general plan, but who knows what might happen on the trip.

DB So when you get up in the morning and start writing about Father Tim, you don't know exactly what he'll be up to?

JK No. I don't want to know. I would be so disappointed if I knew. Sometimes I think I know. But, oh honey, it always takes a turn.

DB It's not like there's this sermon that has to be preached today or some message?

JK No, no, no. These are characters just living out their lives. And I'm just observing. I'm just there. I'm just being there to record it. I feel there's a documentary quality to my work in that I am documenting a true society, a true culture in which I have lived, and where I, to some extent, still live.

DB Henry James talks about the "germ" of a novel, that scene that somehow gives shape to everything. You talk about the dream in which you saw the priest walking down the road. And you've just followed along, looking over his shoulder?

JK Here's my only agenda: to let people know God loves them. That is the only agenda I have. And I don't even work that agenda. It just falls out, you know what I'm saying? It's just going to be there.

DB Because it's who you are?

JK Yes.

DB It's not written on a three-by-five card propped up against your computer screen?

JK No. And God didn't actually speak to me and say, "Go let people know I love them." But I think it's important for people, whether they want a life of faith for themselves or not, to simply see a life of faith. That's all. Just see one. I don't want to ram it down their throats. That's not my job. In fact, the only job I have is to write the best book I can write. That's my only job. Everything else is up to God. People say, "Ms. Karon, I was saved by what you wrote." You know, I don't want to know that. That's His business. They say, "My friend was dying of cancer and I can't tell you how your books ministered to her." Or, "I go to the nursing home every week and I read your books and it's so wonderful what happens." None of that is my job. I cannot make that happen. I'm still thinking about that word *solas* you used before. It would be wonderful to get that from a book.

DB   It comes up in the chorus of the old Christian hymn, "What a Friend We Have in Jesus." "Solace" has a strong religious sense somehow. That hymn is probably the first place I heard the word.

JK   "All our sins and griefs to bear." Ah yes. People don't know what to make of Jesus. And one of the things we need to make of Him is a friend. I love that old hymn. That will have to be His job too. Many of us are still trying to get over that Old Testament God, who is going to kick our rear ends every chance He gets. I'm not ashamed to write books that may offer solace too.

DB   I'm from that part of the South where the subject at lunch is always what you're going to have for supper. A part of the solace in your books is related to food. You have a lot of food in your books.

JK   That is exactly what I write about. You hit the nail on the head. That's what's important in the end. It's not about the war; it's not about the economy. It's about, "Son, what did you have for supper last night? How's the family?"

DB   So you're living out the farm life now, dogs and cats and all the rest?

JK   Three dogs and sheep and chickens. And I've got seven wild cats out there. I would send you home with eggs, but you don't want to go back on a plane with eggs. And I live out here in the sticks, scared to death. But fear is something I fight all the time. In the book I have just sent up to New York, Timothy and Cynthia discuss their fears. They seem to be losing some of their fears. She's no longer fearful that Tim will leave her. He's getting over his fear of flying and actually wants to take her to Ireland, which will give me another book down the road.

DB   So you've just finished the eighth Mitford book, *Shepherds Abiding*?

JK   Yes, the next to the last.

DB   And the last is to be *Light from Heaven* in 2005?

JK   Yes.

DB   Do you think your more recent books are the best of the lot? You've talked about learning to write. Are you getting better at it?

JK   In some ways. Some people say the first book is their favorite. It's like your first love affair, your first sweetheart, your first kiss. I mean it's hard to top your first kiss. But, I guess *In This Mountain* would be my favorite, because it was such a struggle, a book of struggle, and I was undergoing some deep struggle.

DB *Out of Canaan* and *In This Mountain* are deeper somehow, it seems to me. Morris Love is a most complicated and dramatic character in *Canaan* and Uncle Billy's eulogy chapter in *Mountain* is my favorite bit in all of your books.

JK I really love Uncle Billy. I spent a lot of time with him. I think he's a wonderful guy.

DB Well, you haven't been on "Oprah" yet, but this writing thing has certainly changed your life.

JK Oprah. Honey, I just love Oprah. And this house is entirely Mitford, though I do worry about how big hits change people's lives. I don't keep up with the Oprah writers, however. I don't read many contemporary writers. I'm afraid of them.

DB What about the Mitford movie or TV series?

JK We've been approached by many people, but the "Mitford Bill of Rights," as my film agent has titled it, is so stern that it scares people off.

DB And there's talk about a television series?

JK I'm talking with the folks who produced *Touched by an Angel*, which had a very successful nine-year run. Whether that will turn into anything, I don't know. But of all the people who've approached us over the years, this is the one I'm most hopeful about.

DB Do you have connections with other writers who live around here?

JK No, not at all, though this town is just covered up with writers. Rita Dove, Sharon McCrumb, John Grisham — there is a long list. But I don't know any of them, because I work so hard all the time that I don't get out into the community. I do go to Monticello, to the events there. I'm very very involved in what they're doing.

DB Where do you get your fellowship, your support?

JK I have few friends. That's one of my problems. I work almost all the time, and that's a real problem for me. I've fought it and tried to figure it out and I have not solved it. I go to church, but it's not a church that I feel particularly happy in, though I feel it's a place where I'm supposed to be. Very small.

DB Episcopal church?

JK Episcopal church. At the foot of the hill. And I could have a community or more fellowship if I had time enough, I suppose. But I'm just run ragged.

DB In your dedications you have a lot of people to thank.

JK Yes. Every time I ask a question, I have to thank someone. For example, if I've got to fix the brake shoes on the Honda in this book, I have to ask someone, "Do Hondas have brake shoes?"

"Oh yes, ma'am, they have brake shoes."

"Well, where?"

"Well, they mostly have them in the rear."

"Well, what's your name?"

"Silas Marner."

So that becomes a thank-you to Silas Marner. It makes people happy.

DB I know you are working on another Father Tim scrapbook, *A Continual Feast*. Do you get queries from religious publishing houses, particularly for the non-Mitford material?

JK The Christian book publishing community leaves me alone pretty much. I do get inquiries now and again. Somebody I met back at Lion Publishing House was determined to publish me, something I do not want.

DB These are some characterizations of your work. Tell me what you think. "Reads like a small town newspaper." "The most successful writer you've never heard of." "Complete rendering of the American myth." "Comfort fiction." "Does justice to the real experience of most of us."

JK I like that one.

DB "Reflects contemporary culture more fully than almost any living novelist."

JK Can you believe the *Los Angeles Times* said that? That fellow has probably been so ridiculed that he probably doesn't even work there anymore.

DB He was decrying the ascendancy of the Grisham genre that you talked about a while ago. That's a remarkable line.

JK Remarkable. Boy, don't think we haven't milked that one.

DB What about that "complete rendering of the American myth" line?

JK I think that was said by somebody who doesn't realize that Mitford is real.

DB So they think of you as re-creating *Leave It to Beaver*?

JK Yeah, exactly. All we have to do is get out there. Just get out there. I was raised in Mitford. I lived fifteen years in Mitford before I came here. I am documenting what I have seen and experienced. And they say my books are set in the 1950s. No, they're not. They're set in the present day. I just don't have a lot of televisions, fax machines, and cell phones in my books.

DB You do say that Mitford has to be worked at, that for Mitford to survive there has to be this effort made?

DB Right. You hear in music what you bring to it. And you get from Mitford what you bring to it. If you have a giving heart, you'll get it. I mean, you can't miss it if you're willing to look. You know, there's Miss Rose in Mitford. She is a really a pain in the neck. And yet, people have made a place for her. Remember how the mayor, Esther Cunningham, made sure Rose had oil in her furnace. Miss Rose was allowed to direct traffic. That soon ended because she became too feeble to do it, but some had wanted to get her off the street because it was bad for business. Now that debate was from a real circumstance in Charlotte, North Carolina. There was a man who could only speak in rhyme. He told me in rhyme that he had been dropped on his head when he was a baby. But he faithfully stood out in a median strip in the most exclusive section of Charlotte and directed traffic, and people wanted him to be there.

DB How did you hear about him?

JK I used to go to a restaurant that was in the neighborhood, and he would come in after his civic duties. And they would feed him. He lived in a run-down mansion. His parents had been quite wealthy. It looked like something out of an *Addams Family* movie. I never know what life experience is going to end up in a book. That is more direct probably than a lot of the things I write about.

DB   One critic says that Mitford is "out of step with America." I don't think anyone has referred to you as a satirist or as an ironist, but there's some irony here. Sometimes you're joking lightly as when you say the perfect parson is the guy who does fifteen house calls a day and is always in the office. There's a nice little joke. And you do satirize Tennessee fairly often as the land of the wild frontier. But there's also a complex social commentary in your books. For example, sexuality is tied to spirituality, sexuality is the confirmation of the spiritual relationship in the world of Mitford. That strikes me as counter-cultural.

JK   It is. Definitely out of step with the world. But the thing is, there are many communities that remain out of step with the world. My daughter and I were driving through Kansas, through those flat wonderful lands. And we would just take a side road, pop in and see what we could find. Well, we found a diner, sat down and had a nice lunch, and went down the street to a sort of saloon. And there was a little farmer's market, and it was Mitford. It's there. People with the same values. I'm not saying that folks in Mitford haven't slept together before they're married, but Father Tim and Cynthia chose to wait.

DB   And there's a way in which we need to be told that's okay? New York doesn't think that sells, but you've proven that it does.

JK   I like what you just said, that we're just saying it's okay.

DB   One guy says Mitford is "just a nice Peyton Place."

JK   That's an easy line because Peyton Place is a town that became famous in literature. I don't find any particular meaning in that. You know there's some pretty nasty people in Mitford. There's Edith Mallory and her driver who has fallen from grace. He used to be a nice guy. People liked him and would speak to him on the street, but now he's a low-down dirty dog because he's her henchman. But I don't have many mean or bad people in my books, because I don't enjoy their company. If you're going to spend two or three days in their company, it helps to enjoy their company.

DB   But what about the bromide that it is "sin that makes the story"?

JK   Well, now we've gone and had so much sin that we're about to puke.

DB   So you've come along with a theory that's basically saying "we've had a lot of that sin stuff, let's try something else." And it's working.

JK   Amazing.

DB   Most ordinary lives are extraordinary?

JK   Yes, absolutely. Absolutely. Everyone. Remember that old show on CBS? Some guy would throw an arrow at a map. Then he goes to that town and gets out the phone book and he always gets a story. I saw a story this morning about a man in his sixties, in his fourth marriage, who has had a little boy, his first son, who died in a terrible automobile accident. He prayed at that time that God would give him another son, and here, all these years later, he has the most charming little boy. And that was the story. And it was enough. It was enough.

DB   Are all of your books really about redemption?

JK   I can't help it. That's just what comes out of me.

DB   The conversion experiences, particularly the overheard ones, where does that come from?

JK   I don't know. In this last one, I knew George Gaynor was going to talk to Hope Winchester in the hall, and I knew that Hélène Pringle, whom I like a lot, had been suffering. She is Catholic but has not had much church experience. But she wants a God. She's been talking to God behind the curtains for some time, but fearing that He wasn't real, that she was just an old spinster making a fool of herself. So I thought, she's on the stairway. She's going to hear George talk to Hope. She's going to pray that prayer with them. So now Hope Winchester and Hélène Pringle are turned around by the man who was himself in a double-conversion experience. Truth is stranger than fiction. Or fiction is stranger than truth.

DB   Do the letters and cards and meetings that you have with your readers actually influence you?

JK   They try. "Now, Ms. Karon, you're going to be good to Dooley Barlowe, aren't you? You're not going to let anything bad happen to him, are you?" The characters themselves influence me. But I don't let readers push me around. If I let them do that I would be writing this dern Mitford series till I'm 104. They all say, "You can't stop now; you're just going to break my heart." They tell me I can just have Dooley get married to Lace and see how they can raise their children and on and on. And I'm saying, "It's over." I already know the last line of the series. I know the last scene in the last book. It came to me a long time ago. That's all I know.

But I'm far from finished. After Mitford I'm planning two mystery novels. Father Tim has always talked about taking Cynthia to Ireland, back to his homeland. So they're going to Ireland and that's the first mystery. It's called *A Party of Four*. And then that was fun, so Cynthia says, "Let's go see where all the Coppersmiths came from." So they go to the village of Coppersmiths, where everybody seems to be a Coppersmith: the butcher, the rector, and even a graveyard full of Coppersmiths. That one will be *A Family Face*. That's what I'll take up after *Light from Heaven*.

DB Still a few years away but sounds like you're dreaming these books already.

JK Yes. I am excited about them. When I was a kid, I listened to the radio. I loved radio. There was always some married couple who were a sleuth team. A couple sleuth team is just too good.

DB How does Viking feel about the end of Mitford?

JK They would give anything on earth if I would keep going. They call me their "cash cow." It's the second largest publishing house in the world, and I am the "cash cow." That's pretty good.

DB And now another Mitford novel is about to hit. Without giving too much away, can you say if we have the same characters?

JK Sure, you'll find a lot of the familiar folks, but it's a shorter book. It's about 45,000 words compared to say 105,000 or so in a traditional novel. It's an advent Christmas book, and it looks at a period of ten weeks in Father Tim's life, maybe twelve weeks. It is a period in which he learns something new about himself. And it all came about because I was in Blowing Rock. My daughter was home, and we went over to town. In the window of my favorite antique shop we noticed a nativity scene, which looked like it might be two or three different sets, because some of the figures were larger than the others. So it was a bit motley. It drew me in — angels, shepherds, the babe in the manger, the holy family, a camel, some sheep. I bought it. She just let me have it for a steal. She said, "You know we just been putting this thing in the window three years in a row, and we just don't have any place to store it." I said, "Done." So Candace and I were driving down the road, and we start talking about this nativity scene, wondering what would happen if Father Tim were to buy something like this. Candace got excited and the first thing you know I said, "I have got to put another book in this series. It will be a smaller book, but I'm going to tell this story." And that's what I have done. I had the set completely restored so that missing fingers and noses and so forth are back, and we restored a missing wing on one of the angels. They were painted the most horrible colors you can imagine. Not one single thing in that scene looked good. But now they are gorgeous. So that's the book. And Hélène Pringle is only mentioned. We don't really see her much in this book. I don't answer any of the big questions in the book. Will Dooley marry Lace? I still don't know. What will he do with his million dollars? I still don't know. This is just a few weeks in one man's life. And then *Light from Heaven* ties up all those hanging questions.

DB   Will you start immediately on *Light from Heaven*?

JK   I'm going to take six months. No writing for six months. I'm just going to enjoy my home and rest. I need some rest. And I want to spend more time with my family. On October 27 of this year my fourteenth book will be published. I've written fourteen books in nine years. They're not all big books — I'm including some of those little stocking stuffers in that number. But fourteen.

DB   I ran upon a reference to your letter to the Episcopal Church in which you refer to the church as "a bride that's deserted the union." There's a way in which Father Tim's version of Episcopalianism is inconsistent with what most of us think about the Episcopal Church these days. Perhaps, wrongly, we think of Episcopalianism as a cross between Unitarianism and Druidism or something.

JK   The Druids! I love it. That's right.

DB   You elevate Absalom Greer, a down-to-earth Baptist fellow, to something of a hero. And Father Tim gives an altar call in one of the books. There's a basic Christianity present in Tim that suggests maybe some at oddness with the larger institution. What's your take on mainline Protestantism?

JK   Mainline Christianity is deformed — walking on crutches, hobbling, dragging itself along, still managing to survive. The life, the joy, the truth, is just leaking out. It's just leaking out. It's not gone. There are many wonderful, devout, excited true believers among the Episcopalians. But it's just leaking. It's a boat that is taking on water big time. And because they'll just go for anything, just anything. You name it. There's a church in Asheville, an Episcopal church, promoting men and boy relationships. Yes. Yes. Now think of that heresy. It's just a matter of time. It's done. The corruption has run amuck with the Presbyterians, the Methodists, and the whole mainstream. Now Father Tim is a good fellow, an orthodox believer who preaches the truth. I'm just not happy in the mainstream church anymore. I mean it's been years really. Ever since I had a priest who told me that he did not believe Jesus was the divine Son of God. He invited everybody to make up their own creed, just like a creative writing class. Just make up your own creed. And why couldn't he be thrown out of that church? Because he was not accountable to his bishop. His bishop was as rotten and low as he.

DB   We've raised a whole generation of students, kids in their twenties who are spiritually interested, spiritually alive, but institutionally weary. They don't know what to do about church. Clearly you are thinking about that as you write these books. The errors of the institution are among your subjects.

JK   I stumble over it, yes. Susan Howatch deals with the politics of the church. I deal with the casseroles. I like to get right down in the kitchen, to the volunteerism and the "bane and blessings sale," and I get into the politics of the human heart, how people interact with one another on a very simple level because that's just a microcosm for the larger church.

DB How do you know so much about that small-town church world?

JK I just always paid attention. Raised by my grandparents, I sat in the front row at the Methodist church. I paid attention. I was listening. I was listening to the preacher. I was looking around to see what people were doing, how they were dressed. I was seeing their stockings rolled down below their knees. It was wonderful. Just to watch people and watch their faces. And I enjoyed church, but it was a social outing for us because we lived in the country and we were very sheltered. I never had an overnight party, for instance. I never went to spend the night with anybody. I never did anything social. Nobody ever came home from school with me. I never went home with anybody. We just didn't do that. And our faith was Old Testament faith. My grandmother did read to us out of the New Testament some.

DB King James Version?

JK Oh, yes, the King James Version, which is really what I still prefer. I try to like the other versions, but I keep going back to that. I remember one night my sister and I went looking for the dirty parts of the Bible.

DB Song of Solomon?

JK Yes. I think I made a reference to it in one of my books. Who are these people that say that book's about Christ and the church? It is not. Please, give me a break. I think the faith is interesting in more ways than one. I'm curious about it. I get the *Anglican Digest* and I read it. I like to know how clergy think, and I'm curious about clergy and their wives. Do their wives play the piano or the organ? Do they do anything in the church, or do they say, "I'm not having anything to do with that. I am not cooking any spaghetti dinners."

DB Cynthia says that, but then she winds up plugging in.

JK Right.

DB Do you say, "Ah-men" or "A-men"?

JK Well the Episcopalians say "Ah-men," but I mostly say "A-men." You see, I am a Baptist, really, at heart. I'm Episcopalian in Virginia and allied with the church and support this diocese. But in Blowing

Rock I've joined as an associate member of the Baptist church. That drives Episcopalians crazy. The Baptists don't care.

DB Well, it's not a combination that you typically would think of.

JK Well, Father Tim is kind of that way. Raised by a Baptist mother, a cold Episcopalian father, and thinking, as I said in *In This Mountain,* that if he could just become a priest, he could get his father's attention.

DB You remind me of Eudora Welty sometimes. Do you know her work?

JK She scares me a little bit. There's something bizarre there.

DB She's talks about writing as eavesdropping.

JK Oh, I like that, yes.

DB You know she also worked in advertising.

JK Yes, I did know that. That's so wild.

DB She said she had to quit because it was "too much like sticking pins in people to get them to buy things they didn't really need."

JK A lot of writers began in advertising. Dorothy Sayers was in advertising. Peter Male, of course. John Grisham. James Patterson. Salman Rushdie was big in advertising. So, it's not unusual.

DB What's the connection?

JK I think in the beginning it's just easier to get into advertising than it is to write a book. You make good money. If you write a book, you don't even know if it will sell. You might not make any money at all. Advertising pays well. And it teaches you all kinds of things about becoming an author. It teaches you economy for one thing. It teaches you to get to the point. What I find a tremendous challenge for me as a writer is getting to the point quickly and yet seeming to take my time. I want people to find a lot of white space in my books, breathing room. I want you to open a Mitford book and breathe deeply. So I try not to rush people too much through my books. They're stories that go nowhere.

DB So you don't think of them as books that are to be read quickly?

JK No, they should be read in parts. I love it when people say, "Oh, Ms. Karon, I just love to read your books at night. They just put me to sleep." And I say, "Thank you." What a compliment.

DB Now we're looking forward to the last one.

JK My pastoral novel.

DB   Barbara Bush paid you a compliment. She calls you "the happiest of writers."

JK   Yes, I love that.

DB   Somebody on your website refers to a line from Dorothy Sayers: "Where Christ is, cheerfulness will keep breaking in." Do you know that line?

JK   I'm writing that down.

DB   This takes us back to the theory question, but seen through the lens of Sayers's words, it is wrong-headed to label your work as "children's books for adults." You've had an enormous and serious impact. Lauren Winner, for example, in *Girl Meets God*, credits you for part of her move toward Christianity.

JK   Yes, I read her book.

DB   If you put her words from *Poets and Writers* side by side with one critic's rather snide observation that your work is "no more pernicious than sweetened iced tea," you get some disjunction. For Lauren Winner, the idea that love is as real as hate is revolutionary.

JK   Yes. Bingo.

DB   I remember the famous words from the movie about Saint Francis where Pope Innocent III says: "In our preoccupation with original sin we have forgotten original innocence." Have we become so preoccupied with depravity, with our capacities for ill, that we've lost sight of innocence and childlikeness and the best possibilities?

JK   Yes. Good is as real as bad. Day is as real as night.

DB   And that can be talked about?

JK   Yes. And it's okay to be happy. It's okay to be cheerful. It seems unfashionable. It's definitely untrendy and it makes you look like a sap, but it's okay to be cheerful. It's so simple. My books have such a simple message, but it takes a bright mind and searching heart to figure out that simplicity that you just got to right there.

DB   But is that formula fiction?

JK   It ain't formula.

DB   You do have imitators now, of course, and I suspect they'll find the going tougher than they expected. The humor, for instance?

JK   The humor is so important. People have said to me, "Jan, are you really that funny?" And I say, "No, actually I'm not funny. I'm kind of melancholic as a matter of fact." But my characters are funny. You know, they don't even necessarily say funny things. It's just the tension that's funny. The guys at the Grill, for example. What author in her right mind would name somebody Mule Skinner? But I like it. I'm just going to do it.

DB One of the great scenes in *Out to Canaan* is the episode where you take readers back to the Grill via a phone left off the hook.

JK I really had to dig deep for that book. I love that book.

DB Did you have more freedom there because you were in some ways free of the usual cast?

JK I knew I had to get a breath of fresh air. And I knew that Father Tim was doing something that all retired priests do. They go preach somewhere else. That's just what they do. I get enough of my readers sometimes because they whine. "Oh, why'd you take us to Whitecap? We want to be back in Mitford." Well, just get over it. And, "Oh, I don't know why you made us go through that old wedding book again; they were already married." Balderdash. If people are going to commit to a series, they should commit to it. Just go with it.

DB And *Out to Canaan* is the book with the irascible Mona and Ernie and the store divided by the yellow line. Great humor. And Jeffrey Tolson, a sure-enough villain. And Morris Love is a more complicated character than you've probably had before?

JK Absolutely the most, yes.

DB He's the angry atheist with every reason to be angry about the circumstances of his life.

JK He is a dwarf and a victim of Tourette's syndrome, one of the most interesting diseases I've ever studied in my life. But I have to tell you that Morris Love frightened me. He lived behind a wall, and I kept trying to get Father Tim to go over that wall, and I just dreaded it. I didn't know what I was going to find behind that wall. No, it's not formula writing. I had no idea what I was going to do with or about Morris Love. And finally Father Tim went over the wall. And I went as well. Going over that wall has helped me over several other walls in these books. If I had not gone over that wall, this would not be a series I could be proud of.

DB I don't think a reader could actually walk away from *In This Mountain* and label it "sweetness and light." And even before Morris and Jeffrey, you had Buck Leeper.

JK I love Buck Leeper. I was doing a reading outside Durham, North Carolina. We were in a beautiful inn that was once part of a farm — big silos and barns and those belted cows, the Oreo cows. We were in the barn. There were about 500 people there and, after I spoke, almost everyone came through the line. I always like to have a personal meeting with everybody. I noticed a very tall man, probably middle fifties, standing over in the corner just waiting until everybody left. He was the last one in line. He was an attractive man, big and rough-looking. And I took his hand, a calloused, big hand, and he looked into my eyes, and he said, "Ms. Karon, I just wanted to thank you. I was Buck Leeper." I was just blown away. I'd love to see him again. You know he didn't give me his life story: "Oh Lord, I was a miserable alcoholic. I beat my wife and lost my kids and worse." He simply said, "I want to thank you. I was Buck Leeper."

DB Maybe at the core your books are actually about conversion. Do we really still believe in that? We're more into explaining the causes of our disabilities — more therapeutic than religious, perhaps. I found it interesting, for example, that Father Tim is not a very psychological kind of guy. Oh, we hear sometimes of his psychological issues, but in his great crisis, he never really can convince himself to take the anti-depressants. Did you get letters from psychiatrists?

JK Well, I did. People did rap my hands for letting him go off his medicine. But I'm not writing about people who do things to show the world how wonderful they are. This is just what he did. I can't control his character.

DB He prays.

JK Yes. And that will see him through somehow. I believe this because I *am* born again.

DB So Mitford is about changing, becoming different. J.C., the old clown who suddenly starts dressing better because he's met this woman and needs to change. There's all sorts of variations on change from the major conversions of Pete Jamison, Buck Leeper, George Gaynor, and Hélène Pringle. Maybe even Edith Mallory won't hold out forever. Even Father Tim is learning to change.

JK   I think you have hit on something very powerful here. It's okay to change. Conversion is real. Most people just say, "Well, I've just been going to my psychiatrist now for about twenty years. I'm going to get better; we're just doing it in installments. It's a slow process." But Jesus Christ can reach down and grab you up and you're done. Hallelujah. You know a lot of what you learned in church is true. I guess I am a fundamentalist, just like C. S. Lewis.

DB   How do you feel about celebrity? Do you distrust popularity? Does it seem fragile?

JK   It feels fragile. I couldn't have come up with that word, but that's exactly what I would like to have said. It does feel fragile. I don't trust it. I just sent the manuscript of *Shepherds Abiding* to my editor. I told her to call me if she liked it, and not to call if she didn't like it. Well, she hasn't called me.

DB   It's only been a couple days.

JK   That's true. Sometimes I know, I just know when I've written a good book. I know it through every cell of my being. Then there are times when I'm not sure. I'm not sure at all this time. All I can say is I wrote the best book I could write, and that's the truth.

DB   Did you feel the certainty at the end of *In This Mountain*?

JK   I did, but I didn't feel it at the end of this new one. Because I was moving for one thing, fragmented, and torn in so many directions.

DB   Celebrity has meant money, of course, and this big house, but I suspect the money is not all that important?

JK   It's not. It's God's money. My fees for speeches always go to the Mitford Foundation. I'm weary of the speaking, however. In fact I have just about totally quit speaking. I don't even want to do it anymore. I'm just so tired, but Southern women sigh too much, so I won't talk about that. But I'm proud of the foundation, and when I get through with some of my contractual bondage, I will spend time really growing that foundation. And I mean I will be out there asking for money. People ask me for money all the time, so I'm going to be right back at them. Now the house is getting closer to finished and the book is done. I want to channel my time into refreshing myself. The last thing I want to do as an author is get stale. I shudder to think that there could come a day when someone will say, "Well, you know, she's finally fallen in. You know, you can't get through to the end of that series." I just have to do something to keep my mind fresh. Then I just want to pour whatever I've got left of this life into my work. I really love my work.

DB You'll have to watch out for continuators. It has become popular these days.

JK No sir, they'll never do it. It's in my will. I know they did it with Nancy Drew and Laura Ingalls Wilder. Wilder's attorney lived here in this house for ten years. He ran for president on the Libertarian ticket. He had control of Wilder's literary estate, which was said to be the single most valuable literary estate in America at the time. And he continued the series. People can't use the Mitford name unless I allow them to do it. Somebody wanted to name a real estate development Mitford. Can you believe that? I've got a strong will.

DB When you were six you wanted to be a preacher?

JK I did.

DB Did you ever get over that?

JK No.

DB Do you sit in church and think, "Now here's the sermon that I would've preached today"?

JK I do. I edit. It's like, "Come on, already, come on, make your point, get to the point."

DB So the books have let you exercise your preaching instincts. How else have the books changed you?

JK I think they've made me a better person. I think they've made me stronger. I think they have made me examine my faith more carefully. They've brought me into contact with thousands and thousands of people. And I've been able to search out through my readers something more of the kinds of characters I create. I don't exactly know how to put that together, but sometimes I meet people who are not so much my readers as they are my characters. I can look out into an audience and see Miss Sadie. Over there is Esther. And there's Dooley Barlowe. I even talk to them. "Why good gracious, Dooley, I didn't know you were coming today," or whatever. My characters are out there, all across America. They're just you and me. They're just your daddy and your momma and my momma.

DB   It sounds like you've become more and more a writer.

JK   I think I have grown. One thing I'm glad of is that I didn't let Father Tim get stuck. You know that's a thing psychologists like to talk about: "I think you are stuck back when you were four years old," or whatever. Father Tim could easily have been stuck if I had not gone over the wall in *In This Mountain,* for example. My readers didn't necessarily want my books to get deeper. But it was necessary for both of us that he change and grow. The thought of more depth, or more darkness, was alarming to most of my readers. So going over the wall was a good thing in the fiction, and it has been a good thing in my personal life. I went over the wall to buy this house that I knew had problems. I didn't know what kinds of problems, but this has been an experience that has really shaped me in some mighty ways. And I will continue to go over the wall. Life is about taking risks. It just is. I do not want to go to the grave without having lived as fully as I possibly can. I try to take those things which frighten me, and I'm full of fear, by the way, and I try through prayer to cast them off one by one. I pray about it a lot. "Lord, take this fear from me." I fear living alone, and look, I'm living alone in a big house in the country. And that is a hard one for me.

DB   You don't have people coming to your front yard to be married out here, do you?

JK   They did that in Blowing Rock. They were at my front door, and it was miserable. But here, nobody bothers me. In fact, they come over to me very tentatively at a social event and say, "Ms. Karon, I'm sorry to bother you. I just want you to know how very much I like your books." And then they just go away. But one thing I must tell you is that Mitford has greatly enhanced the economy of Blowing Rock. It was already a tourist spot. But now people are coming from further and further away. And that's good because the little town has no industry but tourism. They are very happy about it.

DB   Jon Hassler tells a great story about a plumber who came to fix a pipe explosion in his Minnesota cabin. Down on his knees, cleaning an awful mess, the plumber asks Hassler about his job. Hassler says, "Oh, I'm a writer." "Oh, I don't see how you could do a job like that," says the plumber. It's not always cleaning up messes, but writing is not easy work, as you know. You've talked about the loneliness and the lack of fellowship. Some writers talk as if they're threatened by the celebrity. Do you feel any of that?

JK   Well, actually I don't. I feel very safe with my audiences. But I don't enjoy going out to large events anymore. Not really. I really love to talk to people. I love to get up before people and talk. When I was three or four years old, they taught me how to sing, "A tiskit, a taskit, a green and yellow basket," and they'd give me chewing gum and applaud. "Now do Mae West." "Why don't you come up and see me sometime." "All right," and then they'd set me up on the table and I would dance, you know, so I've always had some desire to be before people because it got this applause. But it takes too much.

DB   So besides the Mitford wrap-up and the mysteries, there's another collection of Father Tim's quotes.

JK   Yes, *A Continual Feast.*

DB   I was amazed at the combination of names in the first book. Leonard Cohen of all people. I expected Oswald Chambers and C. S. Lewis; they're both in the books often. And Chesterton, of course. Pascal is one of your favorites. And Buechner was there, which I was glad to see. Trollope and Bonhoeffer. But no Louisa May Alcott even though you have been compared to her?

JK   I'm flattered.

DB   Several people mention Dora Saint.

JK   Yes, Miss Read. I love Miss Read. She and I corresponded until about a year or two ago. She's quite elderly now. In her late eighties, she was going blind and couldn't write anymore. Her books are like mine only in that they're set in pastoral villages and had interesting characters. But there is almost no faith content in her work. They are simple, but a total joy to read. When I was in advertising and everything was so fretful, I loved to turn to Miss Read. It was solace.

DB   Other names come up: Phil Gulley, Ann Ross, Garrison Keillor. He gave us Wobegon. You gave us Mitford. James Herriot.

JK   I'm always flattered by these comparisons. The Herriot shows were my favorite TV.

DB   Another name in the quotebook is Vance Havner. Where did you hear of him?

JK   When I was saved I went to a wonderful non-denominational church in Charlotte, North Carolina, and they had Vance Havner. Just one of the scraps I've saved. I knew Father Tim kept a quotebook, but I'd never yet mentioned it in the books. That's the kind of fellow he is, and I had kept scraps of paper all of my life. I never actually formally entered it into a consistently kept book. But then I thought, well, why not just get this together and see if they'll publish it. Well, they were very skeptical. "It's not a novel; we'll lose momentum," they said. And I said, "Just do it. It's going to work." Publishing is very very conservative. They were just afraid that it would go out there and sit on the shelves. They just didn't want to be bothered.

DB   Has it sold?

JK   It sold very well. It's not a bestseller, but it's sold very well. And it will sell over time. It will be a consistent gift book.

DB   So of every five people who discover the Mitford series, one of them will probably buy the quotebook.

JK   Yes, so they're willing to do the next one. I'm under contract for *A Continual Feast*.

DB   I think it's a great idea. I read the scrapbook last. I expected it to be material culled out of the books, lines I'd already read. But it works. I found lots of stuff to scribble in my own notebooks.

JK   The funny part was finding someone to write in Father Tim's handwriting. I didn't know exactly how he would write, but I knew I would recognize it if I saw it. So my publisher did an audition, a handwriting audition. And the winner was a thirty-year-old traveling salesman, who wrote just like I think Father Tim would write. And let in a few mistakes, typos and that kind of thing. My hands are on every single thing that happens. I sketch the covers of all the books. I'm very involved in the typeface. I write all the jacket copy. I even pick the dingbats, the little figurative elements that go between the segments. I love making a book.

DB In the early days, you took charge of the marketing and everything?

JK If I hadn't, it would have been over. I had two books out with Lion, the Christian publishing house, before Penguin came along and picked up the third book and brought it out in paper. They had some success and then brought the first two out in paper. *Out to Canaan,* the fourth book, was published in hardcover. Viking published it in hardcover. So that was my first hardcover book. Now of course they're all in hardcover. My biggest dream was to have a book in hardcover.

DB What are your writing routines like?

JK I have to admit that I have no routines. I worked in advertising for so long, and had to be there early and stay late. Now I just give myself the privilege of working when I want. I don't have a schedule. I write in small chunks. I write in large chunks. And I sometimes write in the cracks.

DB You like to have a quiet place?

JK Never play music. I keep it pretty quiet. And I like pictures hanging straight on the wall.

DB Anything you've been reading lately that you really like?

JK Yes. I read *Bruneleschi's Dome* by that Ross King fellow who writes all those wonderfully arcane books. I hardly understood a word of it, but I loved it. I couldn't put it down. It was so compelling. I read *Lamb in Love.* I felt like I'd discovered Carrie Brown, like I felt I had discovered Tony Earley, who wrote *Jim the Boy,* though I didn't discover either of them really. I'm ashamed to admit that I haven't read enough recently, because it is my job to write and to read. It is the job of an earnest author to read. And I've been falling down on the job.

DB   And you are finished with Hallmark?

JK   Yes, that's done. They produced several hundred pieces over a period of three or four years, but then they hired a new leader. Hallmark is still a family owned and operated company. But they hired somebody new, and I'm afraid he didn't think much of Mitford. Although it's perfect for Hallmark. It's perfect, but that's okay.

DB   But no Hallmark movie?

JK   No, that's actually a separate division. Hallmark entertainment is a very different thing. At one point, one of my agents talked to Hallmark, and they didn't think my work was right for them. So strange. It's perfect for them. That's odd. But I figure my patience will pay off. I've never signed a contract, even when we had two CBS contracts on the table. It never felt right, so I never signed anything. If I had signed, they wouldn't have done it anyway, and then I would have been tied to them for four years.

DB   And you wrote for *Victoria Magazine* for a while?

JK   I was writer in residence for them, and they let me do some interesting things. I really enjoyed a piece called "Heirloom Language." I got to talk like my grandmother talks and say things like, "Well, Dale, you just come anytime. You're as welcome as the flowers in May." Now you've heard that before?

DB   Do you "swan"?

JK   I don't ever swan.

DB   Do you "swanee"?

JK   I do swanee sometimes.

DB   I think that means, "I swear."

JK   Oh, that's charming. My mom says, "I'm not going out there; it's black as pitch out there." Just all that colorful language. So I did an article to play with that. I did a three-part Mitford installment for them, which will show up in the *Bedside Companion,* a collection my sister is working on. And I enjoyed my association with them. Now they have gone out of business. It was a wonderful magazine. They had the best photography.

DB   You still seem to like the business of writing on deadline.

JK   Everything to do with writing is on deadline. I was on deadline when I was in advertising all those years, and now I'm still on deadline. I don't think you can sign a contract and not have a deadline. They will not sign a contract in today's world if you just say, "Well, I'm going to give you this book and it's going to be about Father Tim and Cynthia going to Ireland." You can forget getting an advance on that. Of course I'm very driven now to maintain this house.

DB   Your readers are no doubt grateful for that. And you've won awards — the Abby, the Logos, the Gold Medallion, the Christy, *Christianity Today, Parent's Choice*. Quite a list.

JK   You got it.

DB   What do those do for you?

JK   It is very nice. I've never really thought much about awards for some reason. I won a lot of awards in advertising. The *Parent's Choice* award especially pleased me. I was nominated for an Abby three years in a row — the first time that has ever happened in the history of that award — but I never actually won one until 1998.

DB   What about the children's books? They seem to have been inspired by personal and family connections somehow.

JK   I just figured that I wanted to give my daughter something that she could keep forever, and I didn't know how to make a quilt. I didn't have time to make a quilt. I couldn't sew. So I thought, I'll write her a little book. Someone had given me a handmade blank book. And oh the temptation of the blank book. I sat down with a pen. There's a gambling streak in me. I've never actually gambled with money, but I gamble in other ways. I started to write the book without an idea as to where it was going. I wrote in pen, so I could not erase. I wrote all the way to the very last dot of the end paper in the book, and the story ended right there. I did mark through one word. If I got a word wrong, I would just make it work. It was kind of a game. It turned out to be a story about a bunny, even though my daughter was in her thirties at that time. It just turned into a children's story. I couldn't help it. I don't know how to talk about my children's books as well as I talk about my books for adults. The children's books don't seem to have as much rhyme or reason.

DB   Mitford casts a big shadow, of course, but your fundamental themes are there even in the most recent, *The Trellis and the Seed*. Possibility, conversion, change. . . .

JK   Redemption.

DB   And a website too. Do you prowl there?

JK   About once a week. I'll occasionally write a new letter and freshen it up. But I don't pay much attention to it. Have you been there to see what people are saying?

DB   There's the "You Saved My Life Mister" chorus, of course. There's some good readers, people who are caught up in your stories, real book people. A decade ago, so many were predicting the end of book culture. You remember electronic books and all that? You even have Father Tim talking about "the precious few who still love and enjoy books." Yet you've sold 15 million. J. K. Rowling has just moved 9.3 million copies of one book. Are we at the end of books?

JK   No, we're not. People love books. They love to hold them in their hands. I do too. Smell them and touch them. So no, I'm not worried about that. I did sort of get caught up in that and wanted to do an electronic book, but my publisher wouldn't let me. That was good.

DB   I've been inviting writers to a literary festival in Grand Rapids for fourteen years now, and I've noticed that fewer and fewer of them answer their mail.

JK   Every letter that comes in here gets answered. Every letter. Anything else is bad manners.

DB   When I innocently picked up *At Home in Mitford* for the first time a few years ago, I followed my usual practice of scribbling names in the back cover. And I don't think I've ever had a book where I didn't have enough room on the cover. I'm 250 pages in and here comes this new guy. You break all the rules — a cast of hundreds and coming and going all over the place.

JK   You know the town is the main character. If you're going to have a town as your main character, you've got to have a lot of people. And I figured there would be no sense of a village, no sense of a town, if we didn't have lots of people. I didn't realize how many characters I did put there until my sister started compiling the *Bedside Companion*.

DB   Is this a glossary?

JK   It'll be everything: Crossword puzzles, Mitford quizzes, character names, and even the Uncle Billy jokes. She's brilliant at it. It will be fun. And she said, "Janet, guess how many characters you have in your first book?" She said 169. You know the complaint about the Russian novel is that it had too many characters in it. But I've enjoyed building a town. When I started writing the books, I didn't know I was going to create a village. And that just, it just became the thing that was right to do. Mae Benchley writes a book, and you see one circumstance through sixteen different eyes. When I write a book, you see sixteen different circumstances through one set of eyes. We see everything through Father Tim. I believe that consistency has given the books a kind of inner structure. There's a good word for it; it's the thing that goes inside a piece of sculpture — "armature." The armature of all of my books is Father Tim's perspective. The reader becomes familiar with his take on everything. We see everything through his eyes. No surprises. He doesn't suddenly change his mind or go out of character. He's always the same. That makes readers feel secure. It makes them comfortable. I think another reason they like to go to Mitford is because they can trust it. It's just secure.

DB   Where did you get all those names?

JK   Out of my childhood. I didn't actually know someone named Mule Skinner, but I might have known someone named Mule and somebody else named Skinner, and the two names just started going together. I remember when I started writing the series, I had no idea what to call Father Tim. I wanted him to be Southern, and for that, I got down on my hands and knees on a map of the South and looked at all the states. I didn't want him to be from North Carolina; I wanted him to be from away. He wasn't from Tennessee. He wasn't from Alabama. Definitely not Georgia. He was from Mississippi, I finally decided. I went up to Northeast Mississippi and found Holly Springs. I was looking for a name with some music in it. Holly Springs, I come to find out much later, is a town absolutely filled with gorgeous antebellum homes and wonderful history. I'm going out there, by the way. Holly Springs may even show up in the final book. I just know that's going to be a good book. Father Tim is still going to deal with some old issues. In *Shepherds Abiding* he's still dealing with his daddy.

DB   Did the editors balk at so many characters, your rule breaking?

JK   No, they never balked. Here is a secular publisher, second only to Random House in size, and they have never tried to handcuff me. They have never tried to limit me. They've never said, "You cannot talk about Jesus." They've never said, "Get all these Scripture quotes out of there." They have just gotten behind me in such a wonderful way. Only God Himself could have done this. I love my publisher. It was the Christian publisher that was troubling. They never really cared about Mitford. They never got a vision for Mitford. To this day, Mitford has never been a bestseller on their list.

DB   How long did it take you to write that first one?

JK   Two years. When I found that I couldn't write the novel that I thought I'd quit my job to write, I was so devastated. Then one night I had a dream in which I imagined a priest walking down a village street, and I got up that very night and started writing. After a few weeks, I had a simple story going. I didn't know what it was, but I was starting to put some energy in it. I took it to the editor of the *Blowing Rocket*. (Don't you love that name?) He said, "Let's run it." I think he did that really just to fill up space in this little weekly. I think that he was so grateful to get half a page every week. It is true that nothing much happens in a small town. So it ran for two years. And I was on deadline every week, just like I was writing a column. I was Dear Abby. Finally, it started to take form. I wrote that book whether I wanted to or not. If I had not gotten hooked into that newspaper deal, the Lord knew that I would have become very very disheartened. Once I made that commitment, I was not going to disappoint that editor.

DB   Which book was the quickest and easiest to write?

JK   *A Common Life* because it was a love story and because I enjoyed it so much. I could not wait to get to the computer. And that was the book that people liked least because they were so mad.

DB   Well, it's funny, I thought I was going to like that one least because it is a flashback. But you did a couple of marvelous things there.

One was the bringing together all the famous proposal stories. It is more than Tim and Cynthia's courtship. But people still didn't like it?

JK It made them angry because it was out of place. It was still a bestseller. It was still on the *New York Times* list. But it didn't sell as well as the big novels. That was the easiest book for me to write because it was the most fun. It just poured out. The hardest book for me to write was *In This Mountain;* it just about half-killed me. I know people think I write these little sweet stories about this cute little town. I cannot tell you what agony I experience when I write sometimes. I'm not being dramatic. They're hard. I was also going through the agony of this house, trying to get this together, all those distractions, and trying to make that book work, trying to give people something significant, forcing readers to go deeper than they'd gone in the other books. And I was going through a hard time.

DB Was it hard because you didn't want to see your beloved Tim go through the fire or because you were going through the fire?

JK Both. I really suffered with him. You can imagine that these characters are pretty real to me. I wept bitterly over Miss Sadie dying.

DB That's a powerful scene all the way back in the third book?

JK Yes. And that broke my heart. People say, "Well, you're the boss, why did you let her die?" She had to. What can I say? It was her time. When I'm writing, sometimes I laugh out loud, just roar with laughter. I did last night as I edited on this manuscript I've just finished. I thought that was so funny. I'm in there with these people.

DB Miss Sadie is really Tim's advisor, isn't she?

JK One of the things I love about *A Common Life* is that we get to see Miss Sadie again. Remember when he goes up the hill and talks to Louella and Miss Sadie, sits on the porch with them? I loved having her back. I think she's my grandmother, Miss Fannie.

DB You wrote a children's book about her when she was ninety-nine?

JK Yes. And she lived to a hundred.

DB In *A Light in the Window* you had a good bit to say about the dangers of creedal belief. You talked about "being devoted to causes rather than to Christ."

JK Yes, church people instead of people in relationship with Christ.

A Light in the Window was the second easiest book to write, even though I introduced Buck Leeper, my first really difficult character there. I loved that book because of the love letters. I enjoy writing letters in my books. There was a whole chapter of letters. And that was a love story too. So I liked that book. The books started to get really hard for me with *These High, Green Hills*.

DB Miss Sadie's death?

JK Miss Sadie's death and there was a burn scene there with Pauline. I had to go to a burn center and oh my word, what I saw and what I learned.

DB There's also issues about aging and retirement in that book.

JK Yes, and I had thought myself in love while I was writing that book. But I was wrong. Then *Out to Canaan* with the retirement. And, I loved *A New Song* because I enjoyed being down on the Outer Banks. I went down there to research that book. Although I'd been many times, I wanted to go get the feeling of it again. And I so loved writing that thirteenth chapter, which was about his deep-sea fishing experience.

DB Where Father Tim gets sick, eats the Snickers bar, starts feeling better, and everything's okay when he gets back home?

JK I saw a man get deathly ill on a deep-sea fishing trip, and he was a priest. I don't like water and didn't want to be out in the ocean, but I said, "I'm going to do this thing. I've got to know what it feels like."

DB You were doing research?

JK That priest got so deathly ill. I didn't know how he was going to recover. I knew that Father Tim was going to get sick, but seeing that priest suffer helped make Chapter 13 better and funnier. And I had to research that cave business too. It was a chilling experience. I thought it would be like the school trip where we went to a cave with a big entrance and fluorescent lights. I figured we'd just go see the stalactites and stalagmites. Well, it wasn't anything like that. It was in the middle of nowhere. We had this cave person with us. I had on a miner's hat with a light. Spelunking. And we come to this hole in the ground, just a hole in the ground. It looked like a groundhog maybe would go in there. He said, "Well, this is where we go in."

DB   You got that in the book.

JK   I was panic-stricken. My heart started pounding. He said, "Let's just hold hands and pray." We did, and I managed to get down there. I would never do it again for a million dollars. But it was an interesting experience. It was so beautiful down there. But it was scary. He said, "Okay, let's stop now and turn our lights off." Oh boy.

DB   In *Out to Canaan* I like the change versus improvement theme. You even get Thoreau's notions of simplicity into your books via Homeless Hobbes. It is also in *Out to Canaan* that you talk about the choice between "muddling on about the fire" or "noticing the Phoenix rising from the ashes." Do you think of yourself as an optimist? Do you like to be categorized that way? Is this optimistic writing?

JK   I am optimistic, but I struggle. I struggle against my pessimism. I do. I'm aware of my pessimism, and so I often work to be optimistic. But then I can also work myself into believing it. Largely yes, I'm optimistic.

DB   You talk about "corporate indifference" in *A New Song*. You must have felt that in advertising.

JK   I just never liked anything corporate. I mean I do enjoy corporate worship. But to work in a corporate setting is inhibiting. But not everybody's wired that way. Not everybody should be wired that way. I've always been very sociable. And I could be with a lot of people. I'm invited to a lot of events. But I don't go to many. It's too much. I'd rather be home listening to some quiet music than out in the fray; the fray exhausts me.

DB   How about Jeffrey Tolson, a character in that book. Was he tough?

JK   He kind of scared me too. But I needed somebody to challenge Father Tim. He's really angry. He's really had a lot of hurt. He fancies himself. He thinks he's a pretty cute guy, with that poet shirt and his big sleeves and all of that. I always remember him wearing those huaraches. He is a prideful man, and unfaithful to his wife, and he wants to smear it in everybody's face. I've known people like that. And Father Tim just says, "You're out of here." Period. This is one of the places I see the church failing. We are afraid to discipline. I see people getting away with murder. We actually pander to them, "Oh, you bad boy." We ought to be smacking his fanny across the narthex. It's just, anything goes, but Father Tim says, "It's going to stop here. You're out of here."

DB   Until you're ready to come back and repent.

JK   Yes. Until then.

DB   And then on the last page, he does come back. Though you don't name him there. You make the reader realize who this is. In the next book we hear of his gradual change — a different sort of conversion. Again Father Tim's foolishness has proven to be the right way. I do resist talk about Christ figures and all that English class stuff, but would it be a fair summary to say that Father Tim is a "fool for Christ's sake"?

JK   It is very fair. And I think that Father Tim is a Christ figure if you want. I mean just like the lion in C. S. Lewis's *Narnia* series. Father Tim is human, he's flawed, and he struggles. But he represents Christ.

DB   Somebody says "God is the antagonist" of your books and "Satan is the protagonist," but that can be said of almost every really good book. Tim is a Christ figure because of his sacrificial nature, his instinctively right choices, his humility, or what?

JK   In his humility. You know he's the one who is a foot-washer. He never wanted to be a bishop. He never wanted to get on that corporate ladder, and rise to the top. He just wanted to be a pastor. There's a deep and lovely meaning to the words "pastor" and "parson" that we've nearly lost. And Father Tim does love pretty unconditionally, but he also has his limits. And so did Jesus. You know Tim doesn't say, "OK, Jeffrey, that's all right, you come on back, we forgive you, and everything's fine." Jeffrey was eventually forgiven, but everything wasn't fine.

DB   Which is a message that goes down hard these days?

JK   Boy, howdy. Nobody wants any bottom lines. That's why they don't want Jesus, because He insists that they draw a line somewhere or other. It may be a different line for you and me. But He's going to draw a line.

DB   Yet despite his profundity, his simplicity, his humility, there is this darkness in the last book. Even he can't always get it right. The lesson he finally learns is to say thank you even for the darkness. He learns again about grace.

JK   Yes. It is the lesson I'm still learning. It is an essential, central lesson for a believer, to give thanks in everything.

DB   That's where I would start if I were attempting to talk to somebody who categorized Jan Karon's novels as "light." Giving thanks for suffering? Being grateful for all that goes wrong? Sounds like anything but "light." Somehow you've got that grace thing right at the heart of that last book.

JK   I prayed and prayed for that sermon at the end. I didn't know what it was going to be about. I knew I was coming up to the end of the book, and I knew I needed one. I personally needed one, and that book needed a conclusion. And God just gave it to me. It was so easy. I said, "Now wait a minute, can this be? I don't know. I just don't know." Then the more I reflected on it, and my own life and what was going on it, and what had gone on, the more extraordinary I found the wisdom of the line — "In everything give thanks."

DB   Can a good book still make a difference?

JK   Time is running out so fast. It was spring, just a couple months ago, it was last spring two months ago, and I feel the weight of the years. I think it's the move and finishing the book, and I've got a lot ahead of me too. I look in the mirror and I hardly recognize myself. I've always found that age lines come on quickly. You go for a long time, and then, suddenly, there are new wrinkles, new lines in places they hadn't been before. When I was forty-eight, I went in to my boss, whom I admired very much. He was a big name in advertising. I said, "I'm going to have to leave." "You've left me once before," he said. (That was the second time I'd worked for him. And I'd won a lot of awards there and had a good good time.)

I said, "I'm going to be fifty, you know, in just no time at all."

He said, "But fifty is nothing. It's nothing."

But oh, I knew, fifty was something. You better get cracking. That's what fifty is. And then when you're sixty, you better give it everything you've got because you're not going to be here forever. That's the real deadline.

DB Though at the same time you have to extend grace to yourself knowing that you can't get it all right?

JK Absolutely. Yes. Look what a difference Ayn Rand's book has made. I mean in all these years. And I'm not calling that a good book; I'm calling it a dangerous book.

DB *Fountainhead*?

JK *Fountainhead*. Look how many people say that it's changed their life. For what? To what? Look at *Catcher in the Rye*. That book made a difference. *Uncle Remus* made a difference for me. That was one of my earliest, most beloved books. That taught me that dialect is filled with color and life and imagery and warmth. Just Uncle Remus talking about a fire. Huge impression.

DB *Catcher in the Rye* is a book which taught a generation about hypocrites, phonies, and cynics. You see books, maybe one of your own books, as being able to posit another possibility?

JK Yes, simply to posit another possibility.

DB That not everybody's a phony?

JK Yes. And that it's okay to be genuine or happy or cheerful or optimistic. It's okay. Some people probably don't even know what cheerful is until you give them a demonstration. Well all right, here's what cheerful is. Here's how you bake a biscuit. Here's what it means to walk out your faith on a simple day-by-day basis. Remember in school how we would get those wonderful instructional films about how to live our lives as teenagers? My books are about demonstrating just how simple and just how hard it is to have faith in Jesus Christ, how simple and how hard it is to walk it out.

DB There's a notable absence in your books of television shows and movies and the things of modernity. Instead, there's the celebration of simple things, the little stuff, the little stuff that turns out not to be little stuff.

JK Like talking at lunch with your daddy about what you'll have for supper.

SHERI REYNOLDS

Oprah, Jesus Music, and Pressing Stories

1967 — Born in Conway, South Carolina
1994 — *Bitterroot Landing*
1995 — *The Rapture of Canaan*
1997 — *A Gracious Plenty*
2005 — *Orabelle's Wheelbarrow* (play)
2006 — *The Firefly Cloak*

Lives in Richmond, Virginia

Sheri Reynolds hit the jackpot in the mid-nineties, and she's still amazed by it. Reynolds boomed onto the best-seller list after a quiet beginning in 1994 with *Bitterroot Landing*. A second novel in 1995, *The Rapture of Canaan,* seemed destined to follow the sales path of the first. Then Oprah called and *Rapture* became the talk. Reynolds has since added the impressive *A Gracious Plenty* (1997) and *Firefly Cloak* (2006) to a list that has established her as an important force in contemporary fiction. She has also turned to playwriting with *Orabelle's Wheelbarrow* in 2005 and continues to teach creative writing at Virginia Commonwealth University.

Intense during the writing, Sheri Reynolds is also intense about the writing. She speaks of a nearly obsessive flow that has produced novels in less than a month. She talks, too, of a restless period where

stories insist themselves upon her, willing her to at least write them, if only for herself.

A complicated religious background has left this writer with a reservoir of anger, perhaps, but a hopefulness persists. She talks of having felt the nourishment of her soul, the connectedness of all things, and the power of spiritual presences. We had our conversation in the fall of 1998 in Richmond, Virginia, where Reynolds had come to speak and read her work at a local Presbyterian church. Among her comments that day was her feeling about church: "I don't go to church anymore; there just aren't churches that will have me." But, somehow, it was more a question than a conclusion.

DB   Do you enjoy giving readings?

SR   I do as few as I can. I try to accommodate schools where they're teaching my books. And doing a reading myself is all right; I can manage that because I can make that performance art, give people a pretty good time. I understand that most people sitting in those chairs are a lot like me: they're not always engaged with the writing. I get frustrated at other people's readings sometimes. I consider readings mandated daydreaming if it comes to that.

DB   Do you have friends that help with the work?

SR   I do, but it's a much smaller kind of community than you would think. I have individuals here and there that I've come to rely on. Most definitely.

DB   Do you have people who actually read manuscripts for you?

SR   My friend, Amy, is a poet and she's a fiction writer and she reads things when I get them done, and she's the most reliable critic I've ever had because she's so honest. She'll say, "I've seen you do so much more than this. What truth aren't you telling here?" She can say the hard stuff to me. And I have an incredible agent, Candice Fuhrman. She has become much more than an agent to me. She's an important friend, and if something would happen to our business relationship, I have no doubt that we would stay in touch. She's very reliable. I'm always battling the feeling that I should be writing, because I call myself a writer, yet all the books I have published come from a place that don't seem like they came from me. And so I spend time writing these inspired books and then, not only do I have nothing left to say, but I am wiped out. I need to do something else for years before I can come back to it, but in the meantime I feel guilty about not writing. I get ideas for research. I tell myself I'm going to write this or that. I guess I'm learning my process more and more at this point, but Amy and Candice are real good about saying, "No, just quit. Just put it away; it was good for you to do this and you will find your way." And I usually do. Another thing they often do is to point out "Here's what seems authentic in this piece; here's where you want to go." But very often, they've approved maybe three pages of a 300-page book and I just think "No, no, no." So I have a couple of readers. And then I have a few other people scattered here and there, but the longer I've been writing the more solitary it's become. It really has. I've also realized that actually the things that people think are personal questions, maybe too personal to ask, usually aren't the ones that are personal to me. I can say things that some people would consider unthinkable, but the really personal questions are about my writing process, what it means and that kind of thing. It's very hard to share it with somebody else. It's very hard to make myself so vulnerable. You know, there's only a few people you want to be that open with. You know that you're saying more than you're really saying in fiction, so you open yourself up that way and the question is who would you make yourself so vulnerable before?

DB You sound like Walker Percy or Kaye Gibbons. They talk about the psychic toll of creating fiction.

SR It hits me. I hurt, but I don't think I'm mentally ill. If I have to go completely nuts, I hope it doesn't hit me until I'm an old, old lady. A really old lady. Because I have too much I want to do. Writing books is a strange possession for me; it feels like a possession. I mean, I'm only partially in control of it.

DB John Steinbeck talks about a book being "willful." You talk somewhere about the character in *The Rapture of Canaan* who commits suicide. You said you wept and had to call your mother, almost as if you were surprised at that turn in the plot, even though you knew it had to go that way.

SR It's one of the most frustrating and most blessed things about writing. It is existing in two simultaneous and opposite states. I must let go of control and lose all agenda, all deliberate thinking, in order to write. And at the same time, I have to maintain control to sculpt it into this product.

DB Do these characters take on lives of their own in some ways?

SR They do. I mean, I don't know if it will always be this way or if it's just this way for me now. I'm as narcissistic as the next writer, I guess, and I write about me. But not "me" in capital letters, but aspects of me that I can plant in different people and write about the positive and the negative and the things that worry me and the things I'm proud of, and I put that in different places. And then I build the character around that, so that nobody recognizes it as me, I hope. Some characters are more recognizably me than others or have more of me in them than others, but it's within the character.

DB Your novels are self-exploration?

SR In a lot of ways it's almost like dividing up the different archetypes that I live. Or taking the different components of myself, and building on it. So I have a point of contact with the character. I know what that character's going to do under certain circumstances because I know about myself. But then I get to use all kinds of things that I don't know so much about and things that interest me. I can let that character be an expert in something totally other and get that information.

DB So there is a research dimension? Like cemeteries in *A Gracious Plenty*?

SR Exactly. I can start forming stuff where I have lots of knowledge. But when I need detailed knowledge, I just call on my dad or something. It's that simple sometimes. What that does, I guess, is put me in a state when I'm actually writing where I have no skin. I'm just bones. I'm experiencing all these people at one time, not only the main characters, but the minor characters. And it does reach into me.

DB Is that why you have so much sympathy even for your villains finally?

SR I am my villains. When I think about it, even Grandpa Herman in *The Rapture of Canaan* holds my secret self. He holds pieces of me, the part of me that wants to control everything, and if I have to strangle you to do it, then I'll strangle you. I mean, that's very vulnerable stuff.

DB Is there a part of you that wants the world to be simpler than it is?

SR Sure, I'm a little like Reba, in *A Gracious Plenty*. And I grew up with a Grandpa Herman too.

DB Even River Bill, the villain of *Bitterroot Landing*, is tough to hate.

SR I have a real fondness for him — for all three of those characters. I have not really thought about my characters or my books as a collection. But I need to start doing that, because people are starting to ask me questions about all the books. I haven't thought in terms of themes I have going throughout. I hadn't thought about those three characters together, but they're all very sympathetic characters to me. They're all precious babies that grew up hurt somehow or afraid of something. All their meanness has a place. It came from somewhere. And I don't think you get anywhere by blanket condemnations. I mean, what does that do for you? So I want to show both sides of them; they're all real people too. At least they're pieces of people that I love.

DB When did you first start thinking of yourself as a writer? Are you comfortable with saying that? Or do you still say, "I'm a teacher and a writer"?

SR Well. It depends on the situation. Sometimes when I say I'm a writer, I'm saying it to try to convince myself. I have a hard time saying I'm a writer when I'm not writing, and I've also been thinking a lot about what writing demands of your life and what part it wants to play in my life. It is a demanding job now that I have national attention. But it wasn't nearly so demanding before. And it's the other parts of my life that make me have something to say; the writing comes along for the ride.

DB It sounds like you view these books as gifts. They came to you in some ways unbidden.

SR Yes, but I wish I was able to say that I didn't fight for them or didn't fight when they weren't happening, that I just lived my life and down came the angel and kissed me. But that's not how it happened at all. There's a lot of hard work involved and there's also a lot of struggling. In the times when I'm not writing, I'm just wretched. It's like I itch all the time because I think I need to be writing. I'm in such a place now, a place of agitation. I have some ideas about where I'm headed, but nothing specific. When the opening comes to me, it will be done. The book will be done.

DB You have a novel that's brewing right now in your mind?

SR Yes, but I don't know what it is, or whether I'll write it when it comes. Will I recognize it and will I accept it? That's another big thing.

DB Is that a matter of courage or is it a matter of energy or self-revelation? I mean, why would you not write it?

SR I should revise what I said. I'll probably write it — will I share it? That's another thing. I can't imagine not writing it. The energy will have to go somewhere, into some creative form. I think I'll probably write it.

DB I was going to ask about the national attention. You've said that if you were ever on the Oprah Winfrey show it would be under the couch, not on it. So many writers now have to do publicity tours and signing tours and all sorts of self-promotion.

SR I do it. I can turn on the extrovert if I need to. I love meeting people, but I start thinking about who will be there. I wonder who will be at the Borders in Denver, and that's exciting and it's fun. But really, I wouldn't do it if I didn't have to. I wouldn't choose it in a million years. One thing I know is that if I don't write another book, I won't have to tour again. I'm tired. So right now I'm doing more self-preservation, soul work. That's what I've got to do. I got a huge boost early in my career because of "Oprah," and that was good. I believe that it happened because it needed to happen. I believe that I needed to be in the public for some reason, and I hope that when or if that reason becomes evident to me I will be ready to take the next step. I don't have a philosophy. I don't have a plan. I don't want one right now. I don't know why I do what I do. I sometimes use parts of Carol Bly's *The Passionate, Accurate Story* in my classes. I read to students from it. She has this one section about the need to start from a point that is familiar. You need to start from something that you're engaged with, and then you need to give up control and be weak and go to a place that is not conscious. And imagination is the bridge between the places. Even talking about this is really difficult for me. I don't have a vision beyond today, not much of one. There's some things I'd like to do, some things I think I'll probably write about. But I trust that when it's time to say something, the words will come. By the same token, I hope that I won't be trapped in a certain category and that my writing will continue to grow — that my writing will not be trapped beneath an agenda.

DB Being on "Oprah" is like winning the Nobel Prize in terms of your books' sales.

SR Yes, I've sold more books than some Nobel Prize winners.

DB But it's "Oprah."

SR Pop culture, glittery fiction.

DB Oprah Winfrey as arbiter of literary taste does give one pause, but she's chosen many good books. Is there an "Oprah" formula that could become restricting?

SR I haven't read any book because it was an "Oprah" pick. I am honored to be among the writers that she's chosen. But you know I haven't tried to keep up with the "Oprah" stuff. I have tried to stay away from it as much as I could. I do think that she is interested in stories about religion.

DB And there are a lot of young women characters in the books, women who overcome enormous obstacles to find redemption of some sort. I suppose the danger would be if someone tried to write an "Oprah" book to fit a formula.

SR If you were to deconstruct what she's after.

DB In the transcript of the show, it seemed as if you were trying to get a word in now and then?

271

SR   On the show, yes, but there was also that three-hour dinner party, with three readers, Oprah, and me. They did everything they could to make it intimate, but there were camera people all around us, and a bunch of producers. It was bizarre. Right in the middle of conversation, somebody would yell something about needing more tea or whatever. I was very nervous. It was strange with the lights baking down on us. They did everything that they could to make us relax, but it was a long, long conversation. It went on for hours. We covered all kinds of things. Then, of course, what they do is edit all those hours down to a theme. I was on stage with Oprah and they had pieces of the dinner film overhead on this big screen, so the audience was seeing this for the first time. And Oprah would talk to me and then they'd cut to that, and then there'd be a little bit more and they'd cut back to that. It was as edited as anything is edited. I felt a little bit like a Sunday school teacher whose job was to educate non-fundamentalists on the rapture. They had to focus on something and the rapture is what they focused on. That was partially why my book was selected, of course. I didn't talk a lot, but it was okay. It was fine.

DB   And you respect Oprah Winfrey?

SR   I do. And I respect her choice of the book and the choice of questions. What showed up on the show was not a reflection of the conversation that we had. She has integrity. She's a businesswoman and she's not necessarily as she appears to be on TV, but I think that she is doing her best to do her job in this world.

DB   You've had such good fortune. Some of us are wondering where the industry is, about publishing and the future of books. You have a huge readership out there. You can call the editor and say, "Look, publish this."

SR   Yes, it's scary. The year following Oprah has been a time when all the old ways have died. The new ways are not formed. It hit me at a developmental stage, you know. I was twenty-nine years old, so it hit me literally at a time in my life when I was shifting into an adult identity and beginning to rethink some of the things I had always just taken for granted. I could probably just publish pure crap if I wanted to, because they could put "Best-selling author of *The Rapture of Canaan*" on the cover. So I have to become really careful. I know I have some readers who won't let me do that and I'm glad that I have them. But it's dangerous because it could happen.

DB   And you have friends who are writers who have not had such good fortune?

SR   The whole market is so strange right now. Janet Peery, for example, is a brilliant writer and a brilliant thinker. She was nominated for a National Book Award for *The River Beyond the World*. But there are so many people who have never heard of her or seen her books and book stores that don't stock them. I don't know what to make of that. But I have to just stop questioning, because all the questions sidetrack me, I think.

DB   Well, you have to accept what's happened to you as marvelous. Obviously, for you, it is a moment of grace.

SR   But a moment that has also catapulted me into another time of my life that I wasn't really ready for. I'm still not wise enough to understand. Maybe my lack of wisdom shows a weakness in my thinking. Maybe I need to have more answers than I do.

DB   Well, you're still adjusting to this.

SR   Definitely. But one thing that has happened is I know where I'm headed. I know if I choose to write the next book, I know where it's going to go. It's about the Southern woman, how the good Christian woman lives and how a good Southern woman is supposed to behave. I can't be that and be what the world is demanding of me, too. I must say no to things. I must say no to that guilt of "Oh how could I disappoint all these people this way?"

DB   Is it true that, once you start writing, you move very quickly?

SR   Yes, I wrote *The Rapture of Canaan* in about four or five weeks.

DB   It sounds as if there's this whole thing that goes on in your head for a while, and then you sit down and just pour it out.

SR   I wrote *A Gracious Plenty* in under a month of eight-hour days.

DB   Do you feel a fury coming on? Suddenly a cloud bursts?

SR   This is what happens. That's why I talk about being mentally ill, because I go into the state that I'm in right now. I'm in it pretty deep right now. I feel agitated. I know that I'm burning up with themes that I must find a forum for and yet it's not time. And then something clicks, something shifts, and I go in. I am so consumed by the writing. I don't worry about what I'm going to do next in a book — I'm always behind. I'm writing toward what's going to happen maybe about twenty pages ahead of where I am. And it stays about that far. I write toward it, and I write all day. I have so many stupid rituals for this kind of writing. For one thing, I had to start going to the chiropractor when I was doing *The Rapture of Canaan,* because I messed up my neck. And it is somehow very unpleasant. I have to keep a pitcher of water by my desk so I'll at least get up to go to the bathroom. As long as I have a pitcher of water by my desk, I will drink it. So I have to get up about every thirty or forty-five minutes. If I didn't have it there, I wouldn't get up all day.

DB   Obsessive?

SR   It is obsessive. I would go so far as to say it's almost a trance. And I would like to not be that way because it makes me feel so out of control. But at the same time, I'm so absorbed. That's why I go so fast, I have to get in fast and get out fast, because I am living not just my life, but the lives of everybody in the book. I can be writing the character of Ninah's mother, basically a difficult, bitchy, old, unfeeling character, and I'll understand where she's coming from and I know how she talks. She's heartbroken because she has a child for whom she had so many hopes, and I know how she feels. So I get in that intense place and try to get out quickly. I am wiped out after I finish it. It's bizarre because, after I've written these things, it's like I've always known the story. And there are moments that I put in the books that weren't even conscious in my mind but were really me. I didn't know that they were there. But I tap into it and I remember it for the first time. I live it for the first time. They are these tiny pieces that I've collected. One of them in *A Gracious Plenty* is this random little scene about how Finch had a cat that she loved differently from the other cats. She bashes it on the head. And that is a scene from a dream that affected me profoundly, because the cat was my cat that I loved so much. What was true about it, I guess, was the reality of unintentional destruction, meaning to act to make something better but instead making things much worse. I still have this animal, and I love her dearly. But that dream from years before became part of the novel. It's bigger than me.

DB What creates a writer like that? Does it have something to do with your religious past?

SR My religious past has been troubling all my life, even when I was in it. Even as a little kid. Church and the church family, and all that.

DB Do you feel gratitude or anger?

SR Mostly anger. Well, no, that's not true. I feel about it like I do about a lot of things: a lot of anger but also a great deal of love for these people and for the community that I still have some access to. I tried to put that feeling into *The Rapture of Canaan*. But I invented much of the religious experience there. It is an autobiographical book, but only in a sense. I didn't grow up in a community exactly like that, but most meals that I ate with my family were, in fact, for at least twenty people. It was the extended family thing. And there were lots of church activities. The women in my family, especially, were deeply entrenched in the church. Men in my family expected the women to be in church, but the men were outlaws.

DB That's really Southern.

SR It is. They were not in the church, but they would go for special occasions. Here's a good example that I haven't told anybody; I just remembered it not too long ago. I love to sing and apparently I can pull it off all right. We had a youth choir and they made me sing this song that was basically set after the rapture. It was a song about a little girl speaking to her father, saying, "Sorry you can't be with us, but we must sail unto lovely shores. Sorry for we still love you, but you cannot be our daddy anymore." Because, of course, the daddy has not been saved. So they would make me sing these solos, and then they would coerce my dad into going to church because I had a solo. They wouldn't tell him what the song was about. So there I had my daddy, who I loved so much, and me standing up there singing. The whole point for the people who organized it was how to bring this man to Christ. They had no thought of what that situation did to father and daughter. It killed me. I hated it.

DB   And you were how old?

SR   Maybe nine. The seed of *The Rapture of Canaan* that was so true was the stuff about the rapture. I was terrified of the rapture. I would go stand in front of the faucet and think about turning it on. If it was water, I could go to sleep. Most times, I couldn't make myself turn it on; I was so afraid it was going to be blood. And the horrible part was I couldn't get saved.

DB   What would have been evidence of being saved?

SR   Baptism. This was a church where we were exposed to people who spoke in tongues and there was a lot of shouting, a lot of people praying out loud with people leading the prayer. So there would be voices going off all over the church. It was charismatic. You know, the minister with tears streaming down his face while talking hellfire and brimstone. There was praying over people and invitations to come and be saved that would go on for half an hour. If nobody came to the altar and someone felt like somebody should, then we'd stay. Then we'd go into our Sunday school classes and we had to raise our hands if we were going to hell — "sliding sidelong into the lake of fire." Did I put that in my book? I can't remember if I did it or not. They would come into our Sunday school class and make us put our heads down on the table. Then they'd say, "If you're going to hell, raise your hand. If you haven't been saved and baptized in the blood of Jesus, raise your hand." And I'd raise my hand the second time. That meant I hadn't been saved and I was going to hell. There I'd be. Then they'd make the offer. I could go with them and take care of this. And I could not, to save my life. I could not. I was terrified. Everybody thought I was unaffected. I was so affected. But something was wrong; something was always wrong. So I'd ask all these questions and nobody would know the answer and they'd all get upset about it. You know, what about the people who were born in India? What about the people who were born in China? Don't you think it's a problem if we go evangelizing to a country and they don't want to accept Christ and then they've heard about the good news? What do you do then? In Sunday school we had to read a book by Ernest Angsley called *Rapture*. It was so upsetting to me. In that book, he had things about cutting off the limbs of people and throwing them into vats of boiling grease, and people would be hauled off to the beast.

DB And you must have sung "I Wish We'd All Been Ready."

SR "Life was filled with guns and wars."

DB And "Jesus Is Coming Soon" sung with a smile despite the words "Many will meet their doom."

SR Yes, celebrating because we were special. It didn't matter about the others. Annie Dillard in *Holy the Firm* says, if she belongs anywhere, it is in the higher churches with their doctrine and so on. But those folks would be genuinely surprised if God blew the roof off the church whereas in fundamentalist churches you expect it at any moment. And I don't want to be bored out of my mind; I want to feel it. I don't even go to church anymore. I haven't found one that would have me, really. Because I want to feel it, and I felt it growing up. But you don't get both. I've never found both.

DB There's something dangerous about that kind of fundamentalism, obviously. That comes out in *The Rapture of Canaan* but at the same time, as you put it earlier, Grandpa Herman, even with his hypocrisy and false teeth, is wonderful. You demonstrate the trauma of trying to figure out what the Bible means at every turn. At the same time, you get something of the power and the humor. Many of your memories from church in those years are purely funny. So you're soft toward it all too?

SR I'm both. I am angry. It terrifies me. It upsets me. I don't want my niece and my cousins to be afraid of God. I don't understand the point of that. I don't think it's necessary. I think it is, in fact, destructive. I think that you can be a thinking person and a spiritual person, but I was always taught that people who go to college turn their backs on God. If you go there, they will take your faith away. I don't like that mentality, but I did have some wonderful, wonderful times in that community. I love and miss, deeply miss, the family that I had there and choir practice. I miss choir practice. I miss putting on the Christmas play. I miss all these things.

DB And you still got those lyrics and tunes in your head.

SR I would never forget one of them. I'm singing them all the time; I love them.

DB   But then you stop to think about what you're singing and you think "whoa." Do you still stay in touch with most of your family or has this all created a lot of awkwardness?

SR   *The Rapture of Canaan* created some trouble for me. And it was really just between me and my mom. I worked hard to make that book not my family. I really tried. I used all these medieval law codes and that kind of thing. I guess the mystery of the saints and penitence and all that fascinated me. We grew up in such a narrow, "we are the way," world. Catholics weren't going to heaven, so why should we even care who they valued? You know, we didn't deal with saints. So when I got into college, I was amazed at these religious people. I carried around Saint Theresa in my backpack for probably ten years before I put her out. And Julian of Norwich and Saint John of the Cross.

DB   The Christian mystics.

SR   Sure. And always I've intended to study the non-Christian mystics more than I have. But then I was reading medieval law codes, because I was taking a medieval history class and I was interested in that period. And I used ideas from there for the book, so it would not be the church that I grew up in. The one really serious thing that I kept was the rapture, the whole apocalyptic view. I tried to make it different. But my mom thought I was talking bad about Jesus. She only read into the book maybe thirty or forty pages before she quit reading it. She wouldn't keep reading it, and I had been close to her my whole life up to that point. It was very clear when we weren't talking. I mean a week of not talking with my mother was a big, big, big, big deal. I knew that she was upset. My sister was talking to me about it and my grandma. The book is dedicated to my grandmother, and in fact the character of Nanna is the most autobiographical character I've ever made; she's my grandmother. There are some things that aren't literally true in the book, but if they had been literally true, that is her voice that would have responded to them. What Nanna says is what she would have said. And so most of my folks were okay with the book, because they read all of it. My mama thought I was tearing down Christianity, and I really needed her to finish it. I needed her to read it to the end because I didn't mean to be doing that. I was trying to open it up some. She came around; I guess she finished the book, but we never talked about it. But we got through that. Not without some damage, however. She says some things like "*The Rapture of Canaan* is my least favorite book that you've written" or something. She'll say something like that, but it's okay.

DB Given all this, it's interesting that one label given your books is "redemptive fiction." There is so much affirmation, so much salvation, so much redemption, so much okayness in your books. Where does that come from? There's a way in which you've rejected certain kinds of orthodox institutionalism, but. . . .

SR I've kept some things too. I don't know how to name them, but I have held them. I've kept them. I try to pray now only when I mean it and not when I need something, when I'm just insecure or something like that. It's a good time to pray when your airplane's taking off and you've got a fear of flying, as I do. But I try to mean it more than I used to. The contact with the higher power is important to me. I seek transcendence. I hope for transcendence.

DB You still think of yourself in very spiritual terms.

SR I do. I pray a lot, but I try to be conscious. I try to recognize all the things that go into life. When I eat, I try to think about not only the food but also where it came from and who prepared it and who grew it and who stroked that leaf that becomes my salad. I try to backtrack; that's my way. I don't know what I hope to gain from that except maybe just a connection to something bigger than me. Maybe I'm trying to put myself in a place that recognizes how we all touch one another. I pray more to trees than anything else, and I don't know what to think of that to tell you the truth, but I can't not. I meditate on trees a lot. I have to work on not becoming obsessive about this, though, so I don't feel like I need to touch every tree that I pass. But to feel this tree growing here and how solid it stands and how weather stains it and how it is representative. I don't know how to talk about this.

DB Is there a danger in fleeing from a childhood of walls and lines and rules and definition to a diffuse God who becomes anything and everything and therefore nothing?

SR I have a friend who talks about Unitarians, and I like Unitarians. It's so open to many things. But she says Saturn owners have more to rally around than Unitarians. I don't know where I sit right now. I'm at a real transition place. I cannot fit into Christianity. I don't even have hopes for it. I love so many parts of my past, but I'm soured on so many parts and I don't fit within that tradition.

DB Do you get letters from Christians or former Christians? Is that a part of your audience?

SR Yes, it is. I hear from lots of people who say that they grew up this way and that they appreciate what I've said. I have people who are fans, and I have people who write and tell me I'm going to hell. I hate that. Somebody got me on National Public Radio and said something kind of mean to me, and it always hurts my feelings. I never have a response, because I always come from an emotional more than a logical place. I want to say, "I am not going to hell. Don't tell me I'm going to hell." But it's useless to go that avenue. I get people who love my writing and people who hate my writing, strong feeling both ways. If somebody is responding to the religious elements in my writing, they are either grateful or they are defensive and angry with me for the approach that I have taken. And I don't know what to do about that. I guess I hope that God is big enough to embrace more than Southern Baptists or whatever. I hope so; I think so. I don't want to hurt anybody, not even somebody who hates me. I don't want to cause harm. I hope that my writing doesn't cause harm.

DB Well, it's certainly the case that *The Rapture of Canaan* has given lots of people a voice. It has helped them articulate the discomfort they feel about their own sort of cult or sect or whatever it is they're wrapped up in. I want to ask a little bit about *Bitterroot Landing*, the book you started while you were still a student.

SR That was a different kind of book. I wrote it in graduate school.

DB Your main character is Jael, a name that conjures the Old Testament story. What is the connection?

SR Oh, it's so uninteresting. You're going to be disappointed. I was taking a class at Virginia Commonwealth University with Tom De Haven, an incredible teacher. He offered this class called "The Novel

Workshop." It was two semesters long, and there were seven of us, I believe, in the class. And we each committed to drafting a novel. The only rule was that we could not back up. No matter what we learned in the workshop, we had to move forward.

DB   How many got published?

SR   So far two. There were some good books in there; I would not be surprised at all to see some of these other writers coming up. In fact my acknowledgements in *A Bitterroot Landing* are to the class and those people. On the first day of class, he said, "These are the rules; this is what we're going to do. You're going to submit roughly forty pages every couple of months. We'll go through the year. And Sheri, you're up next week." And I didn't have anything. I mean I had nothing and I had forty pages due the following week. What am I going to do? I thought, well, I'm going to explore the story of Jael in the Bible. I'm going to modernize and figure out who she may have been. So that was where I jumped in. I actually wrote the beginning of that book. What did it say — "For as long as I can remember, I have searched for things to worship: bits of rocks, storm fronts, bugs with turquoise glitter on their wings." And I was thinking about who the character was, who this woman was, and by the second page, she was not that character at all. You have her in the beginning hitting Mammy over the head with a mallet and killing her. It moved away from the biblical text almost immediately. I was grateful when the character took the book and I wasn't just trying to rehash the Bible story. But the name stuck. By the end of the first section that's who she was. Nobody in the class even knew the Bible story, so I kept right on going. The original title was "Nails." And when I finished the book, there was not a single nail in the story, and I could get rid of that title, but I didn't get rid of her name. But that's where it came from; that's what I thought I was going to do when I started out.

DB   Well, the whole saga in this first book, and the other books too, is that of a young woman who is abandoned. Often the mother, if she's present, as in *The Rapture of Canaan,* is not very involved. In this novel, she's gone. There's guilt. Jael obviously feels guilt about Mammy's death. But there's also this horrific abuse, and also a deep understanding of the psychology of abuse. How did you know all that? Did you actually go to these meetings of abuse survivors?

SR   I did. Some of it was research; some of it was trying to make sense out of my own past, trying to make things fit, and always trying to deal with the place where my own reaction didn't seem to fit the thing that had happened. There could have been nothing more destructive to me than those years in church of not being able to be saved and believing with all my heart that I was going to burn in hell for all eternity. You know, living in this tension, I was just ripped all to pieces. I was terrified and it was abusive. It was an abusive situation for me to be in. Years later I said to my mom, "How could you put me in a place where there was so much meanness and God was so wrathful and there was so much hate and fear and terror? How could you put me there?" And she said, "Sheri, nobody else reacted that way. The other people in your Sunday school class went, 'Well, gosh, I guess I better raise my hand, but if I go to the altar I'll be saved, I'll be baptized, and I never have to think about it again." There's a man who was a kid in my Sunday school class, who when we were fifteen or sixteen years old, raped a girl. He was saved. The church went with him to court. It was rape. But he was saved; he was a Christian, so they stood behind him: "It will be all right, son. We know you've made a mistake, but you're forgiven, praise God." And he had gone through this thing I could not go through. I tried to live right. So you have this tension, but other people did not internalize this process or worry about it. I worry that some of them do. I worry specifically about my niece, some of my cousins that I love, and I think they think about these things and I don't want this for them. But that was so hugely difficult. Why did I do that? What made me not just take the bait, go along, live my life, finish high school, marry a good Christian man, raise my family right there, and never ever look back? I don't know what that was, but I explore it again in the book.

DB   So you're purging ghosts there?

SR   I hope that at some point I get beyond myself. The only thing that I can say is that I know that other people have benefited, because I get the letters. And I think, okay, well, thank goodness because it was very difficult to do. I'm so glad that somebody else's life came into some clarity, that they felt something lift because of something that I wrote. I feel sort of like a fake sometimes, because I'm writing what I know, and I'm writing what I lived, or I'll find the parallels for it. I don't always tell the truth; I don't really use the twelve-step group I went to for the book. I find the parallel, the perfect parallel, so that my own experience is unrecognizable or at least disguised enough that only people who are very close to me would know it. Every one of my books is autobiographical, completely autobiographical, but not in a literal sense.

DB In *Bitterroot Landing*, readers are forced to wonder how Jael manages to escape. She has read the Bible. She is bookish. Is that part of it? Books and ideas lead you to the sense that it is okay to see things differently from the way your family sees them?

SR I'm not there yet. I've struggled with that. And I guess I am making my own choices about things all the time, but I have felt again and again like I go alone and am often very frustrated and very lost. I'm lost right now. I get to a point of dramatic intensity where I don't know what I'm going to do. Then something, some person, something, grabs me and pulls me up; it's happened again and again and again. I don't know what it is, but I'm starting to trust it. I call it God.

DB It sounds like a statement of belief in Providence.

SR But manifested in the strangest ways sometimes. But yes, grace, or something, gets me and pulls me right where I need to be. And all I can do at this point is say, "I have never been without." I have often been in a place where I felt that my survival was at stake, not just my identity, my living, or dying. For whatever reason, I am preserved, not only preserved but also nourished by something, and guided to the next place I need to be. So I'm learning to let go and just be. It's very hard for me. I'm a control freak. I want to have my thumb on every single thing, but I've learned it with my books, and my teaching. And you know I've written other books, horrible ones. Very often in those in-between stages when I was uninspired, I force myself to start working. And I will write the thing out, but I have my thumb on it the whole time. And it's a loss.

DB Elizabeth Dewberry says something like that. She writes a good book, then a bad one. She goes through the process. She also describes it in terms of control. When it doesn't come from what she calls some deep place within her, then it doesn't work.

SR That's exactly what happens. I find that I need the bad book. I will find what I am supposed to be doing from what I do wrong. It takes that for me to be able to let go of the control.

DB All of your books have jolting moments. I'm reading along in *The Rapture of Canaan,* and I think I know this world, I know these people, and then they go out and dig that hole in the hillside and make somebody sleep in it and I say, "Where'd that come from?" In *Bitterroot Landing,* there's the self-mutilation. Where does that come from? One time you say it is "trying to get the poison out"; another time you say, "This is the way you know you're real."

SR It is. It's also like physical pain versus spiritual and needing a manifestation of what is on the inside on the outside. It's instinctive in my mind. Sometimes you have to go into the madness to come out and make tangible what is intangible. And she puts her name on herself too. You know that's one of the themes I was bothered to find out. It wasn't a part of my plan, of course, when I started writing. I didn't say, "I'm going to write about somebody who's self-mutilating." But in *The Rapture of Canaan,* I have the nettles that they rub on people as punishment. In *A Gracious Plenty,* I have the man who carves up Lucy Armageddon. And there was a failed book before that one in which a woman had the name "Steve" engraved across her chest. She goes to a tattoo parlor and adds a dot so it is St. Eve. And from there she changes her identity. I'm not sure where all this comes from. I know that I don't have scars on myself. And, of course, there's Finch's scars. I don't know what I'm doing with that. I'm almost afraid to go there. Maybe I want a physical representation of emotional pain.

DB Finch Nobles' scar becomes her identity; she's the outcast, the alien, because of that.

SR I knew when I wrote Finch that she was an outsider and that she was scarred. I didn't know that it was physically and outside that she was scarred. I started writing that book not knowing that she was burned, and I burned her on page 3. That wasn't a part of my conscious planning for Finch. I thought she was going to talk to the dead. I knew that she was going to talk to her parents at least when I started the book and I knew that there was something about connection between the dead and living worlds.

DB As you wrote *A Gracious Plenty,* you were dealing with a friend's grief.

SR Yes, I lived with Amy, and she was there in my house with me. But she was not there with me. She had lost a dear friend and teacher and was simply gone.

DB You used to go for walks trying to think what you could say to her?

SR Yes. What can I do? How do I try to get her back? Do I try to get her back? I had lost people, but I had not grieved, not like that. So that's where that book was starting from. I thought this character also has to be scarred somehow and she has to choose between dying or learning to live.

DB Like your other characters, Jael does learn to live. "The Lord knows me well," she says. And here's your first book already, and you're still in college?

SR Yes, I graduated in 1992 and had the draft of that book with my agent.

DB What about sales?

SR It was bizarre. It didn't wow anybody. I had much higher hopes for it, but out on the West Coast it did really well. In San Francisco, it hit the *Chronicle*'s best-seller list for no reason. It had no endorsements or anything except that the sales representatives were excited about it. I got enormous response from readers.

DB It inspired you to go on with writing?

SR I got a contract. When we sold the paperback rights and had a movie deal, Putnam signed me on for two more books. For *The Rapture of Canaan* and *A Gracious Plenty* — that's what they ended up being.

DB What about the movies?

SR They're all under option. I have no expectations whatsoever that *Bitterroot Landing* will ever make a movie. It belongs to Lorne

Michaels, the "Saturday Night Live" guy. But he may have abandoned that by now; I don't even know. *The Rapture of Canaan* was optioned by Jenny Garth, who is a "Beverly Hills 90210" actress; she's just sort of playing around, I think, and learning about movies. So she has the rights to that one. *A Gracious Plenty* actually may end up being a movie, because the script is being written by the guy who did *As Good as It Gets,* the movie with Jack Nicholson. Because the screenplay is getting done by him, there is some good potential with that one. But I try not to think about the movies too much, because I've had to give over so many things. I write books. If they become movies then that's wonderful, and I hope that somebody else has a vision for it that will hopefully bring something good to the world, but that's not my aim.

DB There's so much that runs through all the books about storytelling, about getting one's story out there. All of your characters have to find a way to confess. Jael has to confess to Wallace; she has to find a way to say, "This is my story, and I'm defined by this abuse." Is that a right thing to say about the power of confession and the power of telling the story?

SR I hadn't thought about it that way before, but yes. I am well aware that I don't know why I've done this thing that I have done. I know that anybody who wanted to could find out things about me that I don't even know about myself. I don't know why. It's not something that I chose. I don't know why I do this. I feel like I'm confessional myself. I mean I feel like I'm confessing in these books.

DB And it seems there's something painful in that, too.

SR It is. And I'm saying, "Why do you do this, Sheri? What are you trying for here?" But, I keep on doing it.

DB The grandmother character in *The Rapture of Canaan* finally concludes, however, that storytelling is not enough. She understands that she's never going to get the true story told. She recognizes incompleteness. That's probably what made me nervous about Oprah's summary: "Young woman questions her religious background and brings about change as she discovers who she is." Does that reduce the book in some way or not?

SR   I think it's about more than that. But it does cover one part of it. That whole "Oprah" experience was so surreal to me. There was too much going on for me to keep up with it. I feel perfectly fine about it. I feel like I handled it much better than I thought I would. Everybody said, "I wish Oprah had shut up and let you talk." But it's her show! It foregrounds Oprah and what Oprah has experienced or thinks and all that. I'm grateful for all the good that came of it for me and for my household, and what it was able to do for me. I'm grateful for the readership. It put me on the best-seller list, and I would never have been there in a million years otherwise.

DB   Did you get letters about the child with the joined hands? Did some doctor write you and say "That's impossible"?

SR   That was the place where the book really started. I had a dream, and in it was an image of a child with hands seamed together. I started working backwards asking: Who is this child? Why are his hands seamed together? What do his parents think? Oh, his parents aren't his parents, well.

DB   Why wouldn't the children of the Church of Fire and Brimstone and God's Almighty Baptizing Wind have been schooled in the church community?

SR   I needed to get them in the public school, because I needed to have some other voice to bounce off of them.

DB   And that's where you have the friend who's not of the faith.

SR   Right. And I really needed that; that was important.

DB   There Ninah meets her worldly friend, Corinthian. Was that word "wordly" a loaded word in your background?

SR   Oh yes, you didn't want to be "of the world."

DB   So you had a separatist mentality?

SR   Sure. It was expected that there would people around us who would tempt us and that kind of thing, but we weren't to hang out with them. I mean it wasn't as bad as I set it up in the book, but we knew better than to sit at the back of the bus. We weren't supposed to do that; we weren't supposed to be hanging out with anybody who was going to tempt us.

DB   And of course the big sin in those communities, besides card playing, is sex. It seems that a lot of what's going on in Ninah's head has to do with sex as religion.

SR And the eroticism of Christianity, yes. I have spent years reading the lives of the Christian mystics, and I have found that women often form a religious and ecstatic, or even erotic relationship to the beloved. There are so many of them following in that path. And then when you take somebody like John of the Cross, who does write in terms of having an erotic experience with Christ, he becomes a woman in his poetry to make that acceptable and possible. He takes on the female voice in his poems and writes about the sexual union and at the same time I'm coming up in this world where we can't even say the word "sex." We didn't know what to do with any of this. Sex was saved for marriage. There were these rigid rules that you went through and these stages you went through, and you were supposed to be a virgin and blah, blah, blah. . . . And then I find out that my mom married my father because she was pregnant with me. When she told me that, it was so devastating to her that she wept. It killed her to have to tell me that. Because she wanted me to believe. But three-quarters of the people out there are not living what they say. That's why they can go up to the altar and just say "Yes, Jesus" and never worry again.

DB Much of *The Rapture of Canaan* is about James and Ninah's different reactions to that artificiality. Ninah somehow realizes that she has to go with her natural instincts. There's a level at which she understands that sexual longing is like spiritual longing, that there's a connection. James goes with the community's definition. Ultimately, he has to erase himself because those two worlds no longer fit. Ninah learns that God is often silent. She learns to live with ambiguity, without answers.

SR Without answers, that's right. You live in the tension between the opposites.

DB Ninah learns that her community is living in a lie, the false assumption that God has made it all cut and dried. She discovers it's not that way. So what's going to happen to her? Is she just going to light out for the territories like Huck Finn?

SR   When I was writing the ending, I did not know what was going to happen. I didn't know I was at the end of the book. Suddenly, I thought, Oh my Lord, look where I am. I don't know if she's going to survive." I didn't know what she would do. I mean, at the end of the book, she's fourteen still, so what options does she have? I can say, Okay. She runs away, how far is she going to get? How far is she going to go with this baby at fourteen years old? As little knowledge as she has of the real world, what is she going to do? Then I think, well, she's probably going to kill herself, and I think I'd hate for that to happen. But she would find that to be a release. I don't in any way compare myself to Kate Chopin, and I can't even believe this is about to leave my mouth, but one can read the ending of *The Awakening* as a positive, as the only possible way to persevere. And I'm thinking suicide would not necessarily be a negative thing for Ninah. So I tried to write it that way. But I couldn't imagine that she could actually go through with that. So when she cuts Canaan's hands, it occurred to me that he is no longer the exceptional one. He's just a human baby with human blood splashing the walls as he runs around this room. And then I thought, whatever happens from here on out, she has saved them. They can live somehow. A lot of people have asked me about the sequel to this book. I will never write a sequel. I have a feeling that goes with Ninah. I ended the book where I felt wholly okay. Absolutely okay. She has a father who will support her unconditionally, even though he hasn't needed to yet. And she has changed this community enough to make them already question some of their basic tenets. They're even cutting their hair, and the women are putting on the pants and wearing watches. They're doing some things differently. And she will be all right.

DB   And Grandpa Herman is dead. The great sin has been "to think with one great misshapen mind." And she has shown them that at some tiny level?

SR   Yes. That when this is over, they'll never return from this fauxrapture. They were not left behind. They have a new opportunity, a new day. I do miss Ninah. One of the things that happens to me is I get so absorbed in the characters that I miss them. I feel like they're sisters and brothers. I keep them very close to my heart. It does feel like a small death when you're done with the book. I miss them.

DB Your books also have a Southern feel. That label "Southern writer" is probably no more appropriate than "writer of redemptive fiction" or any other label. And yet it's deeply a part of who you are?

SR Most definitely. I'm proud of that. I have a lot of problems with the South and being a woman in the South. So I struggle. But what incredible writers, remarkable writers. To be a part of that tradition is amazing.

DB Of the three books, *A Gracious Plenty* is my favorite. I'm not even sure why. Maybe it is the title. Finch Nobles has a "gracious plenty of friends," she finally decides. And that's really where we started; all your books are about finding folks to tell the stories to.

SR You want to hear something hilarious? All my books have been titled *A Gracious Plenty*. I finally got to use it. I have two fake versions at home that are entirely different books. *The Rapture of Canaan* was supposed to be *A Gracious Plenty*. It just wasn't.

DB Was this book easier to write?

SR It was a relief to write this book finally. Also I did a lot more playing. I'm growing up, and it's good. I feel fine about it. *The Rapture of Canaan* is the least favorite of my books. I look back at *Bitterroot Landing* and I go, "ugh" about the things that slipped through — very, very young things. Nonetheless, *Bitterroot Landing* will always be very special to me; I love this book because I was so raw. So you have those moments of "ugh," but you also have these moments of "I was not stopped by what a good writer does or doesn't do." It's full of passion; it's full of real stuff. After I wrote *Bitterroot Landing*, Putnam asked me to write in a more linear, plot-driven way. I knew when I was writing *Rapture of Canaan* that I needed to lay off the language and the images, and to try to be linear. I didn't like it, but I still think I maintained my voice. There are some parts that I like very much. Of course, Putnam dropped me after *The Rapture of Canaan* because it didn't sell well enough.

DB And lived to regret it.

SR Yes. With *A Gracious Plenty,* I was at a different place. I was frustrated with the demands, the deadlines, and the business of writing. This was all "pre-Oprah." So I wrote *A Gracious Plenty* the way I wanted to write it. I did not worry about the things that I teach versus the things that I do. I didn't worry about structure; I didn't worry about how I moved myself between scene and summary. I just wrote the book. I was more relaxed in the writing. That one took a little less than a month, and it was burning up in there. It was coming as fast as I could get it down. And it's much more sensory than my other books in my mind; it's got more texture.

DB It's got music in it.

SR I hope. I'm in a good position now, of course, so I could just start writing sequels. I could write a sequel to *The Rapture of Canaan* and get all the *Rapture of Canaan* readers, and I could make a lot of money. But that isn't my goal. I hope that I will write out of something else. I hope that I will put other needs in front of commercial ones. *A Gracious Plenty* was completely something that I needed to do. It was for my soul.

DB Is your mom okay with this one?

SR She's all right with this book. She just can't bear *The Rapture of Canaan*.

DB Besides Finch, there's Lucy Armageddon. She threatens to take over that book. She's a strong character, and she's Finch's teacher with the line about "what your heart is taught to think." She works to overcome what her heart has been taught to think. You don't have to be the way your mom shaped you to be. You can defeat that.

SR I loved writing this book. It was so much fun. That section about how the dead control the seasons was so delightful to write. I just played. I love every time the mediator shows up in the book.

DB Finch is so witty and sardonic and there's a complexity to her that makes her more complete than Ninah or Jael, I think. Is it the role of suffering? She has this awful thing that has happened to her. She's completely isolated. But she also grows from it.

SR They all do. I mean we have to make the best of it. And I personify it differently in each of the books. But suffering and longing — for God and for all the things I want — will just bring me to tears. We all suffer so much whether we're capable of suffering for more than our-selves or whether we're suffering over a tiny, personal thing. And I think there must be something to come of that. There must be.

DB You certainly show your characters as looking for it.

SR I don't think I'll ever write a book where they don't. I don't know how I would survive in the world if I didn't keep that alive, that possibility for there to be meaning.

DB I'm curious about William Blott, the ghost who is full of guilt about his homosexuality. And the mediator says why don't you pon-der a moment what the real sin is? You just sort of leave it there. What is the real sin?

SR I don't know.

DB You leave it that way to suggest that what he's caught up with is not the real problem?

SR Perhaps. I know exactly where that scene is, but that's always been vague to me. When I wrote that line I did not have a real sin in mind. I couldn't say it. I did leave it, though, purposely. When I first put it there, I thought it might be a place holder. But then I left it on purpose. I think it has to do with the idea that everything is punitive. We get caught in thinking that we've done something wrong and have to be punished.

DB Well, it seems like all three of those — Lucy, William, and Finch — have to get to a point where they're not spending their lives look-ing for somebody else. And I think that's one of the lines somewhere near the end of the book: "You can't spend all your life just looking for somebody else." You have to free yourself. Lucy has to free herself from her mother, William has to free himself from his family and from Reba, and then Finch has to free herself from the implications of her ugliness, and so forth. There's a way in which, and I don't want to assume too much, but you end with affirmation. For Finch, there's the promise of touch, the promise of the end of her isolation. Now can I leap from that and say that that's your vision — that there's an okayness, that things will turn out.

SR I do believe that. I think that is there.

DB Is there a spirit of benevolence that pushes us along?

SR I believe so.

DB Even Reba, the religious bigot?

SR Of course Reba! Especially Reba. There is the capacity within her for so much more than she even knows.

DB So she's learned toleration.

SR Maybe only for that moment.

DB But she's come a ways.

SR That's what I find with transcendence. You only get to stay there for a second. You would blaze and singe yourself if you stayed much longer. But for a second, we can be bigger than that. And maybe that's enough, I don't know.

DB What would you want your readers to know about you?

SR As little as possible.

DB You like staying private?

SR I have to fight that. I have a different idea of it now that I've been so public. I feel very ordinary.

DB Do you feel you've been thrust into the spotlight, as it were, for a reason and you're still wondering what that reason is?

SR Maybe. I mean I think that there's always a reason. I believe that.

DB Is there a responsibility that comes with it?

SR There is. And I grapple with that because on the one hand I want to pout, and say, "But I don't want it. No!" But you don't have room to do that. You don't have that option. I don't know what else to do but I just hope that with my writing or whatever else I do — running an antique shop or arranging flowers — I hope that I don't hurt anybody. And I like to think that maybe I could open something up so someone else could see something a little bigger or a little bit more than they did before. And I hope that there is meaning in the things that I do or that I can bring something to the places that I go. And that's my only wish. I told you I'm a sucker for trees. I love them so much and they're probably always going to be in my books. I bought the house I'm living in now for the trees in the backyard. I've been talking to a tree surgeon, a gentle and wonderful man who's been coming to check on my tree. I need to have a woodborer removed.

He's known that tree for thirty years, and somewhere that's going to be in one of my books. I have to appreciate that man who knows my tree. Do you see? The small pieces. I have a tree and a woodborer and a man named Paul who drives up in a yellow pickup to work on my tree. And I remember those things and how connected they are.

DB Sounds to me like you're still writing twenty pages ahead.

SR And trusting that the rest of the world is going on and people are doing whatever they have to be doing for whatever reason. And that it has a pattern.

LEE SMITH

Writing for Joy

1944 — Born in Grundy, West Virginia
1968 — *The Last Day the Dogbushes Bloomed*
1971 — *Something in the Wind*
1973 — *Fancy Strut*
1981 — *Black Mountain Breakdown*
        Cakewalk
1983 — *Oral History*
1985 — *Family Linen*
1988 — *Fair and Tender Ladies*
1990 — *Me and My Baby View the Eclipse*
1992 — *The Devil's Dream*
1996 — *Saving Grace*
2003 — *The Last Girls*
2006 — *On Agate Hill: A Novel*

Lives in Chapel Hill, North Carolina

I met Lee Smith at the Hindman Settlement School on the banks of Troublesome Creek in Eastern Kentucky for our conversation. To get there, I had to pass near Rowdy, Fisty, Talcum, and Dwarf. The town names like the mountains and shaded valleys seemed especially right, because Lee Smith has given us the cadences and rhythms of Southern speech along with the beauty and terror of Southern places.

And her chronicle, in such books as *Fair and Tender Ladies, Oral History, Black Mountain Breakdown, The Devil's Dream,* and *Saving Grace,* captures the courage and character along with the foibles and fun of these mountain folk.

Lee Smith's stories are about remembering where you came from, about enduring, and sometimes even about winning through despite overwhelming odds. She is Grundy, Virginia, and Chapel Hill, North Carolina, and thereabouts, but her work resists the Grit Lit label. Her stories are, finally, about all of us.

Smith's career reaches back to 1968, the year she published *The Last Day the Dogbushes Bloomed,* a story of the complicated life of a nine-year-old girl as told by the girl herself. Written while Smith was finishing her studies at Hollins College, the book won a Book-of-the-Month-Club award and launched a career. Other awards and prizes have followed alongside the ten novels and two short story collections.

The writer now divides her time between working on new stories and talking about the old ones. I caught up with her at the Settlement School where she had come to spend a week reading manuscripts and talking with fledgling writers. She seemed to be glad for all of it — the would-be writers, the demanding schedules, the books both written and waiting to be written, and even my annoying tape recorders.

DB   Well, here you are wearing yourself out teaching in this workshop. And exuberance is certainly one of the first things people notice about you, exuberance for writing and teaching. Why keep writing when the rewards are pretty meager? Where does that energy come from?

LS   I don't know. I started when I was a girl. It's just what I do. It's the way I make sense of my life. I think I write fiction the way other people write in a journal. It's as necessary to me as breathing. And I will sometimes try to not write for a while. I think you can publish too much and all of it's not good. It's just the way I go through my life. It's a way of processing experiences and a way of having vicarious lives. There is no other activity that I have ever come across that I find as intense or as exciting as writing a story. The moment when I'm writing fiction, I'm not really myself. I'm really out of myself into some other realm which is profoundly exciting. And there's nothing like it.

DB   You've called it a process of self repair.

LS   Yes. I think it's therapeutic for me. I think I write for many reasons. I write for intensity and joy. I also write because I think it's therapeutic. For self repair. I think I process a lot of things that I have in my mind. Instead of going to the psychiatrist, I write a story.

DB   You've said that if you hadn't been a writer, you would have been a psychiatrist.

LS   I think so, because what interests me are people and the choices we make, how we try to live our lives, and how we try to do good.

DB   How does your own life come into your books?

LS   It is just part and parcel. I think up the books, and I'm not what you would call an autobiographical writer. I don't write out of exact experience. I have certainly never been a serpent-handling believer, nor have I been an old lady living back in the hills at the turn of the century, but everything I write about is of enormous importance to me emotionally. It corresponds psychologically or emotionally to things I am going through myself. For instance, when I wrote *Black Mountain Breakdown,* which is about a girl who is physically paralyzed and can't take control of her life, I was in a very bad marriage. And I was unable to do anything about it. I was unable to leave. So instead of doing anything, I wrote that novel. The book was an almost unconscious working through those issues of the marriage. Later, I was able to understand a lot of things because I had written that book. The book was like a cautionary tale.

DB   So the book is more autobiographical looking back than you thought it was at the time?

LS   Yes. I didn't think it was autobiographical at all, because there were a lot of things about my situation I was not facing.

DB   When you work with young writers in workshop settings, do you find that this business of autobiography is a problem? Do beginning writers tend to be too close to their own lives?

LS   Most people are writing too close to their own experience when they begin writing, often because they are compelled to write out of pain. So sometimes I know when I'm discussing a story with somebody that the protagonist is really her or him.

DB   Robert Olen Butler says you only begin to be a writer when you can get past that first level of experience.

LS   I think I agree. My first novel, *The Last Day the Dogbushes Bloomed,* has definite autobiographical elements in it. I was an overly imaginative child who found it difficult to grow up. Then there were autobiographical elements in my second novel, *Something in the Wind,* which was horrible. It's a disaster. It's the worst novel ever written. I think I did have to get past myself at that point or I wouldn't have been able to continue writing. It's true.

DB   But the storytelling goes back into your family heritage and especially your Uncle Vern?

LS   Yes. We told stories. There wasn't anybody else in my family writing stories or reading much. My mama was a school teacher, and she subscribed to *Reader's Digest Condensed Books,* so we got books. But neither she nor my dad really read them much. My dad liked to do dramatic readings of Rudyard Kipling. But nobody was reading literature or talking about it. But, boy, they were telling great stories. So to me a story has a human voice.

DB   I wonder how one develops an ear for that? Do you go around with a notebook and listen for the good story? I was talking to my ninety-two-year-old aunt recently, and she told me about finding a bargain on shoes. She bought six pairs of shoes. I thought if you're ninety-two and you buy six pairs of shoes, that's incredible optimism. That ought to be written down somewhere.

LS   Yes. Of course I do write things like that down. I don't carry a notebook with me all the time, but I keep track. A doctor told me the other day the way he could judge the health of his elderly patients. When they came in, he'd ask them if they had planted their gardens.

If they had not, he would know that they were really sick. But if they had, then he would figure they were good for another year. So there's that kind of thing you're listening for all the time. It's just a way you go through the world.

DB This sort of wakefulness ties to religious issues too. Your books seem to be full of an awareness of the significance of faith.

LS Yes. And that goes back to my childhood too. I think it also has to do with my writing, because I first came to appreciate language via the King James Version of the Bible. My whole sense of language, I think, was formed by church, and those responsive readings in the Methodist Church and the Bible and the sermons. It really was. It's just always something that's kind of a given in my childhood and in my background, so I can't really imagine writing a story, particularly set in the region where I'm from, without religion as an absolutely important feature.

DB Do you feel some ambivalence about the church, the influence of the church, as you look back?

LS Not now. But I think some ambivalence shows in "Tongues of Fire." That is my most autobiographical story. I really was very drawn as a child to those emotional services, the Pentecostal kinds of services, and I was a nervous and emotional child. I really did believe that I heard God speak to me at church camp, and they put me in the infirmary. That is true. And several other times I felt I heard God speak to me. And somebody might say I was having a nervous breakdown. I don't believe that. But it scared me.

DB So they might say you were being abused by these religious fanatics?

LS Yes, but I wasn't. I was choosing to go there. I was choosing not to go to my own home church, the Methodist Church, and go into these other churches and get myself all worked up. And I was choosing to read the Bible over and over. I think I did succeed in scaring myself. Not as specifically as in "Tongues of Fire," perhaps, but scary. Then I turned to the Episcopal Church. In those earlier years I had come to associate religious fervor, that kind of intensity, with something scary. So I pulled back from it. My parents sent me off to an

Episcopal school, and I found myself relieved. But I was still always drawn to the more passionate religious expressions, and in a certain way that's why I wrote *Saving Grace*. I don't attend a church where anybody is laying on hands. I don't practice this. But I am certainly a believer.

DB   And you say that writing is like prayer?

LS   Yes, because of this state that I'm talking about when I'm writing, this intensity. I don't get that anywhere else. It's the same feeling in a way, I think, as prayer. I remember Annie Dillard and I were having this conversation one time and I said, "Well, what do you think prayer is?" and she said, "I think it's just when you think real hard." And that's what you do when you're writing. You're thinking so hard that you're sort of outside yourself. You know, there's a similarity there, for sure.

DB   Do you get letters from the fundamentalists who are angry at you for attacking fundamentalism or from the irreligious who wish you wouldn't be so tied up with things religious?

LS   Oh sure. It's very dangerous, I think, to write anything that has to do with religion, because you're going to step on everybody's toes. With *Saving Grace* I had a woman who stalked me. I was on a book tour, and she was in the crowd when I was reading at a bookstore in Memphis. She had a stark, sort of obsessed face. She looked very different from everybody in the bookstore, so I noticed her. Then she disappeared. Then in Oxford, Mississippi, there she was again. And I began to get really nervous. And at the end of the reading she pushed people aside and got in front of the line. She started yelling and said she had come there to tell me that I was going to hell because of what I'd written in *Saving Grace*. And I said, "Have you read the book?" And she said, "I don't read no book but the Bible." It turned out she had read something about the book, some description of it in an ad or something. She didn't want me making fun of snake-handling religion. And then she knocked the books off the table and stormed off.

DB   Do you think much about the audience for your books?

LS   No, that's not something that I think about when I write. Religion, for example, has been such a part of my own life and a part of the country I'm from that it will inevitably work its way into things I'm writing about. But I certainly don't think of myself as writing to a religious audience or something. I guess I don't actually have an audience in mind when I write. I'm just a person who's compelled.

DB You don't have some vision about who goes to the bookstore and buys these books.

LS I don't. And I remember having this conversation with Denise Giardina. She told me that she has in mind the person who walks into the bookstore and picks up the book. I don't have a clue. I don't even care.

DB I've read a good bit about your years at Hollins College with Annie Dillard, Louis Rubin, and "The Virginia Wolves."

LS It was a hotbed for wonderful writing, a very nurturing place. I think a lot of it was simply chance.

DB It sounds like an electric time.

LS It was great. And for me it was wonderful. I always thought that I was weird because all I ever wanted to do was read and write. And I just met these people who were like me. And I wasn't weird.

DB And you really had a singing group called "The Virginia Wolves"?

LS Oh yes. And we were in writing groups with teachers who were also writing, and they were sharing their work with us. There were very few creative writing programs then. And it was in Louis Rubin's Mark Twain class that we decided to raft down the Mississippi and got ourselves arrested. That was the kind of nurturing that we got. And that's why I do think that women's education was something wonderful for me. You know, the idea that if you want to do this, you can figure it out, and you can do it.

DB Were you surprised by the success of *The Last Day the Dogbushes Bloomed,* that first novel?

LS It won some award, but it wasn't successful. Only 3,000 or so were published. It was kind of a fluke, that it was ever published. It had been picked for publication by a very old man, Cass Canfield, who was a famous senior editor at Harper & Row, and he was already on his way out. The book attracted his attention. But other people at the company were not much interested in books that he found. He had had his day in a certain way. And I didn't know anything about this. I didn't know that I should get to know people at the publishing house. And so the book did get a couple of good reviews, but it sank like a stone.

DB What's wrong with it?

LS I don't know. I was just so unaware of publishing at that time. Maybe the publisher did absolutely nothing to promote it. And I did nothing to promote it. It got some notice because James Kirkpatrick, the columnist, wrote a column about it. He did that because I had worked for him in Richmond.

DB You were praised for your skill with the narrative voice, the little girl.

LS I remember at Hollins I kept writing a series of stories that often seemed to be about the same little girl.

DB It gets labeled as a "loss of innocence" novel. Do you get nervous when people start making thematic statements about your novels?

LS No, because I'm in that same business. I'm not able to make those statements very well about my own work. *The Last Day the Dogbushed Bloomed* is so long ago that I can see that. But that's the kind of thing I do when I teach other writers' work.

DB You don't sit down with a book and say, "The theme of this one's going to be this or that."

LS No. I never think about theme. I just think about the stories.

DB *Something in the Wind,* the second novel, really does have that late sixties feel. There's some lovely satire there. My favorite passage is when Brooke is taking notes in Mrs. Poole's English class. She's going along, determined to be studious, and then the notes dwindle off into doodle. There's this sort of college experience that has nothing to do with books. She's really not learning anything in the classroom.

LS Actually I've been taken to task for that a couple times. People say that I make fun of education, that I seem to think that real knowledge is out somewhere among the peasant folk. And the criticism is not entirely untrue. I have known several older mountain women who seem to me so much wiser, wiser than the academics I'm around. I haven't really intended to denigrate educational institutions, but there it is.

DB What is disappointing in *Something in the Wind* when you revisit it?

LS I wasn't ready to write another novel. I had just sort of used up my whole life and my whole childhood in the first book. And I didn't have another story to tell. I just didn't have a novel. I had two separate things going on. I had this sort of supernatural thing gleaned from my summer job down at Carolina where I worked for the Institute for Psychic Research. And the other a sort of story of grief and the college experience and identity and figuring out who you are. And they don't fit.

DB When did you start thinking of yourself as a writer?

LS You know, only very recently.

DB I remember reading about your coming to a point around the time of *The Devil's Dream* when you realized you needed to promote yourself as a writer. Maybe Clyde Edgerton and Susan Ketchin had something to do with this?

LS Yes. And this was amazing to me. What they did for me was incredible because realizing the publisher wasn't going to promote the novel, they said, "Let's just put on a little show." It was great. I just loved it. That was really important to me. You don't have to act like you're a teacher who writes on the side.

DB Do you ever sit down and think, what would it take to write a best seller?

LS I don't think that you can even try to do it. I mean you either have the touch or you don't. And I think I'm too weird and idiosyncratic to fit into any category of genre writing. So if I were to write a best seller, it would be something that would appeal to people out of some merit. I can't sit down and try to do it because I'm unable to fit a formula. And actually I went through several periods where I tried. I was broke, so I tried to do it. And I couldn't.

DB You were interested in the mystery novel?

LS Yes. I have an unpublished mystery novel; it's terrible. It's called *Children of Chronus*. It takes place in an experimental school, where a charismatic mythology teacher is mysteriously murdered during a snow storm. But it just doesn't work.

DB And you can tell that yourself? Nobody needed to tell you that?

LS No. I know that it doesn't work.

DB Some Southerners have expressed concern about the Grit Lit school as employing hillbilly stereotypes to get a laugh. I know that's been something of an issue in your books. I heard some people sharing Jeff Foxworthy jokes last night. Foxworthy has one that says, "You know you're a redneck when you go to your family reunion to meet women." Now that's an interesting kind of joke. It's funny if you're with family and tell that joke. But in another context, that's a cruel joke. It sort of depends on where you are.

LS Oh, yes.

DB The reviews of *Fancy Strut* kept raising this issue. I remember the phrase, "satiric but not mean." You're always walking the line on this — satiric, but not cruel.

LS I don't think of myself as a satirist. I will poke fun, sure. But is it satire?

DB I remember the majorettes in *Fancy Strut,* and Frances says that the most beautiful thing she's ever seen in her life is this line of majorettes marching across the field. And Theresa's title, Miss Fancy Strut, is the greatest thing that's ever happened to her. That's a pretty deep jibe. You're certainly questioning what sort of people these are.

LS Yes, but I understand these people.

DB And you like them?

LS Oh, yes. And I'm trying to go beneath any stereotype. You just have to go deep enough to find out all the ways in which people don't fit the categories we like to put them in.

DB Roy Blount has a famous line about you. He says reading Lee Smith is like reading *Madame Bovary* while listening to Loretta Lynn and watching "The Guiding Light." Does a line like that help or hurt?

LS I think it is helpful.

DB It doesn't make you into the Dolly Parton of the literary world?

LS That's fine with me. I really admire Dolly Parton. Obviously I try to do serious work. But I would like to be read by regular people. I want to be read by people that go to Dollywood, you know, as well as some blue-haired book club or academics and the like. I would really like to be accessible because I think of myself as an average person. When I wrote *Fancy Strut,* I was living in Alabama. I had young children, and I wasn't much aware of all the big issues. I didn't think of myself as having a career, a writing career. I just never thought of it.

DB The race question shows up in that book and in most of your books. Has that been controversial at all?

LS No. Race is a real issue with a lot of writers from the deeper South who can't avoid coming up against it if they're going to be writing honest books about the South. It just hasn't played as much of a part in my life. I grew up in an all white area. But in Alabama I got really interested because I was working for a newspaper. This was just after the civil rights era.

DB Is there a career shift with *Black Mountain Breakdown*? Some critics say it is your most overtly thematic book.

LS I think it is the only one where I was really thinking in terms of theme. It almost killed me. When I was writing it, I was in a women's reading group and all these feminist books were coming out. I had a couple of friends who were all fired up with feminist issues. And I began to get really interested because I was at a point where I had noticed that we had all tried to do what was expected of us and it was kind of falling apart on us. I was raised to fit expectations. I was passive, at least domestically, especially in terms of relationships with men and marriage, and the like. My mother was a home economics teacher, and a lady from eastern Virginia. I was growing up as this girl who wanted to read all night and be a writer, but I had another side who felt that I should have a husband and children and go to church and prepare balanced meals with green leafy vegetables. And I could never make these two sides of myself fit. But I was aware of these expectations and suddenly wasn't able to do them all anymore. *Black Mountain Breakdown* has a lot to do with that.

DB So you were frozen like the character Crystal in the novel?

LS Yes. Crystal was trying to fit everybody else's expectations. She lacked the ability to make up her own mind and take control of her fate. I was, I think, writing a cautionary tale, an object lesson. If we are too passive, unless we decide what we want and go after it, this will happen to us. I didn't really understand that I was writing about myself.

DB But she's also dramatically victimized by others, by the awful uncle, Devere, especially.

LS I guess a writer should never admit this sort of thing, but in the first draft she was not victimized by Devere. In the first draft, he didn't rape Crystal. Nothing like that happened; he was just a feature of her childhood. I have to confess I put that in because my editor suggested it. The book had been rejected twenty times, you know, and suddenly here was an editor who wanted to publish it, but she just felt like there wasn't enough motive for Crystal's being like she was. I could see how it would work, thematically, but I didn't really think that it was necessary. I felt that most girls raised in the South would understand that passivity anyway.

DB There's the father's dreaminess that seems to contribute to the passivity.

LS I had read a book on family therapy which said something that is just a quirk in one generation will become a neurosis in the next, and maybe even a psychosis in the next. It's like a breakdown in music; every time you do it, there's a slight variation. So I was playing on all those things. But when I talk about it, you can see that I was thinking more thematically, too thematically. And my editor kept wanting reasons for that passivity. But I think it's just innate in girls raised a certain way.

DB You really have a good eye, too, for pretension. The most pessimistic thing in the novel as I read it is Agnes. She could be the prodigal son's elder brother. And Crystal is literally in her hands when the novel ends.

LS Yes. It is a disturbing novel.

DB But things seem to fall together for you in the early eighties. There's the wonderful Flora of *Cakewalk* and, of course, *Fair and Tender Ladies*. Did you get some sense that you were catching a following wind at last?

LS No. I was just teaching school, raising my children, and writing. And I wasn't aware of anything. But I think what's happening there is a move away from self focus. The books up to *Black Mountain Breakdown* show a lot about me. I was just paralyzed at the end of *Black Mountain Breakdown*. Afterward, though, I began to get more of a sense of myself as a person who could be in the world and do things. And I think that's reflected in the women characters that come after that.

DB Dorothy Hill's book on you gets to this feminist business.

LS I haven't read it. I'm afraid it would stymie me. It's dangerous to bring a point of view to texts that way, adapting a way of reading a woman's work and then applying it broadly.

DB And finally, with *Oral History,* you got a royalty check?

LS *Oral History* was the first one that earned back its advance. I got a small advance for the others. *Oral History* actually earned back its advance.

DB Were you intending to satirize the oral history craze of the early eighties?

LS Yes, and mostly because I knew an old man who took great pleasure in bilking the historians. People were always interviewing him, oral historians, and he'd just make up stuff. Then he would tell me what he told them, and I thought it was hysterical. But again, I don't know that I intended to satirize. I just wanted to write about it. I wasn't intending to satirize so much, just comment on it. I did a good bit of the material of that book without any intention to publish. I had been doing a whole lot of taping with my father and different people in my family. I never took a course in oral history, but I had been poking around in old papers and stuff like that. And I had come to doubt that there was any objective story to be found. The most interesting thing to me was who was telling the story. The story depended on who the teller was. I did a series of interviews on the subject of the last man hanged in my county. I interviewed people that had been there, people that had heard about it from their families, and everything. And I got all these different stories. He was tall, he was short, he spit tobacco from the scaffold, he sang a hymn, he did this, he did that; these stories were completely different. The whole process was interesting to me.

DB   With *Oral History,* you cultivate what you began in *Fair and Tender Ladies,* finding dignity and multiple dimensions in your mountain characters.

LS   That was hard to get at because the first drafts of *Oral History* were in third person.

DB   Then you went back and decided on multiple narrators?

LS   Yes. Because the characters were so diminished without their wonderful speech. I really wanted to document, use, and preserve their speech and to contrast it with the modern speech.

DB   How is it that you, a town girl, understand these people from the hollows?

LS   I don't know. I was an only child. I spent a lot of time with my friends in school, and I went home with everybody. I spent a lot of time in other people's houses. I had really good friends. I had cousins that lived in the coal camp. My granddaddy was the county treasurer for forty-eight years and he was always doing a lot of politicking. Every Sunday afternoon I would go out politicking with granddaddy and my father. We went up in every holler; we went everywhere. And the whole genesis of *Oral History,* in fact, was a time when I went up the holler with granddaddy. We would eat Sunday dinner with everybody. We would eat Sunday dinner about seven times. One Sunday, sitting down to eat with some family, a man there pointed to a pie safe, a big piece of furniture in the corner. "Don't be surprised," he said, "if you hear a big knocking coming from that pie safe."

I said, "Why?" And he said, "Well, there was a little blonde girl just like you who came up this holler one time. She was playing and playing and she got in that pie safe and she suffocated in there. Now every time another little girl comes, she just wants to get out and play."

Nobody else said anything. We went on eating, but then all of a sudden there was a loud knocking sound. It was the man, of course, knocking under the table. But I was terrified and I ran out of the room. I never quite got over it. And lots of stuff like that happened as I went around with granddaddy.

DB   And *Family Linen* comes next. That was the novel you hoped would be a commercial breakthrough?

LS   I hoped it would, but who cares? I knew it really wouldn't because it had too many narrators and it was too quirky. It was a lot of fun to write. I had already tried to write detective fiction, a murder mystery, so this was my version. But I just never seem to fit within the parameters of what is necessary to be commercially successful.

DB   Is it true that you bought a pack of letters at a garage sale for seventy-five cents and with those came to life the idea for *Fair and Tender Ladies*?

LS   Yes. It was a sale in Greensboro. The mother of these three sisters had died and they were selling all of her stuff, the tupperware, the furniture, things you'd expect. But they were also selling this box of all their mother's letters. They were not the letters she'd written, but the letters she'd received. They were all tied in little ribbons and arranged by the year. Their mother had kept them so carefully, but the daughters hadn't even read them. They thought I was a fool for buying them. I read the letters. I was really interested. None of the writers of those letters was literary in any way at all, but suddenly I had a whole life there. Plenty of epistolary novels have been written, but I never sort of understood how well they could work. I had the sense, not only of this one woman, but also of the people that were writing to her. I could see this was a way to do the book.

DB   Is *Fair and Tender Ladies* the book where you got in everything you knew?

LS   Yes, and it is my favorite, I guess.

DB   And how many children have been named Ivy in admiration for the book's main character?

LS   Five or six.

DB   But you do get angry letters from people about the episode where Ivy goes up the mountain with Honey Breeding?

LS   Yes, some people read it until then and then put it down. Several times I've given readings or gone to women's book groups or something where somebody will come up specifically to tell me that they were enjoying the book until that point.

DB Well Ivy is so much tied to Sugar Fork and yet wants to leave. There's this I want to stay, I want to leave ambivalence. And where does Ivy's ambivalence about staying in or leaving Sugar Fork come from?

LS That was me. I've felt that way. You can't grow up in this mountain place and not feel some of that. It's that same little downtown and the straight up mountains. You can't grow up here and not be really affected by it. I was not only surrounded by the mountains, but by all my relatives, lots and lots of them. I was an only child, but there were lots and lots of others there. And I did feel this need to go away. But there was always the tug to come back.

DB And Ivy struggles with God as well. She finally decides just to be what she is. Is that a fair summary?

LS I think it is. The only church she knows is Oakley's church, a church that wants women to stay in their places. So she makes up her own version of things, and it's a more nonsectarian belief. And the book of Ecclesiastes, of course, forms the basis for the final monologue, for the whole end of the book. She learns an acceptance of the seasons and changes in life, but she sees them in particularly religious terms, biblical language and biblical terms.

DB Why do so many of your characters, particularly the women characters, feel condemned? They so often seem to think of themselves as bad people.

LS I don't know. I think it does have to do with the way we were brought up, or the way I was brought up. To be sexual, to feel yourself as a sexual being as a woman was to be dirty and to be bad. And religion was all about sin. In the Methodist Youth Fellowship, they were always lecturing us about not petting and all that.

DB It's almost like many of your characters have an internalized fundamentalism.

LS Oh they do. That's very good. And I do too.

DB They can't quite kick the feeling that maybe the preacher who said I'm going to hell is right?

LS Oh yes. It's just like I cannot possibly go to sleep at night if I haven't washed the dishes. I really do still have it, this whole internalized guilt thing.

DB You obviously know Denise Giardina's work, and like her you are aware of this history of the injustices in the mining region.

LS Yes, except that I think of her as a political writer. And I admire her greatly. I think before she began writing those books she was seeing the world in which she had grown up in political terms. She was an activist. I was not. I grew up in the coal region, in Grundy, West Virginia, but my father had the dime store and my uncle owned stores in town. And I was not nearly as aware of the injustices. My family wasn't going down into the mines. In my books I am letting the characters go and exploring personal psychology and personality and the like. I think Denise is very specifically thinking politically. I think she's getting a real following.

DB How is *The Devil's Dream* different from your other books?

LS I've always been a great fan of country music and I've always been around it. And I knew that real fans, the people who know the music, really know it, would also know if I got it wrong. So I had to do a lot of research. That was new to me, and I just loved it. I had the best time doing it.

DB Have you heard from Hollywood on that one?

LS Oh sure. But nothing has ever happened. I've sold options on a number of my books and several of them seem to have come close. PBS was going to make a four-part miniseries of *Oral History*. It was a very serious project for a while. They had a great script. *Family Linen* was supposedly going to be a NBC movie, and it had a wonderful script by the woman who wrote *Blue Sky,* the movie for which Jessica Lange won the Best Actress Academy Award. This stuff keeps happening, but I don't believe a word of it. And there's not a lot of money in acquiring an option until they get to a certain point.

DB Do you still have trouble with endings? I'm thinking particularly of the ending of *Devil's Dream*. In a piece you wrote for *The Writer* years ago, you spoke eloquently of beginnings.

LS And I didn't have anything to say about endings. I cannot end a book. I just can't.

DB I remember my surprise when Katie, at the end of *The Devil's Dream,* is recording gospel songs. She's had some religious experience?

LS Yes, and it is absolutely true and real. And I was happy with that ending.

DB And *Saving Grace* has that surprising circling back in the ending too. Do you get letters about *Saving Grace*?

LS I've gotten a number of letters about it. A lot of letters I get are from people who grew up in holiness families. They talk about what they felt as children on that religious roller coaster ride.

DB Is there anything in Virgil Shepherd, the preacher of *Saving Grace,* that we should admire?

LS I think there is. And I'm not so sure that I was actually successful in getting that into the book. He's pretty despicable, I guess, as it comes through in the book. But it's hard to convey a character like him, because I do not think he is a complete charlatan. He's not totally cynical and he's not putting on a show. There's a part of him that really does believe what he's doing. And I don't think that I was very successful in portraying that. He's not a con-man. He backslides and he's irresponsible and he's manic, but he is not entirely a con-man.

DB But there are those who would read the book and say, this kind of religion is just pathological. Snake-handling for goodness' sake?

LS I don't believe it is at all. I believe it's a real expression, a valid expression of religious belief.

DB I'm sure some people read this book and thought this an unreal situation. And then came the incident in central Tennessee where a snake-handling preacher's wife died from a snake bite. Social services took the children away from the preacher, and there was a legal battle.

LS Yes, I contributed to his defense fund. I was very much aware of all that, and it does confirm some of the issues of my book. But I wish I'd been more successful in drawing Virgil Shepherd. Particularly those people outside this culture are horrified by him. It becomes too easy to view him as a complete villain, and I didn't mean it that way.

DB What about your writing routines. Don't workshops and publicity tours throw you off schedule?

LS No, because I don't write everyday anyway. I sometimes have to try not to write. And I love the teaching too. When I'm writing I like to closet myself away. But it's really fun to interact with a bunch of people as I'm doing here in this workshop. I liked being a newspaper reporter. I like being out and about in this world.

DB   And you must take great pleasure in your work here at the Settlement Camp. I've heard about your work with Florida Slone, the woman you met in the camp's literacy program.

LS   Oh yes. That's been wonderful. She's learned to read and write, and now her songs are published. She tells me she's had two proposals of marriage since her book came out. She says she's not going to marry either of them, because she doesn't want to take care of some old man. She's great. And I have much enjoyed this work.

DB   And you like doing readings, going around to bookstores?

LS   That gets to be too much. I really enjoy it when I do it, but if you do it as much as people want you to, then you don't have time to read. And you don't have time to hang out and talk to people that you care about, and you don't have time to write. When I go somewhere, I tend to throw myself into it and really enjoy it, but I say "no" an awful lot these days.

DB   I know you have many close friends who are writers, people like Clyde Edgerton, Susan Ketchin, and Doris Betts. Do you read one another's work?

LS   Never. We don't ever read each other's work, nor do we talk about writing too much. You know, we don't talk shop, which, I think, is one reason why I am so comfortable with the writers' community in North Carolina. A couple of times I've gone to publishers' parties in New York where people are asking what kind of an advance you've made or telling catty tales about other authors or talking about their agents. We never do that. We're always just telling stories.

DB   What comes next?

LS   Well, I have a book coming out in the fall, *The Christmas Letters.* It's a novella. It is in the form of those Christmas letters people fold into their cards.

DB   Is this what you've called a collapsed novel?

LS   Yes, a little cut, not quite a novel.

DB You've said that a short story is a young writer's form. Do you still think that?

LS I do. I think this all has to do with energy which is one reason I don't go around to as many places as I might. Writing takes enormous energy. And you put the same energy into a lyric poem or short story as you do in a novel. There is the conception of it and the search for the image — that initial creative rush. When you're young, you've got a lot of those, and then you start using it up. I think that's why the novel is the older person's form, because you just have to think of it once and then you can write for a long time with what you have thought up.

DB And yet your recent story in *The Atlantic*, "Happy Memories Club," is wonderful.

LS Well, I did hear from a lot of people on that. But the older folks hated it. They do want things to be a little smoothed over, a little rose-colored. They prefer to have a little sugar coating on their pills. So I've realized that's not the story to read at the retirement communities.

DB I figured you got letters from people who said, "Wow. Thanks for satirizing this awful place which I live."

LS No. I got those letters from other people who had mothers and fathers in retirement homes.

DB At the end of *Saving Grace*, in the postscript, you say, "Writing is a lifelong search for belief."

LS Yes. I think I use the writing as a way of examining the feelings and things and beliefs that are most important to me. That's my form. I started doing it when I was so young that that's my sort of proving ground. That's what I do.

DB At the same time you are wary of faith. You describe religious devotion as "compelling and desirable and terrifying."

LS Yes. But as I get older, I'm more drawn to church, to the more organized, traditional kinds of religion that I had gotten away from for a while. I never got away from thinking about moral issues. But now I find myself more drawn to the Episcopal Church and even the Unitarian Church.

DB Well, what about all the comparisons to people like Faulkner, Welty, and O'Connor?

LS That's ridiculous. Forget it. If I had to consider myself anything, I would have to consider myself an Appalachian writer. That's why I like to come here to eastern Kentucky. I like to get back into the coal fields.

DB So this is like coming home?

LS Exactly.

DB And being called a regionalist doesn't bother you?

LS I love it. I think I'm lucky to be from somewhere.

DB And you don't worry about who might come across your stories?

LS I don't care. I don't care much about critics either. I just do this. This is the way I live my life. And I like to teach. I do like to encourage other people. I think writing is a valid thing to do. It's wonderful for so many reasons, the least of which is publication. I always try to tell my students to keep their day jobs.

DB And soon you'll be back teaching at North Carolina State?

LS Yes. And I love it. It's the land grant university and it has the kinds of students I like, both adults and kids off the farm. I will teach graduate creative writing and probably another course. So I'll just teach half-time. I'll just teach one semester a year. Because I like it. I want to. I would really miss it if I didn't do it. Such interesting people come into those classes, and my writing is better for it.

DB You're dismissive of audience and critics, but you've learned a lot from your characters?

LS Yes, I have. I've learned a lot from my life too.

DB Have you ever thought about returning to a character, revisiting a place to see what happened to them after a book was finished?

LS Sure, but I've got all these books in my head all the time. It's like those games at the fair where you hammer down one thing and another one pops up. Stuff is always popping up for me. Most of my ideas are probably not very good. I have too many. I think you can write too much. I've probably already written too much. I do it because it's fun.

DB   Years ago in *Harper's,* you said you fear you might have "Southern Door Disease." What is that?

LS   That is the inability to shut up. I come from this tradition of big talkers in both the mountain and the eastern Virginian part of my family. My husband, Hal Crowther, made it up. As a non-Southerner, he's always been fascinated by us. I will say that we have to leave a party at such and such a time, and then we'll stand at the door and talk for forty-five minutes. That's the way to do it here. He calls that "Southern Door Disease." He says it's an affliction that strikes Southern white women. And it has sure struck me. He's right.

Acknowledgments

Excerpts of these interviews have appeared in the following publications:

"A Faith to Live and Die With." *Sojourners Magazine*, May-June, 1998: 52-56.

"A Lesson for Living." *Sojourners Magazine*, September-October, 2002.

"Called to Write: An Interview with Jan Karon." *Radix*, Spring, 2004:14.

"David James Duncan: River Mud, Mysticism, and Corvette Stingrays." *Cimarron Review*, Winter 2000: 122-151.

"Oprah, Jesus Music, and Pressing Stories: An Interview with Sheri Reynolds." *The GSU Review*, Fall 1999: 6-25.

"Ron Hansen: Participating in the Divine." *Sojourners Magazine*, December 2005.

"Tar Heel Profile: The Voice of a Story Teller." *Our State*, November, 1997: 64-66.

"Terence Faherty: Doggedly Low Key." *The Mystery Review*, forthcoming.

"Silas House: Incredibly Blessed." *The Southern Ledger*, web magazine, November, 2006.